ALPINE PASSES
BY ROAD BIKE

ALPINE PASSES BY ROAD BIKE

100 ROUTES THROUGH THE ALPS AND HOW TO RIDE THEM

RUDOLF GESER

B L O O M S B U R Y

LONDON · NEW DELHI · NEW YORK · SYDNEY

Published in 2013 by Bloomsbury Publishing Plc
50 Bedford Square
London WC1B 3DP
www.bloomsbury.com

First published in Germany in 2005 by Bruckmann Verlag GmbH, Munich under the title
100 Alpenpässe mit dem Rennrad.

Acknowledgements
All photos by the author Rudolf Geser, except: Gunda Amberg: p. 7; Hans-Joachim Arndt: pp. viii, x, 2, 8, 14, 66, 68, 86, 87, 93, 132, 133; Catherine Avak: pp. 5, 25; Bildverlag Wilfried Bahnmüller: pp. 105, 114, 251, 252, 253, 256, 258; Martin Barnack: pp. 156, 183, 184, 185, 204, 205 top; Heinrich Bauregger: pp. 10, 54, 59, 82, 83; Peter Dinter: p. 76; Robert-Felix Dodu: pp. 32, 33 right, 102, 136, 261; Don Fuchs: pp. 72, 254; Gerold Jung: pp. xiv/1, 12/13, 18, 58, 80, 142, 179; Bildverlag Klammet/ Bahnmüller: pp. 116, 250, 257; Torsten Köhler, www.quaeldich.de: p. 52; Iris Kürschner: pp. 46/47, 73, 79, 129, 131, 154, 165, 166, 170, 180, 193 bottom, 201 top, 202, 203, 212, 220, 223, 237, 242; MOUNTAIN PICTURE/Martin Siepmann: pp. 26, 40/41, 44, 141, 143; Thomas Rettstatt: pp. 125, 124, 224, 228, 229; Oskar Schraml: pp. 36, 38, 53, 78, 89, 90, 94, 95, 130, 138; Jan Sahner, www.quaeldich.de: pp. 102, 103; Stefan Stickler, www.quaeldich.de: p. 22; Klaus Tödt-Rübel: front cover, pp. xi top, 240, 243, 244, 245, 246, 247; Ulrich Vormbrock, member of www.quaeldich.de: pp. 151, 168; Michael Waeber: p. 265; Niklas Wellmann, www.quaeldich.de: p. 122; original cartography: Achim Norweg, Munich

Designed by James Watson
Translated into English by Rosemary Dear

Typeset in 9.5pt on 11.5pt Eurostile and Myriad by seagulls.net
Printed and bound in India by Replika Press Pvt. Ltd.

10 9 8 7 6 5 4 3 2 1

CONTENTS

FOREWORD

Any cyclist who has ridden through the Alps on a road bike will understand the fascination of mountain roads and passes. Some, like the Großglockner High Alpine Road, the Stelvio Pass, the Col du Galibier and the route up to the Alpe d'Huez, are legendary in cycle sport circles, their names spoken with reverence and respect. Others, such as the Sella Pass, the Jaufenpass and the Mendel, are so physically demanding that amateurs will need to train hard if they want to tackle them. Other beautiful, demanding and difficult routes of note include the Sölden Glacier Road, which climbs from the Ötz valley to a height of 2829m, the highest point in the Alps accessible to the public, the Oberjoch in Allgau, a mere hill by comparison but boasting more bends than any other German pass, and the nearby Riedberg, at 1420m Germany's

highest alpine crossing. A whole series of other well-known and not so well-known climbs await your pedalling pleasure: in the east, the Hahntennjoch road in North Tyrol, the Zillertal High Road over the Zillertal, the Penser Joch down to the Falzárego Pass and the Giau Pass in the Dolomites; and in the west, the high passes of the Col d'Iseran, the Col de Restefond and the Col de la Bonette passes in the French Maritime Alps.

This guide selects and describes the 100 most beautiful alpine passes and other mountain roads for cyclists. It begins with the Roßfeld Mountain Ring Road in South Bavaria and goes over the other side towards Austria where the Turracher Mountain Road awaits anyone who considers a 23 per cent gradient possible. Anyone who disagrees can take on the more moderate Nockalm

One for the album on the Gardena Pass, 2137m high, in the Dolomites (Tour 25).

Mountain Road and work their way along to the Großglockner High Alpine Road. A short detour takes us to Slovenia, to the Julian Alps and the less well-known but nonetheless stunning Predil and Vršič passes.

Then to Italy, offering rich pickings from the Staller Sattel to the Sella Pass in the Dolomites, the Gardena Pass and the Pordoi Pass to the Passo di Costalunga, the Stelvio Pass, and the Gavia Pass to the Campo-Carlomagno Pass in the Brenta Dolomites, once traversed by Charlemagne. Switzerland welcomes us with the Umbrail Pass, which goes over the Bernina Pass into the western Alps and further down to the Côte d'Azur, where the Alps near Nice seem to plunge into the Mediterranean.

The rides kick off less dramatically in Switzerland, where in Appenzellerland the almost leisurely Wildhaus Mountain Road and Schwägalp Pass offer cruising as well as climbing. Things soon become mountainous with the Klausen Pass, and the St Gotthard Pass gives an insight into Switzerland's geology. On the way to the Große Scheidegg you can see famous but also feared mountains such as the Jungfrau, Mönch and Eiger, though cyclists have less to fear than mountaineers, other than the 28 per cent gradient between Kiental and Griesalp. There are more pleasant climbs over the Mattertal Road to Zermatt at the foot of the Matterhorn and over the Anniviers and Zinal High Road to the Zinalrothorn.

Then it's off to France and the second highest pass in the Alps, the 2770m Col de l'Iseran. Nearby is the Col du Galibier, also known as the Roof of the Tour, at 2646m usually the highest point of the Tour de France. That it's also the hardest you can discover for yourself if you cycle up the Col de la Croix de Fer or the Col du Glandon or take the climb up to the Alpe

A narrow route cut from the rock face on the west side of the Albula Pass (Tour 54) in the Bergün Gorge.

d'Huez, perhaps the best-known mountain stage finish on the Tour.

There are surprises on offer on the climb to the Col d'Izoard, whose almost moonlike landscape is unique in the Alps. The highest point, at least in numerical terms, is the Col de Restefond/Col de la Bonette, at 2802m the highest alpine pass open to the public. Also in France, you can do a circuit of the Verdon Gorge, Europe's largest, and conquer Mont Ventoux, known variously as the 'Giant of Provence' and the 'Mountain of the Winds' – nicknames to note.

As varied as these 100 passes and mountain roads may be in their scenery, location and route profiles, they have in common their status as the most beautiful and worthwhile cycling challenges that the alpine region has to offer. I hope you have a great time riding them and above all I wish you an accident-free journey.

Rudolf Geser

KEY TO ROUTE INFORMATION

Start
The ride's starting point, and its altitude.

Directions
The quickest way to the starting point is given, assuming the journey is made by car.

Level of difficulty/maximum gradient
We give an overview of the gradient, and always include a maximum. This is useful for assessing whether you are fit enough to tackle the climbs, but the level of difficulty is more informative because it describes the whole of the route rather than individual and sometimes only short sections of it. Three levels of difficulty are generally given: easy, medium and difficult. Three tours are rated as very difficult: the Nigerpass road (Tour 30) with a maximum gradient of 24 per cent, the Turracher Mountain Road (Tour 6) with a maximum gradient of 23 per cent and the Kiental with Griesalp Mountain

Road (Tour 71) which includes a massive 28 per cent gradient that should only be attempted by riders who have trained exceptionally hard. These three tours aside, the difficulty rating is based on objective data such as a route's length, total vertical climb and maximum gradient. This is the only effective way to calculate difficulty levels as so much depends on the physical abilities and training level of the individual.

Easy
Easy routes make no particular demands on fitness, either on the basis of the gradient, the length of the route or the vertical climb. Longer, flatter stretches predominate. They can be tackled by riders who have not put in much training. However, there are very few easy tours in the alpine region and they shouldn't be attempted without any preparation at all.

Medium
Cycling a tour classified as medium requires a basic level of fitness and regular training totalling 3000–4000km a year. Gradients of 10 per cent or more over longer stretches have to be overcome. Medium tours are the norm in the Alps and can be used as training runs for difficult tours.

Difficult
On difficult tours, a maximum gradient of 10 per cent or more persists for long stretches interspersed only rarely with flatter sections. Routes are 20km and over. Difficult routes should only be attempted by riders who have prepared thoroughly, who do more than 4000 training kilometres a year and have plenty of experience of cycling over passes.

On the south side of the Campolongo Pass.

If you've trained well you can take part in this amateur race on Mont Ventoux.

Length

The length in kilometres corresponds to the route as measured by my cycle computer. It might deviate slightly from measurements published elsewhere, e.g. on maps.

Total ascent

This has been calculated on the basis of official information given on maps and in guidebooks. Minor climbs and descents have not always taken into account.

Time

The journey time given is based on actual times recorded by myself and other riders and allows only for time in the saddle; stops are not included. It should be regarded as a guide – how long a route takes to complete will vary widely depending on the age and physical condition of the individual and their form on the day, among other factors. A range is provided, assuming a rider is in medium shape and not carrying luggage. Riders in peak form should be able to complete the route in less than the minimum time, while those who only ride occasionally may exceed the maximum. But it should be possible for every ambitious rider to complete the tour within the time range given.

Gearing

The biggest sprocket available is on a Campagnolo 10-speed cassette of 13 – 14

– 15 – 16 – 17 – 19 – 21 – 23 – 26 – 29. Campagnolo's 9-speed range includes a 28-tooth sprocket in a 13 – 14 – 15 – 17 – 19 – 21 – 23 – 25 – 28 set. Either of these two 'mountain' set-ups should take you up most of the passes in the Alps. A difference of one tooth makes hardly any noticeable difference in my experience, but the psychological effect should not be disregarded; just as I would rather use a 26-tooth sprocket than a 25-tooth one without being able to explain why, there are riders who are convinced that they'll manage much better with a 29-tooth sprocket than a 28-tooth one.

Shimano's biggest sprocket on an 8-speed cassette has 'only' 26 teeth (13 –

The centre of Wildhaus is also the top of the Wildhaus Pass. In the background is the Schafberg (Tour 58).

The eastern ramp of the Maloja Pass, here with Lake Silvaplana at the foot of the Piz Corvatsch, doesn't boast any appreciable inclines (Tour 44).

gradients of over 12 per cent, such as the 16 per cent of the Gavia Pass (Tour 41).

For climbing extreme gradients such as the 24 per cent on the Nigerpass (Tour 30), the 23 per cent on the Turracher Mountain Road (Tour 6) and the 28 per cent on the Kiental with Griesalp road in Switzerland (Tour 71) we are in unknown territory, athough I do know amateur cyclists who have got up these with a 39/26 set-up.

Suggested gearing

This should be taken only as an indication. The ideal set-up varies widely according to your physical capabilities, your style of riding and your personal preference. For example, two equally well-trained riders may have different cadences but will average the same speed. For pass riding I generally recommend a rear cassette maxing at a 28-tooth sprocket paired with a 39-tooth chainring. You generally won't need to use the 28-tooth sprocket but when your strength is ebbing on a long climb it's good to be able to change gear one more time. Only riders at peak fitness will get away with a 26-tooth sprocket as the biggest.

Route

Here the towns and villages along the route over the pass are listed, with their distance from the starting point.

Road conditions

This section notes the condition of the road surface, along with hazards such as cattle grids, narrow sections and poor visibility. Do ride more defensively and carefully than usual on passes and if visibility is poor ensure your stopping distance is within your range of vision. Expect obstacles on the road such as potholes, small stones, boulders and grazing livestock around every bend. The greatest care should be paid to cattle grids

14 – 15 – 17 – 19 – 21 – 23 – 26), and its 9-speed max is 27 teeth (12 – 13 – 14 – 15 – 17 – 19 – 21 – 24 – 27). This is enough for gradients of up to 10 per cent, though above this it will be difficult. Here it seems more useful to fit a triple chainset with a 30-tooth smallest ring.

If you don't have a triple chainring on your bike and don't fancy converting it, you could fit Shimano's 8- or 9-speed mountain bike cassette ring to a Shimano Road Hub. The biggest sprockets here, depending on the cassette, are a 28, 30, 32 or even a 34-tooth one in the XT or XTR group. That way you may actually be able to solve all gradient problems. The best advice though of course is to consult your bike mechanic or dealer.

Inclines of up to 12 per cent as a rule require a 28-tooth sprocket and if you can manage the likes of the Großglockner High Alpine Road (Tour 9) or the Stelvio Pass (Tour 40) on 26, your ride fitness must be exceptionally good. A 28 will also allow you to ride strongly up shorter which can be dangerously smooth. Don't brake here or take at an angle. Extreme care is also needed in tunnels and galleries (open-sided tunnels) which are often unlit. In tunnels, potholes, water on the road and, particularly in spring, traces of snow and ice are a source of increased danger. Remember that your eyes take time to become accustomed to the changing light conditions as you ride into and out of tunnels, so reduce your speed.

Pass open
The official opening period is given here. Note that weather or road maintenance may require short-term road closures even during this period, or extend it. Enquire locally for road conditions.

Things to see
For those who are interested in local history and culture, places of interest in towns and villages and along the route are noted.

Maps
Taking along a large-scale road map is not only a good idea for navigation, but interesting for interpreting the landscape. I recommend the Euro Cart Regionalkarte RV-Verlag series, on a scale of 1:300,000, available to buy locally. The scale allows a large area, sometimes a whole country, to be covered on a single map. In the UK, Stanfords (www.stanfords.co.uk) is the best place to shop for maps.

Notes
Here we state whether it's advisable or necessary to take lights for use in tunnels or galleries – but it's always a good idea to have front and rear lights with you, primarily for safety reasons but also so that in an accident in a tunnel or at twilight you can't be accused of negligence and held wholly or partially responsible.

Road sign glossary

Italy
Deviazione	Diversion
Tenere la destra	Keep right
Rallentare	Slow
Senso unico	One-way street
Sbarrato	Road closed
Curva pericolosa	Dangerous bend
Strada stretta	Unmade road
Caduta sassi	Falling or fallen rocks

France
Rappel	Reminder – watch your speed (mostly referring to speed limits)
Ralentir	Slow
Déviation	Diversion
Passage interdit	Road closed

Germany
Umleitung	Diversion
Rechts fahren	Keep right
Langsam fahren	Slow
Einbahnstraße	One-way street
Gesperrt	Road closed
Gefährliche Kurve	Dangerous bend
Unbefestigte Straße	Unmade road
Steinschlag	Falling or fallen rocks

These three riders seem to be taking their time, pedalling regularly on the south side of the Great St Bernard Pass.

ALPINE PASSES IN GERMANY

TOUR PROFILE <<

Roßfeld Mountain Ring Road: 1540m

Start: Berchtesgaden, 573m

Directions: A8 Munich–Salzburg, exit Knoten Salzburg Süd or Hallein – Marktschellenberg – Unterau – Berchtesgaden

Difficulty/Maximum gradient: Medium, with a maximum gradient of 14 per cent for about 2km between Unterau and Oberau

Length: 34.5km

Total ascent: 1175m

Time: 3–5 hrs

Suggested gearing: 39/28

Route: Berchtesgaden (0.0km) – Unterau (3.5km) – Oberau (5.5km) – North tollbooth/Pechhäusl (10.5km) – Roßfeldalm (13km) – Roßfeld ski lodge (13.5km) – Hennköpfl/Roßfeld car park (14.5km) – Ahornbüchsenkopf (16.0km) – South tollbooth/Ofnerboden (22.0km) – Hotel General Walker (23.5km) – Scharitzkehlalm (27.5km) – Hinterbrand (30.5km) – Vorderbrand (31.0km) – Berchtesgaden (34.5km)

Road conditions: Well-constructed roads

Pass open: Open all year

Things to see: Berchtesgaden: castle and museum, local history museum, salt mine; excursion to Königssee

Map: Euro Cart regional map 1:300,000, RV-Verlag, sheet 12 Bavaria

The Watzmann towers over the floor of the Berchtesgadener Ache valley, just before Unterau.

In the south-east corner of Upper Bavaria, right on the border of with Austria's Salzburg province, lies the Berchtesgaden region – one of the most beautiful landscapes in Bavaria, if not the whole of Germany. The Watzmann peak and Königssee lake are its best-known attractions, but we are interested in something quite different: the Roßfeld Mountain Ring Road. Set in beautiful scenery deep in the Berchtesgaden Alps, it's Germany's highest mountain road, peaking at 1540m. Offering a 1000m climb to tackle and gradients of up to 14 per cent, it's also a great sporting challenge – and so a route to be recommended.

Start at the market in Berchtesgaden and take the B305 towards Marktschellenberg for 3.5 flat kilometres to Unterau. Alternatively, if you really want to punish yourself, branch off to the right to Obersalzberg just before you leave town. But be warned: you'll have barely crossed the bridge over the Berchtesgadener Ache before the road starts to climb at a heart-pumping gradient of 24 per cent and it won't let up until you reach the Obersalzberg car park a good 2.5km later. At a crossroads there you can either turn left and head for Oberau along an easy route, to continue the tour as described below, or you can keep climbing and reach the

Roßfeld over the western route. Is this alternative climb to Obersalzberg worth doing? Actually, only by those who like to push themselves to the limit, because torturing yourself isn't much fun. At this gradient, your thighs will ache and your lungs burn even in the lowest gear, and you'll be pedalling unevenly and straining hard on the handlebars.

You needn't worry that the standard route won't be demanding enough: from Unterau (3.5km) to Oberau (5.5km) the gradient is a consistent and quite noticeable 14 per cent. In Oberau you can take a quick breather as the gradient decreases, but as you leave the town it's back up to 12 per cent.

The view's on the up, also. To the west, the tops of the Lattengebirge and the Reiteralm are visible, while to the north stretches the Unterberg Massif. Legend has it that here Charlemagne sleeps on his throne in a palace of polished marble surrounded by his entourage, waiting until his beard has grown three times around the table in front of him. At this point he will awaken and crush his enemies in the greatest battle ever seen.

The gradient lets up slightly to between 8 per cent and 10 per cent towards the north tollbooth/Pechhäusl (10.5km). If you're hoping for a brief respite you'll be disappointed: it increases again to 10–13 per cent and after 12.5km, if you've got good eyesight, you'll spot a sign noting an altitude of 1400m. There's still another 140m to go, past the Roßfeld ski lodge (13.5km) up to the Roßfeld car park (14.5km) – the highest point of the climb – which the route approaches in wide loops, reaching a gradient of 13 per cent again towards the top. You're rewarded with a dramatic ride beneath the mighty rock faces of the Hoher Göll for about a kilometre towards Eckersattel,

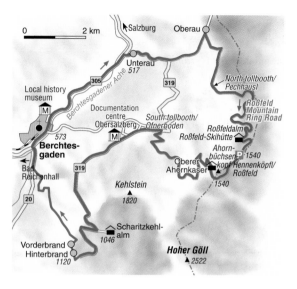

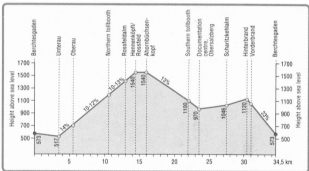

after which the road curves down a descent of up to 13 per cent. At the crossroads after the south tollbooth/Ofnerboden (22km) you can go straight on to Obersalzberg, riding the brakes down a descent of up to 24 per cent to the B425 to Berchtesgaden (25.0km). Another possibility would be to keep to the right and follow the B319 back to Berchtesgaden (30.0km) past Oberau and Unterau. The third and last alternative is to keep left on the B319 and follow it back to the starting point (34.5km), via Hinterbrand (30.5km) and the Gasthof Vorderbrand (31.0km), with a final descent of up to 23 per cent.

2 WINKLMOOS MOUNTAIN ROAD
South Bavaria

TOUR PROFILE <<

Winklmoos Mountain Road: 1210m

Start: Reit im Winkl, 695m

Directions: A8 Munich–Salzburg, exit Bernau – Grassau – Marquartstein – Reit im Winkl

Level of Difficulty/Maximum gradient: Medium, with a maximum gradient of 18 per cent over two stretches 700m and 450m long

Length: 9.5km

Total ascent: 450m

Time: 1–1¼ hrs

Suggested gearing: 39/28

Route: Reit im Winkl 763m (0.0km) – main car park, Seegatterl (5.0km) – Winklmoosalm (9.5km)

Road conditions: Well-constructed roads

Pass open: All year

Things to see: Reit im Winkl: parish church of St Pankratius (1393) with a noteworthy Way of the Cross and beautiful glass paintings from the second half of the 18th century

Map: Euro Cart regional map 1:300,000, RV-Verlag, sheet 12 Bavaria

Notes: Take care on the return journey because of cattle grids and the steep descent. There is a lot of traffic at the weekend.

In the midst of the wonderful scenery of the Chiemgau, near the well-known tourist town of Reit im Winkl, lies the Winkelmoosalm, an alpine region at the foot of the 1247m Sonderberg peak that's particularly popular with hikers. It's also much used by skiers and cross-country skiers, as it has the deepest and most reliable snow in the whole of the Bavarian Alps. The Winklmoosalm is not quite so popular in cycling circles, being hardly known above local or regional level. So, very few people undertake this tour unless they're staying in this part of the country already. But those who do tend to get quite a surprise. The climb to Winklmoosalm may not be all that long at 4.5 kilometers and not all that high with a total vertical climb of 450m, but it boasts a gradient of 18 per cent and will really make you sweat. In addition to your training kilometres you should also bring a 28-tooth sprocket, to avoid making things unnecessarily difficult. If you have kilometres in your legs and that large sprocket then you can confidently follow the signs to Ruhpolding in the pretty tourist town of Reit im Winkl, leaving the town in an easterly direction on the B305. For the first 5km to the main car park in Seegatterl you can bowl along sedately and if you want you can fortify yourself in the alpine guesthouse of the same name.

Just a few metres after going through the tollbooth things really get going. The gradient increases suddenly to 18 per cent and continues that way around a 700m hairpin bend. Depending on your gearing and your fitness, you'll notice here just how long 700m can drag on, and you'll be grateful when you realise that the gradient has decreased to between 10 per cent and 12 per cent. Even this is difficult enough and only those who have trained hard will dare to change up to a smaller sprocket.

On the wooded northern slopes of the Sondersberg the road winds up over a series of bends, with only occasional short flatter sections to allow you to recover a little, until you reach a small cattle grid (7.7km). This marks the point at which the gradient decreases and the first difficulties lie behind you. A small clearing opens up and you can almost cruise for a little. However, you should stay on the small chainring as you'll need it again in a moment. At the end of the clearing the gradient increases again to a hard 14 per cent and although this only lasts for 50m, it's enough to force most of us out of the saddle.

Now the gradient decreases, allowing us to regain our strength or take a swig from our water bottles. Then once again it's really hard work. The gradient increases to 18 per cent and stays there for at least 450m until the first car park (8.8km). While tourists in cars stretch legs tensed from the accelerator pedal, we can also let our burning thighs relax. Past the town sign Reit im Winkl – 'District of Winklmoos' (8.9km) to swoop into a wonderful alpine area

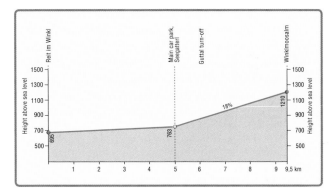

surrounded by a circle of dark woods. Creature comforts are also catered for here in the many guesthouses and hotels. You might want to pay a visit to the small chapel (9.5km) just below the valley station of the Dürrnbacheck chairlift, but you'll have to ride a little further up. There, you'll be rewarded with the most beautiful view of the Loferer Steinberge in the east.

Under no circumstances when descending should you try to recoup the time you've lost by climbing. Slow down, especially at weekends when the route is very busy with traffic, and follow the cars back down. Don't put yourself or others in danger on the sometimes narrow roads through reckless overtaking manoeuvres.

Don't be fooled by the idyllic surroundings, the descent to Winklmoosalm has a gradient of 18 per cent.

TOUR PROFILE <<

Tatzelwurm and Sudelfeld Saddle Road: 1097m

EASTERN SIDE – Start: Niederaudorf, 476m

Directions: A12 Rosenheim– Kufstein (Inn Valley Autobahn), exit Brannenburg – Niederaudorf

Level of Difficulty/Maximum gradient: Easy to medium tour with a maximum gradient of 14 per cent for 1.5km at the beginning. Gradients of up to 12 per cent for 2km in the hairpin bends after the Tatzelwurm car park

Length: 16.5km

Total ascent: 625m

Time: 1¾–2½ hrs

Suggested gearing: 42/26

Route: Niederaudorf (0.0km) – Agg (1.0km) – Berggasthof Hummelei (2.5km) – Wall (3.5km) – Seebach (5.5km) – Rechenau (6.5km) – Gasthof Feuriger Tatzelwurm (8.0km) – main car park Tatzelwurm (8.5km) – Sudelfeld saddle (16.5km)

WESTERN SIDE – Start: Bayrischzell, 800m

Directions: A8 Salzburg, exit Weyarn – Miesbach – Hausham – Schliersee – Bayrischzell

Level of Difficulty/Maximum gradient: Easy, with a maximum gradient of 11 per cent for 1km between Bayrischzell and Sudelfeld saddle

Length: 4.5km

Total ascent: 300m

Time: ¾–1 hr

Suggested gearing: 39/26

Route: Bayrischzell (0.0km) – Sudelfeld saddle (4.5km)

Road conditions: On the lower part of the eastern side the road narrows in places, particularly through villages

Pass open: All year

Map: Euro Cart regional map 1:300,000, RV-Verlag, sheet 12 Bavaria

Things to see: Bayrischzell: parish church of St Margaretha

The Sudelfeld is an extensive, almost treeless alpine meadow region at the foot of the Wendelstein in the Schliersee Alps – also known as the Mangfall range, which stretch between Bayrischzell in the Lietzach valley and Brannenburg in the Inn valley. It's an area steeped in folklore and legend: the Tatzelwurm that gives its name to the starting point of this ride was a fire-breathing dragon said to have made its home in the region. Although the ascent of nearly 300m in the 4.5km from Bayrischzell to the Sudelfeld saddle means hardly anything to the well-trained rider, the eastern side, offering a good 600m of vertical climb, a distance of 16.5km and gradients of up to 14 per cent, is more enjoyably challenging.

Eastern side

In Niederaudorf (0.0km) we follow the signpost 'Bayrischzell über Tatzelwurm/Sudelfeld' and pedal full steam ahead to Agg (1.0km). The road is narrow and climbs up to Berggasthof Hummelei (2.5km) at a gradient of 14 per cent, after which the most difficult part of the route lies behind us. It's only a gentle climb through Wall (3.5km), Seebach (5.5km) and Rechenau (6.5km), and no more difficulties are in store on the way to the Gasthof Feuriger Tatzelwurm (8.0km). Behind the hotel a short forest trail leads to a rocky gorge with a roaring torrent rushing through it, which is said to be the home of the aforementioned Tatzelwurm, and worth a diversion.

Past the hotel the road climbs briefly at 12 per cent, then the gradient decreases to 7 per cent up to the Tatzelwurm car park (8.5km). This is where the most beautiful scenery of the climb starts to reveal itself in a series of hairpin bends at a gradient of 10-12 per cent. At the end of this section (11.5km) the view opens out over the Sudelfeld and during a 1km descent into the Arzbach valley (13.0km) we drop down a few more metres before going up again

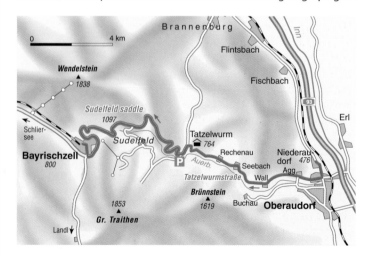

The view from the Sudelfeld saddle over the Kaisergebirge.

at around 9 per cent and then on to the top of the pass (16.5km).

Western side

Though the western approach makes noticeably fewer demands on your cycle computer, it's well worthwhile from the point of view of its scenic attractions. This is obvious from the moment you get to Bayrischzell – one of the best-known tourist destinations in Upper Bavaria – situated peacefully and idyllically at the foot of the Wendelstein, not far from the Bavarian–Austrian border where the Ursprung valley meets the Leitzach valley. Many of the locals might regard that 'situated peacefully' from a different perspective: the B307 which bypasses the town in a wide loop is very busy, particularly at weekends and is very popular with motor cyclists. Be prepared to have your pride a little dented when they pass you with ease on the 11 per cent gradient.

After the first few kilometres the gradient decreases a little, you reach the first hairpin bend (2.0km), soon followed by another, and now all the hairpin bends of this climb are accounted for. The road

turns to the east and we lose the view of the rocky south side of the Wendelstein. It climbs at a steady 9 per cent to 10 per cent in a fairly straight line, and soon the Schliersee mountains come into view to the south. There are cliffs on the left-hand side of the road protected by wire netting, which add to the feeling that you must have reached the high mountains by now, and then there it is, a sign marked Sudelfeld, announcing the end of the climb. A few metres of more moderate gradient bring us to the highest point (4.5km), then the route sinks around a narrow bend to the car park at the Café Kotz (5.0km).

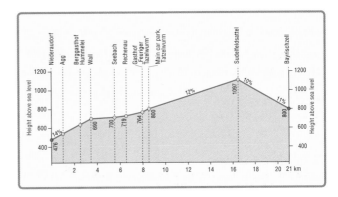

7

4 OBERJOCH PASS
South Bavaria

TOUR PROFILE <<

Oberjoch Pass: 1150m

SOUTHERN SIDE – Start: Hindelang, 820m

Directions: A7 Ulm–Kempten, exit Allgäu – Waltenhofen – Sonthofen – Hindelang

Level of Difficulty/Maximum gradient: Easy, with a maximum gradient of 9 per cent

Length: 8.5km

Total ascent: 330m

Time: ½–1 hr

Suggested gearing: 39/23

Route: Hindelang (0.0km) – top of the pass (8.5km)

NORTHERN SIDE – Start: Wertach, 915m

Directions: A7 Ulm–Kempten, exit Oy/Mittelberg – Wertach

Level of Difficulty/Maximum gradient: Easy, with a maximum gradient of 8 per cent

Length: 14.5km

Total ascent: 280m

Time: ¾–1½ hrs

Suggested gearing: 39/23

Route: Wertach (0.0km) – Jungholz (7.0km) – Unterjoch (10.5km) – top of the pass (14.5km)

Road conditions: Well-constructed roads; southern side has a large number of bends

Pass open: All year

Things to see: Hindelang: town hall from the year 1660 with a council chamber and opulent baroque furnishings

Map: Euro Cart regional map 1:300,000, RV-Verlag, sheet 12 Bavaria

The south side of the Oberjoch pass road has the greatest number of bends of all the pass roads in Germany.

The Oberjoch, which stretches for 23km from Hindelang in the Ostrach valley to the Wertacher Hörnle, is infamous as the pass with the most bends in Germany. Because of this we can overlook the fact that at 1150m it's not particularly high and, given that the valley village of Hindelang in the south is 820m above sea level and Wertach in the north is 910m above sea level, can't boast much of a climb.

Southern side

If you want to enjoy the stretch of bends at the beginning, start the tour in Hindelang (0.0km) over on the south side. The road rolls along straight through the town with gradients of 8 per cent, interrupted by a descent of exactly the same value; the bends and climbs section begins by the Gasthof Letzter Heller as you leave town. There's little to say about the gradient, which over the next 8.5km up to the top of the pass never exceeds the 9 per cent mark, but doesn't drop below it either. Time, therefore, to deal with the bends, of which there are said to be 106. You either believe it or you don't, because you can't count them. The whole route is one big

wiggle in which one curve follows another, but real, clearly defined hairpin bends are few and far between. The village of Oberjoch, which you reach after 8.5km, claims the title of the highest mountain pass village in Germany. For us it's just the end of the southern climb up to the pass where we can start the journey back down the slope we've just come up, or the descent over the north side down to Wertach.

Northern side

The north side of the Oberjoch pass doesn't have any outstanding features. It is, in contrast to the south side, completely without bends and with a total vertical gain of only 280m over 14.5km also without significant climbs. With a maximum gradient of 8 per cent, and that only in short stretches – it's mostly much less than this – it doesn't require much power and so turns into a rather leisurely tour. However, the level of difficulty can be increased markedly by a detour into the eastern Austrian enclave of Jungholz, where the gradient increases to 12 per cent over long sections.

We leave Wertach (0.0km) on the wide, well-constructed B310. The valley of the Wertach soon narrows into a gorge and after riding just 2km we see the turning up to Jungholz. Even though the gradient increases to 12 per cent, the detour is to be highly recommended. The enclave (7.0km) is only joined to the Austrian motherland by a 1m-wide strip of land that stretches to the foot of the Sorgschrofen. This area, lying completely within German territory, came to Austria through land purchase by a Thannheim landowner back in the 14th century, where it has remained until this day in spite of violent border disputes. But there is no direct road from here to Austria, so the 300 or so inhabitants are forced to take

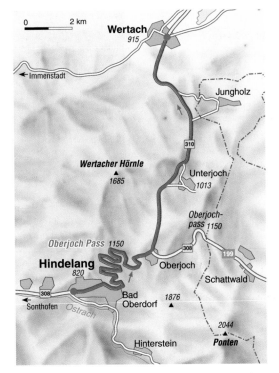

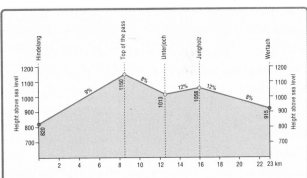

the circuitous route through German territory. The road has a downhill gradient of 12 per cent back to the B310, which climbs up again at a steady 8 per cent gradient to Unterjoch (10.5km). In the hilly landscape of the surrounding area only the wooded summit of the Sorgschrofen is worth mentioning, so there is little variety on offer on the well-constructed road up to the top of the pass.

9

5 RIEDBERG PASS
South Bavaria

TOUR PROFILE <<

Riedberg Pass: 1420m

WESTERN SIDE – Start: Hittisau, 790m

Directions: A7 Ulm–Kempten, exit Allgäu – Waltenhofen – Immenstadt – Bad Oberstaufen – Hittisau

Level of Difficulty/Maximum gradient: Medium, with a maximum gradient of 16 per cent on several 100m sections between Balderschwang and the top of the pass

Length: 20.5km

Total ascent: 670m

Time: 1½–2¼ hrs

Suggested gearing: 39/26

Route: Hittisau (0.0km) – turning to Sibratsgfäll (3.5km) – former customs post at Schönhalden (10.0km) – Balderschwang (12.0km) – top of the pass (20.5km)

EASTERN SIDE – Start: Fischen im Allgäu, 761m, about 6km south of Sonthofen; direction: A7 Kempten, exit Waltenhofen – Immenstadt – Sonthofen – Fischen

Level of Difficulty/Maximum gradient: Medium, with a maximum gradient of 16 per cent on two sections 700m and 500m long

Length: 8.5km

Total ascent: 660m

Time: 1–1¾ hrs

Suggested gearing: 42/26

Route: Fischen (0.0km) – Obermaiselstein (2.0km) – top of the pass (8.5km)

Road conditions: Dimly lit 50m tunnel on the way to Obermaiselstein. Take care on the descent here. Otherwise, well-constructed roads

Pass open: All year

Things to see: Fischen: parish church of St Verena with noteworthy carvings; Lady Chapel from the 16th century with a high altar and paintings by Johann Caspar Sing well worth seeing

Map: Euro Cart regional map 1:300,000, RV-Verlag, sheet 12 Bavaria

Almost there – nearly at the top of the Riedberg Pass, at 1420m the highest pass road in Germany.

The magnificent scenery of the Allgäuer Alps, through which the Riedberg pass takes us, would be worth the journey on its own. What's more, at a height of 1420m, it's considered to be the highest pass in Germany, which should provide an additional incentive. To avoid any disgruntled emails, the Roßfeld mountain ring road in the Berchtesgaden Alps (Tour 1) may be higher at 1540m, but it isn't a pass that connects two valleys over a saddle, just a scenic road leading back to the starting point.

The ride offers almost exactly the same total vertical climb whichever side you set out from: 659m on the east side and 666m on the west. But the western approach, at 20.5km as opposed to 8.5km from the east side, is considerably longer and thus more varied.

Western side

We start in Hittisau (0.0km), on a road that climbs at a rather leisurely 8 per cent, which once past the turning to Sibratsgfäll (3.5km) becomes an easy descent. Cross the Bolgenach (4.5km) and ride into the Balderschwang valley. Short ascents of up to 6 per cent alternate with flatter and even level sections, making for swift progress. A bridge (8.5km) marks the border between Germany and Austria; from here the road climbs to the former customs post at Schönhalden (10.0km). Past Balderschwang (12km) it hardly ascends at all until it reaches the head of the valley (16.0km). Here a low gear is needed: the route profile is almost like a flight of stairs, with gradients of between 12 per cent and 16 per cent, some of them 600m long, running all the way to the top of the pass (20.5km).

Eastern side

To conquer German's highest pass from the east, start in the town of Fischen in the Iller valley. Following the signpost Balderschwang/Riedbergpass, cross the broad valley floor on a flat road and enjoy beautiful views of the mountain scenery of the Allgäu Alps. You'll quickly reach Obermaiselstein (2.0km), where leaving the village and entering the Schönberger Ache valley is rather difficult because of a dimly lit 50m tunnel. A difficulty of another kind awaits after a further 2km at a gradient of 8 per cent. A road sign marked 16 per cent (4.0km) gives a clue, but even without this confirmation there would be little doubt in your mind about said difficulty from the amount of effort required from now on. This steep section goes on for almost 700m, then the climb flattens out, but only temporarily before returning to gradients of between 14 per cent and 16 per cent. A small bridge (6.0km) provides another brief flat section, and as the route progresses, short climbs of up to 12 per cent alternate with longer, flatter stretches. The valley is narrow, with no views, but you would hardly enjoy them since once again a 500m section with a gradient of 16 per cent requires your complete concentration and maximum effort. Once you've negotiated this the top of the pass is only 1.5km away, but it's a difficult 1.5km: climbs of up to 12 per cent allow hardly any rest. Then the route is finally over and a sign announcing 'Riedbergpass' announces the end of your battle.

The pride of having overcome the highest pass in Germany is some consolation for the rather limited view, but further to the east you can admire the Nebelhorn, while the immediate area is dominated by the rugged mountain crest of the Besler and the plateau-like Gottesackerwände.

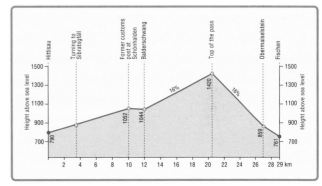

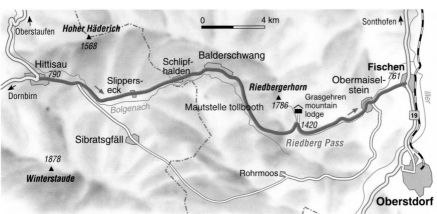

11

ALPINE PASSES IN AUSTRIA

Like all the other passes, the Turracher-Höhenstraße has two sides. But in this case there's not just a northern and a southern side, but a fairly difficult and a more difficult side, or to be more precise, a very difficult side. The northern approach winds its way over almost 20km from the upper Mur valley near Predlitz to the top of the pass, climbing some 840m en route. Gradients reach 12 per cent, but most are well under, so progress isn't too difficult.

It's an entirely different story on the southern side. Here the top of the pass is reached from Patergassen in the Gurk valley over 13km of road – and an epic climb. The gradient reaches a maximum of 23 per cent, and not just for a few metres, but, over several sections, as much as 2km.

Southern side

If you're driven to conquer this magnificent climb, you'll be glad to hear that the first stretch, from Patergassen (0.0km) to Ebene Reichenau (5.5km), is flat – use it as a warm-up to prepare your muscles for the rigours ahead. The 200m climb at up to 12 per cent that starts as you leave the village past the Nockalm–Höhenstraße junction (7.0km), shouldn't give you too much to worry about. But the following section will. You cross a little bridge, popularly known as Devil's Bridge – and if the name makes you fear the worst, you won't be too far wrong. The 23 per cent gradient that starts here can only be described as hellish, and the ensuing kilometres will give you plenty of opportunity to atone for all your sins, particularly

TOUR PROFILE <<

Turracher Mountain Road: 1763m

SOUTHERN SIDE – Start: Patergassen, 1020m

Directions: A10 Salzburg–Villach (Tauern Autobahn), exit Spittal/Millstätter See – Seeboden – Millstatt – Radenthein – Bad Kleinkirchheim – Patergassen

Level of Difficulty/Maximum gradient: Very difficult, with a maximum gradient of 23 per cent on three sections of 1km, 500m and 700m

Length: 13.0km

Total ascent: 745m

Time: 1–1¾ hrs

Suggested gearing: 39/29 or a triple chainring

Route: Patergassen (0.0km) – Ebene Reichenau (5.5km) – turning to Nockalm-Höhenstraße (7.0km) – top of the pass (13.0km)

NORTHERN SIDE – Start: Predlitz an der Mur, 927m

Directions: A10 Salzburg-Villach (Tauern Autobahn), exit St Michael im Lundgau – Mauterndorf – Ramingstein – Predlitz

Level of Difficulty/Maximum gradient: Medium, with a maximum gradient of 12 per cent for 4.5km after you leave Turrach

Length: 19.5km

Total ascent: 840m

Time: 2–2½ hrs

Suggested gearing: 39/26

Route: Predlitz (0.0km) – Turrach (13.5km) – Gasthof Badwirt (18.0km) – top of the pass (19.5km)

Road conditions: Well-constructed roads

Pass open: All year

Map: Euro Cart regional map 1:300,000, RV-Verlag, Austria sheet

if they include doing too little training or carrying too much weight.

A 300m stretch of almost flat road will seem like paradise, but the respite is short-lived. The 600m climb that follows may be only 18 per cent, even 'flattening' to a relatively merciful 10 per cent, but then you're up against another hard 500m section at 23 per cent, and even when that's out of the way there's one more 700m stretch with a gradient of 23 per cent waiting, which really separates the wheat from the chaff. You reach the only hairpin bend (12.5km) on this side of the climb, finally the gradient decreases a little and then you're soon at the highest point(13.0km), and you're finished – literally.

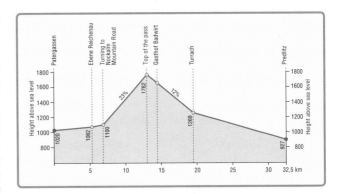

Northern side

Compared with the southern side the northern approach is a walk in the park. A 100m unlit tunnel leads from Predlitz in the Mur valley (0.0km) into the Turrach valley, also known as the

Predlitzwinkel. Follow the course of the stream as it climbs gently. A short stretch at 8 per cent after 6.5km is the only uphill worth noting until the gradient increases to 12 per cent after Turrach. At Gasthof Badwirt (18.0km) you reach the first of two hairpin bends. Once you've conquered these the gradient decreases to 10 per cent and you reach the Sporthotel Turracher Höhe, where a sign marks the top of the pass (19.5km). A few metres further on and the tour ends at the attractive recreation area around the Turracher Lake.

Tip: Climbs of comparable difficulty to the southern approach are rare. For more, see Tour 1 (between Berchtesgaden to Obersalzberg), Tour 30 (the Nigerpass road in the Dolomites) and Tour 71 (the Kiental with Griesalp Mountain Road in Switzerland).

On the northern side the Turracher Mountain Road appears moderate, but be careful, with its maximum incline of 23 per cent the southern side ranks as one of the steepest Alpine passes of all.

7 NOCKALM MOUNTAIN ROAD
Carinthia

TOUR PROFILE <<

Nockalm Mountain Road: 2040m

SOUTHERN SIDE – Start: Patergassen, 1020m

Directions: A10 Salzburg–Villach (Tauern Autobahn), exit Spittal/ Millstätter See – Seeboden – Millstatt – Radenthein – Bad Kleinkirchheim – Patergassen

Level of Difficulty/Maximum gradient: Difficult, with a maximum gradient of 12 per cent over long sections

Length: 32.5km

Total ascent: 1515m

Time: 2¼–3½ hrs

Suggested gearing: 39/26

Route: Patergassen (0.0km) – Ebene Reichenau (5.5km) – turning to Nockalm Mountain Road/Turracher mountain (7.5km) – tollbooth (10.5km) – Schiestelscharte (19.5km) – Sackl car park (26.5km) – Karlbad (29.0km) – Eisentalhöhe (32.5km)

NORTHERN SIDE – Start: Kremsbrücke, 952m

Directions: A10 Salzburg–Villach (Tauern Autobahn), exit Rennweg– Kremsbrücke

Level of Difficulty/Maximum gradient: Medium, with a maximum gradient of 12 per cent over long sections

Length: 18.0km

Total ascent: 1090m

Time: 1¾–2½ hrs

Suggested gearing: 39/26

Route: Kremsbrücke (0.0km) – Innerkrems (9.5km) – Gasthof Zechneralm (15.5km) – Eisentalhöhe (18.0km)

Road conditions: Between Kremsbrücke and Innerkrems the road is at times narrow with lots of bends. Otherwise, well-constructed roads

Pass open: Late spring to 31 October

Map: Euro Cart regional map 1:300,000, RV-Verlag, Austria sheet

North of the Millstätter See stretches an extremely attractive highland landscape known as the Nockberge, whose characteristic humpback hills are among Carinthia's most beautiful scenery, and are protected by the national park. A 41km panoramic road that winds its way from Patergassen to Innerkrems with a vertical gain of 1500m and gradients of up to 12 per cent provides access.

From Patergassen (0.0km) the road runs almost flat along the green Gurk valley floor as far as Ebene Reichenau (5.5km) before a short 12 per cent climb up to Winkl (7.5km), where our uphill route takes us left (the road straight ahead is the Turracher Mountain Road, Tour 6).

The 12 per cent gradient in the Winkelbach valley soon decreases and as far as the tollbooth (10.5km) short climbs of up to 10 per cent alternate with longer, flatter sections. A group of hairpin bends with a gradient of 8 per cent passes quickly (12.0km), then the road gets tougher as it climbs on up at 12 per cent and hardly falls below 10 per cent until you reach Schiestelscharte (19.5km). Then there's a long descent at 12 per cent down to the Grundl valley, where after crossing the Stangbach (26.5km) the road suddenly turns uphill again, at 10 per cent. Karlbad (29.0km) is home to the last mineral spa in Carinthia, where warm water heated by stones is carried by wooden channels into wooden troughs, just as it has been for hundreds of years.

The climb (gradients of up to 12 per cent) finishes at the Eisentalhöhe (32.5km), the highest point of the ride, from which the road descends via many hairpins at 12 per cent to the Gasthof Zechneralm (35.0km). The toll road ends in Innerkrems (41.0km) where it goes downwards for just under 10km to Kremsbrücke in the Lieser valley.

The Nockalm Mountain Road leads through an attractive highland landscape, but requires a great deal of effort given the maximum inclines of 12 per cent.

The gradient doesn't increase (to 6 per cent) until you reach Dellach (79.5km), where you'll need to change down.

The hamlet of Krems on the Northern side.

From here to Radenthein (88.5km) gradients of up to 8 per cent alternate with similar descents, then the slope gets noticeably steeper through the village of St Peter (92.5km), with a 2km long 10 per cent section. The climb continues at gradients of between 8 per cent and 10 per cent to Bad Kleinkirchheim (95.5km), and then you've reached the last climb of the day and can zip down the last 8km to Patergassen (103.5km).

You can return to Patergassen the way you came, which means another 41km with a vertical climb of 1052m, or via Krems, Gmünd, Seeboden, Millstatt and Bad Kleinkirchheim, first along the Lieser valley and then beside the Millstätter See. At 60km this route is much longer, but has a climb of only 370m.

Start by following the meandering, sometimes narrow (barely two-lane) road along the Kremsbach downhill to Kremsbrücke (50.5km) and then a gently descending road and the rather narrow and dark Lieser valley towards Gmünd (60.0km). This medieval-style little town is the site of a Porsche museum where you can marvel at one of the most beautiful cars ever built, from its early development through to the present day. Gmünd is also the starting point for the Malta Alpine Road, which leads into the heart of the glaciated Ankogel mountains. It climbs for just under 29km with a total vertical ascent of 1190m and is described in Tour 8.

A few climbs are in store on the return to Patergassen, too, but not straight away. The road through Seeboden (73.5km) and along the Millstätter See to Millstatt (76.5km) is almost flat, and you can confidently push the large chainring.

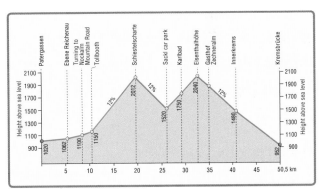

8 MALTA ALPINE ROAD
Carinthia

TOUR PROFILE <<

Malta Alpine Road: 1920m

Start: Gmünd, 730m, about 10km north of Spittal an der Drau

Directions: A10 Salzburg–Villach (Tauern Autobahn), exit Gmünd/Maltatal

Level of Difficulty/Maximum gradient: Medium, with a maximum gradient of 13 per cent over two short sections and two sections almost 1.5km long

Length: 28.5km

Total ascent: 1190m

Time: 2¼–3½ hrs

Suggested gearing: 39/28

Route: Gmünd (0.0km) – Malta (5.5km) – Koschach (10.5km) – Falleralm tollbooth (14.5km) – Gmünder Brücke restaurant (19.5km) – Gasthof Almrausch (24.5km) – Sporthotel Maltatal (28.5km)

Road conditions: Well-constructed roads

Pass open: 1 June to 31 October

Things to see: Gmünd: Porsche Museum, medieval buildings

Map: Euro Cart regional map 1:300,000, RV-Verlag, Austria sheet

Notes: Lights are necessary for the tunnel

In addition to the Nockalm Mountain Road (Tour 7) and the Turracher Mountain Road (Tour 6) the region around the Millstätter See offers a third opportunity to indulge a passion for cycling in the mountains. This is the little-known Malta Alpine Road, outside the borders of Carinthia, which leads up to the Ankogel mountains from Gmünd, north of the Millstätter See. It offers an attractive alternative to the two preceding tours, since it's scenically completely different – in contrast to the green summits of the Nockberg it leads into the heart of the glaciated alpine region. With a total climb of almost 1200m over a route of 28.5km it's also a little easier than the Nockalm Mountain Road – and anyway the 23 per cent gradient of the southern side of the Turracher Mountain Road isn't everybody's cup of tea. The catch is that several tunnels, some of which are one-way, aren't necessarily what you want when you're on a bike. Nevertheless, you can tackle them with decent lights.

Our starting point of Gmünd (0.0km), lying in the Lieser valley, was also known as Rothenburg in Carinthia because of its medieval buildings. The town walls defied the invading Turks. However, the classic cars on show in collector Helmut Pfeifhofer's Porsche museum are of a somewhat later date.

After all that sightseeing, leave the town in a northwesterly direction, following the Malta valley. For the first few kilometres to Malta (5.5km) and Koschach (10.5km) the road is more or less level along the wide valley floor, bar a few easy climbs and descents. The enormous Fallbach waterfall, which roars down over the mighty

The Kolbrein reservoir at the end of the Malta Alpine Road lies deep in the mountains of the Ankogel group.

rock face into the Malta river near Koschach, gives a foretaste of the primordial landscape that awaits.

We have to pay for our enjoyment of the scenery with hard work after the Falleralm tollbooth (14.5km), where the road suddenly goes up a gradient of 13 per cent. This climb lasts for 1.5km, then a long, almost level section, interrupted by short uphills of up to 10 per cent, allows us to progress in a more relaxed manner. Soon we reach the Gmünder Brücke restaurant (19.5km) – but also a climb of 11 per cent and a 527m unlit tunnel through rock. The stretch of hairpin bends that follows, with a gradient of 13 per cent, is one-way, with the direction of flow controlled by traffic lights (it's not a good idea to jump them). Unfortunately over the next 1.5km three more unlit tunnels await us, the longest at least 300m long, no more as pleasant to go through against oncoming traffic than the first one.

This stretch leads to a little high valley (23.5km), which you cross on an almost level road to the Gasthof Almrausch (24.5km). As you can see on this route there is no lack of tunnels and quite a few sections for one-way traffic. After the hotel the gradient increases to 10 per cent, with the exception of one flatter section, and rock faces loom threateningly. The road is protected from them by a short avalanche gallery, but this is followed by a rather unpleasant 348m unlit tunnel (26.5km). Once you've negotiated this another section with a gradient of 13 per cent awaits over two wide hairpin bends, after this you are faced with another set of traffic lights (27.5km). These control entry into the 345m tunnel at the summit, which really is the last obstacle on the ascent. The 10 per cent downhill that follows over the last few kilometres

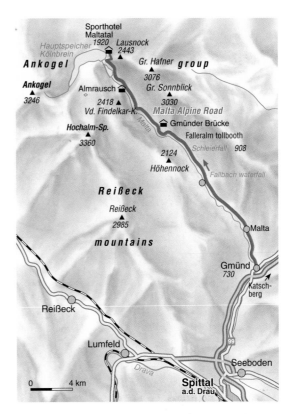

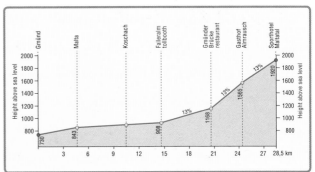

to the Sporthotel Malta are then quickly dealt with.

The tour ends in the mountain restaurant at the edge of the Kölbrein dam, the biggest in Austria, with a view over the deep-blue Kölbrein Lake, in which the glaciers of the Ankogels are reflected.

9 GROßGLOCKNER HIGH ALPINE ROAD

Salzburg province/Carinthia

TOUR PROFILE <<

Großglockner High Alpine Road:
2505m

NORTHERN SIDE – Start: Bruck an der Glocknerstraße, 757 m

Directions: A8 Munich–Salzburg, exit Traunstein/Siegsdorf – Inzell – Unken – Lofer – Saalfelden – Zell am See – Bruck an der Glocknerstraße or A10 Salzburg–Villach (Tauern Autobahn), exit Werfen or Bischofshofen – St Johann im Pongau – Schwarzach – Lend – Bruck an der Glocknerstraße

Level of Difficulty/Maximum gradient: Difficult, with a maximum gradient of 12 per cent for about 12.5km from the Ferleiten tollbooth to Fuscher Törl. Detour to Edelweißspitze, 14 per cent maximum gradient for about 1.5km. Detour to Franz-Josephs-Höhe, 12 per cent maximum gradient on short sections

Length: The route from Bruck to the Hochtor tunnel is 33.5km. The detour from Fuscher Törl to Edelweißspitze is 2km for the ascent. The detour over the glacier road from the turning at Guttal to the Franz-Josephs-Höhe, 8.5km for the ascent

Total ascent: Bruck to Hochtor 1885m; detour from Fuscher Törl to Edelweißspitze 170m; detour from the turning at Guttal to Franz-Josephs-Höhe 510m

Time: Bruck to Hochtor 3¼–5 hrs; Fuscher Törl to Edelweißspitze ¼–½ hr; turning at Guttal to Franz-Josephs-Höhe ¾–1½ hrs

Suggested gearing: 39/28

Route: Bruck (0.0km) – Fusch (7.5km) – Ferleiten tollbooth (14.5km) – Piffalpe (17km) – turning to Edelweißspitze (27.0km) – detour to Edelweißspitze and back 4km – Fuscher Törl (27.5km) – Fuscher Lacke (29.0km) – Hochtor tunnel (33.5km) – descent to turning for Guttal 6.5km

Near the Fuscher Törl at a height of 2405 m.

Tourist brochures call the Großglocker-Hochalpenstrasse the dream road of the eastern Alps. A description which, considering its wealth of variety and the jawdropping scenery of the High Tauern through which it runs, doesn't seem particularly exaggerated. It certainly counts as one of the most beautiful alpine passes, but for anyone who intends to tackle it on a bike it's also one of the most difficult.

Strictly speaking there are actually three high roads between Bruck in the north and Heiligenblut in the south, because in addition to the actual pass over the Hochtor there are two spur roads: the Edelweißstraße, which is about 2km long and climbs from just below the Fuscher Törl to the 2571m Edelweißspitze, the

highest point of the route, and the glacier road up to the 2370m Franz-Josephs-Höhe. This ends right at the foot of the Großglockner with the rugged ice floe of the Pasterze glacier and forms the most imposing point on the Glocknerstraße.

The climb starts in Bruck (0.0km), first along level roads and for the opening few kilometres you can even use a cycle path on the left-hand side of the road. The gradient doesn't increase until after Fusch (7.5km), by the Embach chapel, when it goes up to 10 per cent and stays there until the Ferleiten tollbooth (14.5km). The pyramid-shaped tip of the glacier of the Großes Wiesbachhorn to the west is impressive, as is the gradient, which increases here to 12 per cent and, as might be expected, hardly decreases over the next 12.5km from Törlgrat to Fuscher Törl (27km). Past the Schleier waterfall and the Hochmais services the route spirals up to the Hexenküche (witches' cauldron) rockfall area. During construction work here in 1977 17th-century chains and neck irons from prisoners brought here as slaves from Venice were found. We, on the other hand, put ourselves through a great deal of torment voluntarily, the best-trained of us with a 23-tooth sprocket and most of us with a 26-tooth mountain set-up, but even a 28-tooth one is no shame here.

At Törlgrat the gradient finally lets up – unless, that is, you want to add in the 2km up to Edelweißspitze, which feature six cobbled hairpin bends with a gradient of 14 per cent. If you don't fancy this then just after the turning you'll come to the Fuscher Törl (27.5km), with its stone memorial to the lives lost during the building of the road. From here you go down to Fuscher Lacke (29.0km) before climbing again up gradients of between 8 per cent and 10 per cent through the 117m Mittertörl tunnel (30.5km) to the

north entrance of the 311m Hochtor tunnel (3.5km). At a height of 2504m, this is the top of the pass, but, the glacier road to Franz-Josephs-Höhe awaits. There's a

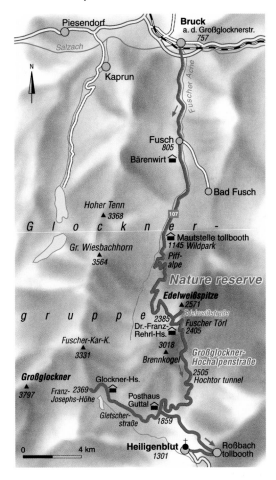

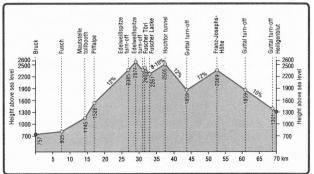

TOUR PROFILE <<

SOUTHERN SIDE – Start: Heiligenblut, 1301m

Directions: A10 Villach–Salzburg (Tauern Autobahn), exit Spittal/Millstätter See – Möllbrücke – Obervellach – Außerfragant – Winklern – Mörtschach – Döllach – Heiligenblut or from the Puster valley through Brunico – Dobbiaco – Sillian – Lienz – Winklern – Mörtschach – Döllach – Heiligenblut

Level of Difficulty/Maximum gradient: Medium, with a maximum gradient of 10 per cent over long sections. On the detour to Franz-Josephs-Höhe there is a short section with a maximum gradient of 12 per cent

Length: 15.0km

Total ascent: 1205m

Time: 1¾–2½ hrs

Suggested gearing: 39/26

Route: Heiligenblut (0.0km) – Roßbach tollbooth (1.5km) – turning to Guttal (8.5km) – (detour to Franz-Josephs-Höhe) – Hochtor tunnel (15.0km)

Road conditions: Well-constructed roads. On the climb to the Edelweißspitze there are some cobbled hairpin bends

Pass open: 1 May to 1 November. Climb to Edelweißspitze and Franz-Josephs-Höhe, 15 May to 1 November

Things to see: Ferleiten tollbooth: wildlife park; Edelweißspitze: panoramic views; Franz-Josephs-Höhe: view of the Glockner, descent by funicular railway to Pasterze glacier; Heiligenblut: parish church of St Vinzenz

Map: Euro Cart regional map 1:300,000, RV-Verlag, Austria sheet

Notes: On the climb over the northern side lights are advisable because of the 117m Mittertor tunnel and 311m Hochtor tunnel

Opposite: A breathtaking view from the Edelweißspitze to the Fuscher Törl and the hairpin bends of the Großglockner High Alpine Road.

A breathtaking view from the Edelweißspitze to the Fuscher Törl and the hairpin bends of the Großglockner High Alpine Road.

6.5km ride down to the turning to Guttal (40.0km), where the climb to the glacier road begins. It's 8.5km long and climbs 510m at up to 12 per cent (but is mostly well below that). At the end of the road the Großglockner rises in front of you, almost within reach. There's a large car park for the funicular railway that could take you the 200m or so down to the bottom of the Pasterze glacier, the biggest ice floe in the eastern Alps. Since you're probably not properly equipped for this it's better to ride back down to Guttal and end the tour with a further 8.5km descent with gradients of up to 10 per cent to the parish of Heiligenblut, the southern end of the Glocknerstraße.

Heiligenblut's parish church, St Vinzenz, with its impressive, towering Gothic steeple visible for miles around, is one of the landmarks on the Glocknerstraße. It's also notable for a small phial, which according to legend contains the blood of Christ. It's placed next to the high altar, which at 11m high demonstrates imposing dimensions even by church standards.

TOUR PROFILE <<

Kitzbüheler Horn: 1966m

Start: Turning from the B161 shortly after leaving Kitzbühel in the direction of St Johann, 763m

Directions: A93 Munich–Kufstein and A12 (Inn Valley Autobahn), exit Kufstein Süd – Scheffau – Elmau – Going – Kitzbühel

Level of Difficulty/Maximum gradient: Medium at first, with a maximum gradient of 16 per cent on the climb to the Kitzbüheler Horn alpine lodge. Further on, the road to the lodge at the summit is difficult, with a continuous gradient of almost 14-16 per cent and two short 18 per cent sections in the last 2.5km

Length: 8.5 or 11km

Total ascent: 901m or 1205m

Time: 1½–2½ hrs

Suggested gearing: 39/29

Route: Kitzbühel (0.0km) – tollbooth (3.0km) – Obernaualm (5.0km) – Kitzbüheler Horn alpine lodge (8.5km) – lodge at the summit (11.0km)

Road conditions: Well-constructed roads on the climb to the Kitzbüheler Horn alpine lodge. Paths up to the lodge at the summit are narrow with some surface damage

Pass open: All year

Map: Euro Cart regional map 1:300,000, RV-Verlag, Austria sheet

The resort of Kitzbühel in the Austrian Tyrol is already very well-known already to tourists. But how did it come by that fame? There are many contributing factors - the beautiful location in the wooded foothills of the Kitzbühel Alps, its picturesque old town with interesting houses and its sophisticated gastronomy. However, the main reason is something else entirely - the downhill ski race known as the Streif that takes place annually, from 1665m up the Hahnenkamm down to the town. The Streif, rightly known as one of the most difficult and dangerous ski races in the world, has gained real cult status and expanded to become an event which is unparalleled anywhere in the world.

Less well-known, on the other hand, is the Kitzbüheler Horn, lying to the north-east of the town, whose ski slopes can't compete in steepness with the Hahnenkamm. However, the Kitzbüheler Horn is much more interesting for cyclists. A toll road leads 1670m upwards to the Kitzbüheler Horn alpine lodge, and here you can follow a summit road that's closed to traffic up to the lodge at the summit with its ORF (Austrian State Broadcasting Company) transmitter. There are inclines of between 14 per cent and 16 per cent to be tackled up here, even reaching 18 per cent briefly.

To get a better look, ride from Kitzbühel in the direction of St Johann, which you reach just after you've left town. The ride proper begins just after crossing the Kitzbüheler Ache at the start of the Kitzbüheler Horn toll road (0.0km). Follow Kitzbüheler Horn signposts through a tunnel under the railway. Once you're past the last few houses at the edge of the town the gradient increases to 10 per cent. A kilometre or so further on you can make out a white stripe on the road surface which marks the start of the cycle race that takes place here, organised by the local cycling club.

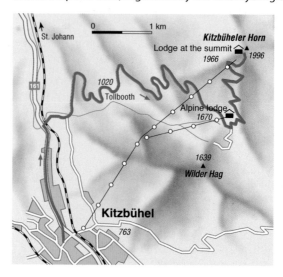

Even though the road climbs up to the Kitzbüheler Horn in wide loops, with inclines up to 16 per cent you'll be sweating hard.

In the 1980s this race was dominated by pro cyclists against whom the hobby cyclists could match themselves. Even the author took part in it a long time ago. At that time the Swiss professional Beat Breu won the race up to the alpine lodge, with a time well under 29 minutes.

So check your watch – and shift to a lower gear, for the gradient is increasing to 14 per cent. It lets up briefly just before you get to the tollbooth (3.0.km), but immediately rises to 14 per cent again. The route winds its way upwards over wide hairpin bends, with signs at the side of the road every half kilometre marking the distance from the start.

The exhausting road continues upwards, with hardly any flatter sections to speak of, just a 300m or so 8 per cent stretch after a cattle grid (4.0km) and a few metres at the Obernaualm (5.0km), and that's about it. Between 6.5km and 7.5km the gradient increases once more, up to 16 per cent, before the last 5km lead up to the Kitzbüheler Horn alpine lodge (8.5km) at an almost moderate gradient of 12 per cent. Glance at your watch again and don't be shocked when you compare your time

with that of Beat Breu, even the author took a lot longer.

The hard graft isn't over yet. The summit road begins by a gate (8.5km) and takes off at a 16 per cent gradient for 300m between two hairpin bends (9.2km). If the slight easing to 14 per cent up to the Raintal chairlift (10.2km) isn't much of a relief, the next 400m at 10 per cent are rather more so, but you'll need the breather: the approach to the lodge at the summit (10.8km) cranks it up to 16 per cent.

If you haven't had enough yet you can follow the two short 18 per cent ramps until the entrance to the ORF transmitting station definitively puts a stop to your forward trajectory.

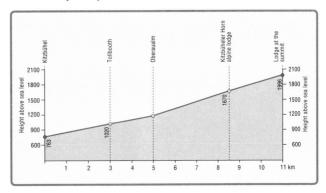

TOUR PROFILE <<

Zillertal: 2133m

NORTHERN SIDE – Start: Ried im Zillertal, 573m

Directions: A12 Kufstein–Innsbruck (Inn Valley Autobahn), exit Achensee Zillertal – Straß – Fügen – Ried im Zillertal

Level of Difficulty/Maximum gradient: Difficult, with a maximum gradient of 20 per cent over short sections plus 18 per cent over about 2km and 15 per cent over several kilometres

Length: 25.0km

Total ascent: 1870m

Time: 2¾–4 hrs

Suggested gearing: 39/29

Route: Ried (0.0km) – Tollbooth (7.0km) – Kaltenbacher ski hut (10.5km) – turning to Aschau/Zemmbach (14.0km) – Hirschbichl Alm (21.5km) – Arbiskopf Pass (25.0km)

SOUTHERN SIDE – Start: Ramsberg im Zillertal, 580m

Directions: Northern side as far as Ried im Zillertal, then further on the B169 as far as Ramsberg in Zillertal

Level of Difficulty/Maximum gradient: Difficult, with a maximum gradient of 17 per cent

Length: 14.5km

Total ascent: 1555m

Time: 2–3¼ hrs

Suggested gearing: 39/29

Route: Ramsberg (0.0km) – Arbiskopf Pass (14.5km)

Road conditions: Narrow roads, sometimes very narrow (occasional passing places). Blind bends and cattle grids (take care in the wet!). Surface damage in places

Pass open: 1 June to 31 October

Map: Euro Cart regional map 1:300,000, RV-Verlag, Austria sheet

The scenery isn't particularly spectacular, and the Zillertal mountain road is narrow, full of bends and has an incline up to 20 per cent.

The Zillertal river, which runs into the Inn valley from the Zillertal Alps and forms the boundary between the Kitzbühel Alps and the Tux Alps in the west, is one of the best known alpine valleys. Riders would really be better off avoiding this very busy valley, were it not for the panoramic Zillertal mountain road, which winds more than 2100m up the slopes of the western side of the valley between Ried and Hippach. Here's a real insider tip: it's narrow, full of bends, steep and very quiet, gradients of up to 20 per cent and a total vertical climb of 1870m also have to be tackled. So anyone who sets out on this road, in addition to being very fit, should also be equipped with a 28 or 29-tooth sprocket; a triple chainset wouldn't come amiss either.

The little village of Ried im Zillertal (0.0km), some 14km from the entry into the Ziller valley near Strass, is our starting point. The signpost to the Zillertal mountain road is easy to find and the road soon narrows to a width of perhaps 2.5 to 3m. This wouldn't be so bad if it weren't also climbing at 15 per cent and doing so for a long time, until you reach the tollbooth (7.0km) that is, where the incline increases to 18 per cent. For almost 2km you struggle on up and anyone who has ignored all the warnings and only has a 26-tooth sprocket will pay the price here.

Once you've crossed the tree line the gradient finally decreases and with the gradient at 10 per cent you can finally afford a glance at the beautiful scenery. You can take a break by the Kaltenbach ski hut (10.5km) to enjoy the view of the glaciers in the Zillertal Alps to the south which will hopefully be sparkling in the sun, the whole thing being much more fun in good weather.

Until you reach the Aschau/Zemmbach turning (14.0km) the road runs downhill and in the unlikely event that you've had enough you could comfortably cruise back down into the Ziller valley. But if you've decided to go on, then follow the mountain road in the Hippach/ Schwendberg direction. To begin with it runs along on the flat, with the silvery ribbon of the Ziller shining below; then after 18.5km it begins to climb again. The gradient now reaches 20 per cent but fortunately this is the maximum and lasts for short distances only; longer flatter sections are noticeably more common. Nevertheless, it's not easy to cope with and you'll be glad when you've reached the Hirschbichl Alm (21.5km). The rustic mountain guesthouse provides a welcome opportunity to rest, and although there's only another 3.5km to go before the end of the climb at the Arbiskopf Pass, it won't be all that easy, so a stop is recommended.

From the guesthouse the road goes downhill for a short distance before going up a 15 per cent gradient on the slopes of the Rauhenkopf to a magnificent vantage point (23.5km), from where you can see the Zillertal mountains and the main range of the Tux Alps lying before you in all their glory. But this isn't yet the ride's highest point: you still need to make one last effort to get up to the Arbiskopf Pass (25km) at a very impressive height of 2133m. Impressive, too, are the yeasty dumplings at the Atlas-Sport-Alm, and if these aren't substantial enough to replenish your lost calories, the menu will certainly offer something suitable.

It would be best not to have an alcoholic drink, because on the next downhill section towards Ramsberg total concentration will be needed. The little road is very narrow again in places, and winding, with a downhill slope of up to 17 per cent or more. You will have to brake for a vertical descent totalling 1550m down into the valley bottom and

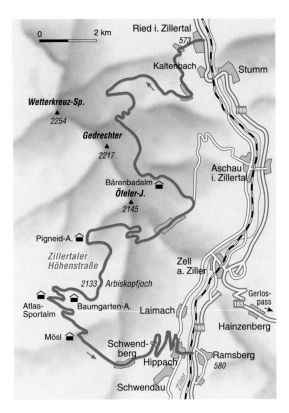

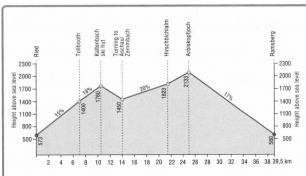

unfortunately you'll likely have to deal with short stretches of repair works all along the route.

Fortunately, once in Ramsberg (39.5km) the traffic on the B169 won't be much of a problem but it's sadly unavoidable on the return journey to the starting point of Ried (53.0km).

TOUR PROFILE <<

Kühtai Saddle: 2020m

WESTERN SIDE – Start: Oetz, 820m

Directions: A12 Innsbruck–Landeck (Inntalautobahn), exit Ötztal – Oetz

Level of Difficulty/Maximum gradient: Medium, with a maximum gradient of 16 per cent over a 1km stretch, 14 per cent over the first kilometre, however, and several shorter sections up to 12 per cent

Length: 18.5km

Total ascent: 1200m

Time: 2–3 hrs

Suggested gearing: 39/28

Route: Oetz (0.0km) – Ötzerau (3.5km) – Ochsengarten (10.0km) – Dortmunder mountain chalet (17.5km) – Top of the pass (18.5km)

EASTERN SIDE – Start: Kematen, 600m

Directions: A12 Innsbruck–Landeck (Inntalautobahn), exit Zirl/West – Kematen

Level of Difficulty/Maximum gradient: Difficult, with a maximum gradient of 16 per cent over 500m in Gries am Sellrain. But long stretches at 10 per cent

Length: 23.5km

Total ascent: 1420m

Time: 2¼–3½ hrs

Suggested gearing: 39/26

Route: Kematen (0.0km) – Gries am Sellrain (12.5km) – St Sigmund (17.0km) – Top of the pass (23.5km)

Road conditions: Well-constructed roads. However, caution is needed on the descent because the route is occasionally full of bends, with a steep slope and also several cattle grids

Pass open: All year

Map: Euro Cart regional map 1:300,000, RV-Verlag, Austria sheet

The western side of the Kühtai Saddle winds up over many bends with inclines of up to 16 per cent from the Ötz valley to the top.

The road over the Kühtai saddle connects the Ötz valley with Innsbruck, the regional capital, through the beautiful northern Stubai Alps. Kühtai was once a hunting ground for the Tyrolean princes and one of Kaiser Maximilian's favourites. Even today brutal sporting events take place in this high alpine landscape, but with bikes instead of guns. This pass is just one of four that features in the annual Ötztaler cycle marathon (the others are the Timmelsjoch [Tours 13 and 36], the Jaufenpass [Tour 35] and the Brenner). Competitors face a total vertical climb of 5,500m over 238km, so not for nothing is the Ötztaler known as one of the most difficult events of its kind.

Even the Kühtai on its own is no picnic. The climb over the western side from Oetz in the Ötz valley still presents a vertical climb of 1200m over 18.5km. The maximum gradient of 16 per cent lasts for a kilometre, and there's another kilometre section at the beginning of the tour with a slope of 14 per cent, plus several short 12 per cent climbs – so this is proper alpine riding.

In Oetz (0.0km), close to the entrance to the Ötz valley, follow the signposts for Sellrain/Kühtaiand and get stuck into the first

climb: 14 per cent in the first kilometre. The gradient then maintains a fairly even 10 per cent to 12 per cent until Ötzerau (3.5km), where it crosses an old wooden bridge into the Neder valley. Then it follows a series of hairpin bends at much the same gradient as far as Ochsengarten (10km), where the incline eases off briefly, only to shoot up again to 16 per cent for a 1km stretch. Idyllic as the high valley may be, as you ride among pines and spruces, the route remains difficult with gradients of up to 12 per cent, despite offering some flatter sections as far as the Längental reservoir. After the Dortmunder mountain chalet (17.5km) there's a last climb of 12 per cent before you reach the saddle (18.5km).

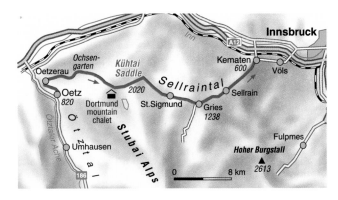

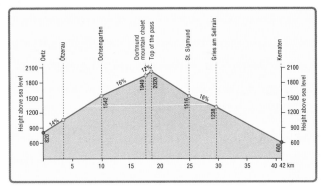

This forms part of a rather desolate high mountain region of strange charm, over which a multitude of hotel buildings is scattered. Head for the descent, where the slope is at first a moderate one you can pedal down easily. The road offers a quick view to the south to the Gaißkogel, the northern spur of the Stubai Alps, which rises to a height of 2820m.

We've arrived in the little village of Haggen, at 1646m, and now wind our way over a little valley floor via a single hairpin bend on this side of the pass to St Sigmund (25.0km), lying 100m lower down. Then comes a stunning section of the route by the side of the Zirmbach river with its still crystal-clear mountain water. Don't let yourself get distracted, because a 500m downhill stretch to Gries am Sellrain with a gradient of 16 per cent requires your full attention.

This leads to the Lüsen valley, which gives you a magnificent view to the south to the Lüsener Fernerkogel in the Stubai Alps, rising to an impressive height of 3299m with some slight glaciation. The road then rolls further downhill alongside the Melachbach, but

soon becomes so flat that you can only achieve a respectable speed by pedalling. Once you get to Kematen you'll have put 42.0km behind you and you can start to consider how to get back to the starting point of Oetz. You can either turn around and return via the same route or do as the participants at the start of the Ötztaler cycle marathon do, and go on to Innsbruck, from there going over the Brenner Pass down to Sterzing, then over the Jaufen Pass to St Leonhard in the Passeier valley and over the Timmelsjoch, now reopened to cyclists and finally back to Oetz. The fastest participants manage this in under eight hours.

If you enjoyed your taste of the Ötztaler, and would like to join the race, find more information at www.oetztaler-radmarathon.com.

13 ÖTZTAL AND TIMMELSJOCH ROAD
North Tyrol

TOUR PROFILE <<

Ötztal and Timmelsjoch Road (northern side): 2509m

NORTHERN SIDE – Start: Oetz, 820m

Directions: A12 Innsbruck-Landeck (Inntalautobahn), exit Ötztal – Oetz

Level of Difficulty/Maximum gradient: Difficult, with a maximum gradient of 12 per cent on two sections of 3km and 4km. However, there are longer sections with a gradient of 10 per cent

Length: 54.0km

Total ascent: 1815m

Time: 5–7 hrs

Suggested gearing: 39/26

Route: Oetz (0.0km) – Habichen (1.0km) – Tumpen (3.0km) – Au (14.5km) – Längenfeld (17.0km) – Aschbach (25.5km) – Sölden (29.5km) – Zweiselstein (34.5km) – Untergurgl (41.5km) – Timmelseck junction (42.5km) – Tollbooth (47.5km) – top of the pass (54.0km)

Road conditions: Well-constructed roads, apart from some narrow bridge crossings

Pass open: 15 June to 15 October. The border crossing is closed from 8pm to 7am

Map: Euro Cart regional map 1:300,000, RV-Verlag, Austria sheet

Notes: Lights are vital for the descent on the southern side of the Timmelsjoch (Tour 36)

SOUTHERN SIDE: see Tour 36

With a length of almost 50km the Ötz Valley is one of the longest side valleys in the Alps.

The Ötz valley, which runs south from the Inn valley not far from Imst and so separates the Stubai Alps in the east from the Ötztal Alps, stretches for nearly 50km and is ranked as one of the longest side valleys in the Alps. The Timmelsjoch joins the Ötz valley and leads up to the pass of the same name, which forms the border between Austria and Italy.

We begin our tour in Oetz (0.0km), which we quickly reach from the Inn valley via Ambach and speed along to Habichen (1km). We quickly deal with two hairpin bends with a gradient of 10 per cent and soon reach Tumpen (3.0km), where it's flatter again. Now and then there are gradients of up to 6 per cent, though most of them are less then that, and in places an even flatter road allows us to make very quick progress through tourist villages such as Au (14.5km), Längenfeld (17km) and Aschbach (25.5km) to Sölden (29.5km), the main town in the valley. Those for whom the journey here was too easy can consider following the Sölden glacier road, which branches off in Pltze just after Sölden. This is described in Tour 14 and takes you up to a height of 2829m, the highest point which can be reached by bike on public roads in the whole of the Alps.

Those who can do without that can go up over inclines of up to 10 per cent, but mostly less than that, to Zwieselstein (34.5km), where the gradient finally increases to a challenging 12 per cent for about 3km before dropping down a little on the approach to Untergurgl (41.5km). At the next junction you can take a short detour to Obergurgl. This village is the highest parish in Austria, and in addition to the beautiful Gothic church of St John of Nepomuk, it also boasts an impressive panoramic view of the mountains. It hit the headlines in 1931 when the aviation pioneer Professor Auguste Picard had to make an emergency landing on the nearby Gurgler Ferner in his hot-air balloon. In March 1999, Picard's grandson, Bertrand Picard, along with the Briton Brian Jones, successfully completed the first round the world flight in a hot-air ballon. We're not aiming to cycle around the world, but just to get to the top of the Timmelsjoch. The ascent begins at the junction with the road to Obergurgl, which is called Timmelseck (42.5km), and offers four hairpin bends with a gradient of 12 per cent, numbered and furnished with altitude markers. At Hochgurgl, the highest settlement inhabited all year round in the eastern Alps, we ride past the tollbooth (47.5km) and then lose height once more on the 2km downhill stretch into the Timmel valley. We have to work hard to regain this height over the next climb. At first the road goes straight up along the Timmelsbach with a gradient of 10 per cent, before a sign for Hairpin Bend 5 (51.0km) shows a height of 2262m. We now have to contend with six hairpin bends at a steady 10 per cent gradient up to the top of the pass (54.0km), which forms the only glacier-free crossing of the alpine crest between the Brenner Pass in the west and the Reschen Pass in the east.

Until recently this was the end of the ride for cyclists, but now things have changed. In 2000 the southern side was reopened to cyclists and we can now descend to St Leonhard im Passeiertal. However, lights are vital here as there are a few unlit tunnels to ride through on the upper part of the route. You should test your brakes are in good working order

because there are hairpin bends to tackle, too, and the road surface is damaged in places – go slowly. But the scenery and the route, which is described in Tour 36, are a delight.

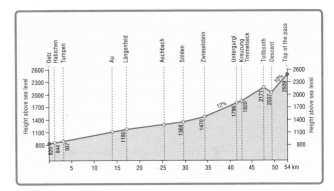

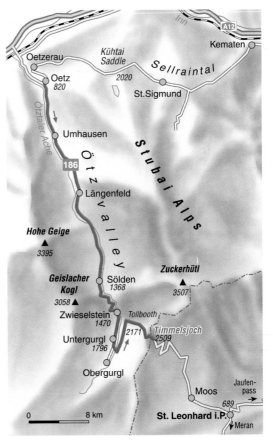

14 SÖLDEN GLACIER ROAD
North Tyrol

TOUR PROFILE <<

Sölden Glacier Road: 2829m

Start: Pitze im Ötztal, 1459m, just outside Sölden

Directions: A12 Innsbruck–Landeck (Inntalautobahn), exit Ötztal – Oetz – Umhausen – Längenfeld – Sölden – Pitze

Level of Difficulty/Maximum gradient: Difficult, with an almost continuous maximum gradient of 13 per cent

Length: 13.5km

Total ascent: 1380m

Time: 2–3 hrs

Suggested gearing: 39/28

Route: Pitze (0.0km) – Turning to Hochsölden (3.0km) – Tollbooth (6.0km) – Rettenbachferner valley station (12.0km) – Tiefenbachferner car park (13.5km)

Road conditions: Well-constructed roads, but the tunnel at the end of the route is narrow, with an uneven surface and rocks and meltwater in places

Pass open: 1 May to 31 December

Map: Euro Cart regional map 1:300,000, RV-Verlag, Austria sheet

Notes: Lights are essential for riding through the 1700m tunnel

If you want to set a new altitude record on your bike most people would tell you to look no further than the Col de Restefond/Col de la Bonette in the French Maritime Alps. At 2802m this is officially the highest publicy accessible point in the Alps reached on tarmac. However, that would be to overloook the Sölden Glacier Road. This ends at a car park in the valley station of the ski lift to the Pitztaler Jochl at a height of 2800m, just shy of the Restefond/Bonette, but about a kilometre further down, at the Rettenbachferner restaurant, you can follow the road leading up to the car park at the Tiefenbach restaurant. This ends at a height of exactly 2829m and can thus indisputably claim the title for itself. The reason for this alternative not being well-known among cyclists is that it has a 1.7km tunnel, the highest road tunnel in the Alps, at the end of the climb.

If this doesn't put you off and you want to go for the record, then follow the signposts to Gletscherstraße Tiefenbach/Rettenbachfernerin Pitze (0.0km), just after leaving Sölden, the main town in the Ötz valley. Then select an appropriately large sprocket because a gradient of 13 per cent starts immediately and doesn't let up until you get to the car park at the ski lift station to the Pitztaler Jochl, which is exactly 13km. Worth mentioning en route are the turning (3.0km) to the tourist village of Hochsölden, situated at a height of 2090m, and the tollbooth, which at 6km (just before the halfway mark) for a few metres offers the only flat stretch. Not to forget the turning at the Rettenbachferner restaurant (12.0km). That's where, at a height of 2673m, you'll find

The Sölden Glacier road leads up to a height of 2829m and is therefore the highest point in the Alps accessible to the public, at least on tarmacked roads.

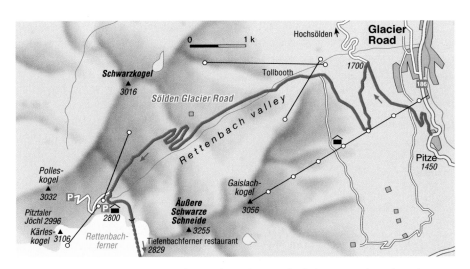

the northern entry to the Tiefenbach tunnel, which is what now separates you from the highest point, at 2829m, in the Tiefenbachferner car park.

This tunnel is 1700m long, dead straight and with a continuous gradient of 5 per cent. Inside it's roughly hewn and the road surface is uneven, in places covered in rocks. Water drips from the roof of the tunnel and meltwater running through it makes things rather unpleasant. Is this unlovely ride worth it for the prize of those last few metres of vertical climb? You decide.

After the climb, a quiet moment to oneself.

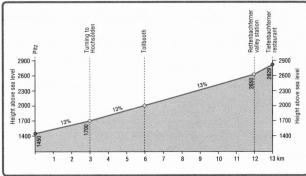

15 HAHNTENNJOCH
North Tyrol

Hahntennjoch: 1894m

WESTERN SIDE – Start: Elmen, 978m

Directions: Füssen – Reutte – Weißenbach am Lech – Stanzach – Elmen

Level of Difficulty/Maximum gradient: Medium, with a maximum gradient of 18 per cent over a 2km stretch at the beginning of the climb. 15 per cent gradient over a good kilometre just before Pfafflar

Length: 17.0km

Total ascent: 920m

Time: 1½–2½ hrs

Suggested gearing: 39/28

Route: Elmen (0.0km) – Bschlabs (7.5km) – Pfafflar (13.5km) – top of the pass (17.0km)

EASTERN SIDE – Start: Imst, 828m

Directions: A12 Innsbruck–Landeck (Inntalautobahn), exit Mils – Imst

Level of Difficulty/Maximum gradient: Medium, with a maximum gradient of 15 per cent over 800m in Imst. Longer sections with a gradient of 13 per cent

Length: 14.0km

Total ascent: 1070m

Time: 1½–2½ hrs

Suggested gearing: 39/26

Route: Imst (0.0km) – top of the pass (14.0km)

Road conditions: Well-constructed roads. However, care is needed on the descent as there are some cattle grids

Pass open: 1 May to 31 October

Map: Euro Cart regional map 1:300,000, RV-Verlag, Austria sheet

The Hahntennjoch is a thoroughly alpine connection between the upper Lech valley in the west and and the Inn valley at Imst in the east. Scenic charm is provided by the Lechtal Alps, the largest range in the eastern Alps, which is named after the river Lech, although this rises a little further to the west in the Lechquellen mountains. The two approaches are comparable both in the beauty of the landscapes they traverse and in the technical challenge they present. Where the 14km climb from the eastern side has a vertical gain of just over 1000m and gradients of up to 15 per cent, the 17km western approach has a maximum gradient of 18 per cent and a vertical climb of just under 900m.

Western side

Right at the start of the ascent at Elmen (0.0km) you come up against a gradient of 18 per cent, which lasts for the first couple of kilometres. Once you've dealt with that the most difficult part of the climb is behind you – which isn't to say that the rest of the route is a breeze, although things do ease off slightly for a while. The stretch to Bschlabs (7.5km) has an initial gradient of 10 per cent, which then decreases.

You could have a rest at the Gasthof Zur Gemütlichkeit before following the almost level road to the entrance of the Plötzig valley (9.5km). This is where the comfortable riding comes to an end, with two hairpin bends that climb at 12 per cent. Up to the turning to Hahntennjoch/Imst (11.5km) the rate of gradient decreases again, only to soar to 15 per cent on the way up to the alpine huts at

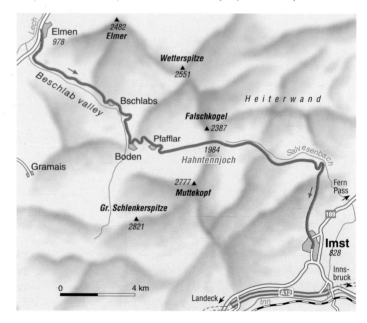

Pfafflar (13.5km). This collection of old wooden huts dates in part from the 13th century, which puts them among the oldest houses in the Tyrol. The top of the pass (17.0km), to which the road climbs up at a consistent 10 per cent, first over two hairpin bends, then along a straighter section, unfortunately offers little in the way of a view.

Eastern side

Imst (0.0km), on the sunny side of the Inn valley at the foot of the mighty Tschirgant, is the starting point for the climb up the eastern side of the Hahntennjoch. It's a pretty little town clearly enjoying a prosperity that at one time was due to the mineral deposits of the surrounding area but now is due primarily to tourism. Striking features include the beautiful old townhouses and numerous fountains that used to serve as drinking troughs for the teams of horses passing through, and which we can now use to fill our water bottles. The Gothic spire of the church of the Assumption of Our Lady is 83m high; just past it green information signs point the way to the pass. Just as on the western side you hit the maximum gradient right at the start: 15 per cent over an 800m stretch.

The first hairpin bend is reached at 1.0km, with a gradient of 10 per cent, and the second at 1.5km (8 per cent). There's a cattle grid as the road leaves the village, after which the gradient goes up to 10 per cent but soon decreases again to 8 per cent and lets us progress a little more easily.

The next hairpin brings us not only a wonderful view back to the formidable Tschirgant mountains in the east, but also an 11 per cent gradient, and after one more hairpin (5.5km) it decreases a little. We ride over a cattle grid (6.5km) into the Salvesen valley and anyone who

has saved their strength on this relatively level section has been wise because the gradient now increases to 13 per cent. The well-maintained road offers little variety in the scenery. To the north you can see the grey rock faces of the Heiterwand, but nearer at hand the view is mostly interrupted by wooden fencing at the side of the road.

The testing gradient is maintained for a good 2km before it finally decreases to 10 per cent, and then alternates with flatter sections. There's even a long near-level stretch allowing you to gather strength for a final burst of speed, or, depending on your level of fitness, just refresh your legs enough to tackle the final 10 per cent climb to the top of the pass (14.0km). You won't find a wonderful view or even anywhere to stop coming from this side, and the top is unremarkably indicated by a cattle grid and a sign saying 'Height 1894m above sea level'.

The Hahntennjoch, here the western side, is an attractive and not too busy connection between the Lech valley and the Inn valley.

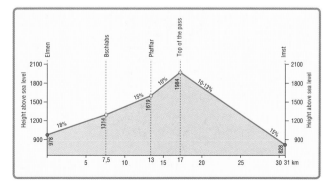

TOUR PROFILE <<

Silvretta High Alpine Road: 2032m

EASTERN SIDE – Start: Pians, 859m, about 6km west of Landeck

Directions: A12 Innsbruck–Bludenz (Inntalautobahn), exit Zams/Landeck-Ost – Landeck – Pians

Level of Difficulty/Maximum gradient: Medium, with a maximum gradient of 11 per cent over about 5km at the end of the climb

Length: 42.5km

Total ascent: 1180m

Time: 2¾–4 hrs

Suggested gearing: 39/26

Route: Pians (0.0km) – See (6.0km) – Nederle (17.0km) – Ischgl (22.5km) – Mathon (27.5km) – Galtür (32.0km) – Tollbooth (35.0km) – Top of the pass (42.5km)

The Silvretta High Alpine Road offers a panorama of attractive landscapes. It connects the North Tyrol Paznaun valley with the Montafon valley in the Vorarlberg, running between Landeck in the east and Bludenz in the west. It leads right into the heart of the heavily glaciated mountains of the Silvretta group, which reach their highest point in the Piz Buin at 3312m.

With a total vertical climb of just under 1200m on the eastern side and not quite 1500m on the western side the Silvretta doesn't rank as a difficult tour, but it rates highly from a scenic point of view and sheer enjoyability. That is to say, it's generally considered to be the second most beautiful, technically interesting and scenically diverse high mountain road in Austria, after the Großglockner High Alpine Road. To test this claim out, we'll start the tour in Pians near Landeck and end it in Bludenz, 88km away, of which just under half, 42.5km, is uphill.

In Pians (0.0km), located about 6km away of Landeck, follow the signposts for Silvrettaride into the Paznaun valley. Enjoy the gentle start: the road doesn't begin to climb noticeably until after 2.5km and reaches the village of See (6.0km) with little difficulty apart from a few short climbs with gradients of up to 8 per cent. From See to Nederle (17.0km) riders who have put in the training can ride on

The Silvretta High Alpine Road is rated the second most beautiful Alpine road in Austria after the Großglockner High Alpine Road (Tour 9).

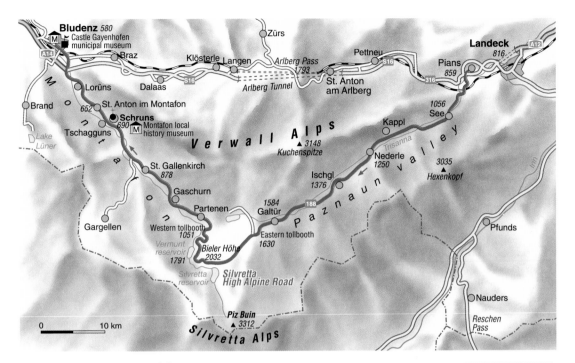

the large chainring most of the time. But from here to Ischgl (22.5km), the biggest village in the valley, the slope goes up to around 8-10 per cent, so you'll be back on the small ring.

The length of the climbs now increases, but flatter sections always allow for a change in tempo which allow us to reach Mathon (27.5km) and the village of Galtür (32.0km) relatively quickly.

If you've been wondering why we haven't described any hairpin bends, that's because there haven't been any so far on this side of the route. You can look forward to these later on. Now the landscape changes to the high mountains as you ride past the tollbooth (35.0km) and over from the Paznaun valley into the Kleinvermunt valley. Then the moderate climb becomes a little more interesting as it rises to 11 per cent after 37.0km. Almost at the end of the climb the road builders have succeeded in

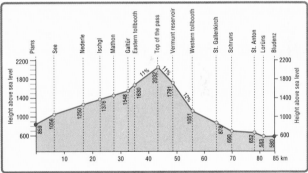

incorporating two hairpin bends as a final flourish, over which we reach the top of the pass (42.5km).

Instead of an impressive mountain panorama the top of the pass offers a view of the shimmering green Silvretta reservoir, which is fed by glacier water. This is the highest reservoir in Austria and if you like, you can swap your bike for water transport, because in season you can take a trip on an impressively large pleasure boat.

TOUR PROFILE <<

WESTERN SIDE – Start: Bludenz, 580m

Directions: A12 Innsbruck–Bludenz (Inntalautobahn), exit Bludenz/Montafon

Level of Difficulty/Maximum gradient: Medium, with a maximum gradient of 12 per cent

Length: 45.0km

Total ascent: 1455m

Time: 2¾–4 hrs

Suggested gearing: 39/26

Route: Bludenz (0.0km) – Lorüns (1.5km) – St Anton im Montafon (4.5km) – Schruns/Tschagguns (12.5km) – St Gallenkirch (18.5km) – Western tollbooth (29.0km) – Vermunt reservoir (33.5km) – Top of the pass (42.5km)

Road conditions: Well-constructed roads

Pass open: 1 June to 15 November

Things to see: Bludenz: historic old town with a town museum, Gayenhofen Castle; Schruns: beautiful townscape with Montafon farmhouses, Montafon local history museum, parish church of St Laurentius.

Map: Euro Cart regional map 1:300,000, RV-Verlag, Austria sheet

At the start of the descent you cross not only the state boundary between the Tyrol and Vorarlberg, but also the watershed between the Danube and the Rhine rivers, and in addition to that the linguistic border between the Alemannic and Tyrolean dialects.

The ascent may not have had many hairpin bends, but there's no shortage of them on the way down. Straight off, there are five of them in quick succession, with a slope of 11 per cent , taking you down to the Vermunt reservoir (48.0km), which is fed by the glaciers of the Litzner-Seehorn range, of which the Gross Seehorn is the highest peak at 3121m.

You then plunge down the side of the valley over 25 – yes, 25 – hairpin bends with gradients of up to 12 per cent and into the Montafon valley, which means that in a very short time you've descended no less than 800m. After that it's almost a surprise to have to pedal again, once you've passed the western tollbooth (56.5km). Just for a while after St Gallenkirch (67km) the road drops down a little more steeply and all the way to the twin towns of Schruns and Tschagguns (73km). Here it levels off and requires stamina again, something that writer Ernest Hemingway also needed when he spent the winter of 1925/1926 here in the renowned Hotel Traube and went skiing in the surrounding Verwall Alps and the Rätikon.

For an insight into the history and culture of the valley, pay a visit to the Montafon local history museum on the Kirchplatz in Schruns, before having to deal with an easy short climb at St Anton (81.0km). Then, after Lorüns (84.0km), the outskirts of Bludenz (85.5km) are quickly reached.

You can take a boat trip on the Silvretta reservoir at the top of the pass on the Silvretta High Alpine Road.

Opposite: There are 25 hairpin bends here on the western side of the Silvretta High Alpine Road down into the Montafon valley.

ALPINE PASSES
IN SLOVENIA

17 PREDIL PASS
Friuli/Slovenia

TOUR PROFILE <<

Predil Pass: 1156m

NORTHERN SIDE – Start: Tarvísio, 751m

Directions: A2 Klagenfurt–Villach, exit Tarvísio–North

Level of Difficulty/Maximum gradient: Easy, with a maximum gradient of 10 per cent

Length: 15.0km

Total ascent: 405m

Time: 1–1½ hrs

Suggested gearing: 39/26

Route: Tarvísio (0.0km) – Cave del Predil (10.0km) – Top of the pass (15.0km)

SOUTHERN SIDE – Start: Bovec, 483m

Directions: A23 Udine–Villach, exit Udine – Cividale del Friuli – Matajur – Kobarid – Trnovo ob Soci – Zaga – Bovec

Level of Difficulty/Maximum gradient: Easy to medium tour with a maximum gradient of 12 per cent

Length: 17.0km

Total ascent: 715m

Time: 1¼–2 hrs

Suggested gearing: 39/26

Route: Bovec (0.0km) – Turning (1.5km) – Log pod Mangartom (10.0km) – Top of the pass (17.0km)

Road conditions: Slight surface damage

Pass open: All year

Things to see: Old fort from the First World War just outside Bovec

Map: Euro Cart regional map 1:300,000, RV-Verlag, Slovenia sheet

Notes: Lights are advisable for the hairpin bends through tunnels on the northern side

This ruined fort keeps watch over the climb over the southern side of the Predil Pass.

In the Julian Alps, the independent Republic of Slovenia has its own small but very attractive corner of the Alps. The most beautiful and unspoiled part, the region around the 2864m Trigla, has even been designated a national park. Of course there are pass roads here too, and one of them is the Predil Pass, which leads us up to this region from the meeting point of three countries – Austria, Italy and Slovenia.

Our departure point is the lively little town of Tarvísio (0.0km), in the Italian region of Friuli, situated in a wide, enclosed valley surrounded by the Karnic Alps to the west, the Karawanken mountains to the east and the Julian Alps to the south. Following the signposts to Cave del Predil we leave the town and are soon relieved to find that once we enter the Slizza valley the noise and traffic of the little border town have been left behind. We make good progress up the moderately climbing road, and a hairpin bend (7.0km) with a 10 per cent gradient only slows us down for a

little while before the gradient drops again up to Cave del Predil (10.0km). The village used to be called Raibl, taking the name from the 14th-century Raibl family who lived there, just as nearby Lake Raibl did, which has preserved its original name.

A short 10 per cent gradient out of Cave del Predil becomes a gentle downhill slope and after a 180m hairpin tunnel Lake Raibl lies in front of us. It's at its most beautiful in late summer or autumn when the shallows gleam turquoise-green and the deep waters are inky-blue, with beeches and sycamores dotted among the pine forests that cling to the limestone cliffs. Its awesome beauty helps you face the unrelenting 10 per cent climb with its many bends and hairpins to the top of the pass (15.0km) and the border post.

Now you roll and can zoom down descents of up to 12 per cent, in Slovenia now, to the bottom of the Koritnica valley, surrounded by the Mangart mountain range, where the western slopes of the Jalovec and the northern slopes of the

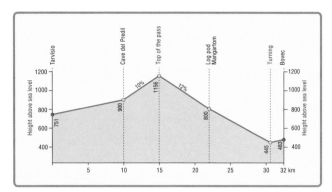

Bretterwand make one of the most beautiful heads of the valleys in the Julian Alps. After Strmec a series of hairpin bends forces you to brake, before the road runs in a straight line down to the green floor of the Koritnica valley to Log pod Mangartom. Then a 300m climb with a gradient of 10 per cent is all that separates you from the end of the pass road in Bovec.

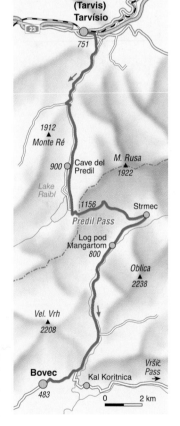

Lake Raibl on the northern side of the Predil Pass.

TOUR PROFILE <<

Vršič Pass 1611 m

SOUTHERN SIDE – Start: Bovec, 483m

Directions: A23 Udine–Villach, exit Udine – Cividale del Friuli – Matajur – Kobarid – Trnovo ob Soci – Zaga – Bovec

Level of Difficulty/Maximum gradient: Medium, with a maximum gradient of 14 per cent

Length: 32.5km

Total ascent: 1170m

Time: 2¾–4 hrs

Suggested gearing: 39/26

Route: Bovec (0.0km) – Turn-off (1.5km) – Kal Koritnica (2.5km) – Soca (10.5km) – Trenta (19.5km) – Top of the pass (32.5km)

NORTHERN SIDE – Start: Kranjska Gora, 810m

Directions: A2 Villach–Ljubljana, exit Jesenice – Mojstrana – Kranjska Gora

Level of Difficulty/Maximum gradient: Medium, with a maximum gradient of 12 per cent

Length: 11.5km

Total ascent: 805m

Time: 1¾–2½ hrs

Suggested gearing: 39/26

Route: Kranjska Gora (0.0km) – Mihovdom (6.0km) – Kocana Gozda (7.5km) – Top of the pass (11.5km)

Road conditions: Considerable surface damage in places

Pass open: 1 May to 31 October

Map: Euro Cart regional map 1:300,000, RV-Verlag, Slovenia sheet

In the Triglav National Park there are still real ibexes, but we'll hardly ever see them as we ride over the Vrsic Pass.

The Triglav National Park is an area of wild beauty with low wooded mountain ranges, open alpine pastures, clear mountain lakes and romantic valleys in which silence and solitude reign, something you seldom come across anywhere else in the alpine region. The Vršič Pass Road, running from Kal Koritnica in the south to Kranjska Gora in the north, opens up the region for us. It's close enough to the Predil Pass (Tour 17) to be ridden in conjunction with it, if you have enough stamina.

The wonderful situation of our starting point, Bovec, in the middle of a wide, enclosed valley with the Soča river flowing through it and framed by impressive mountain scenery in which the highest peak is the 2587m Kanin, gives you an idea of the glories to come. We leave the village, whose facilities we have to share with kayakers, rafters, mountaineers, mountain bikers and paragliders, and after a short ride reach the gateway to the Triglav Park at Kal Koritnica (2.5km). Over the first kilometres to Soča (10.5km), and then as far as Trenta (19.5km), the route keeps to predominantly flatter sections on the floor of the Soča valley, give or take a few short climbs. If you want to, you can stop to visit the botanical gardens, founded in 1926, near the church, or the Museum of Natural History and Ethnography in the national park information centre. The steep-sided rocks crowd onto the road and we're riding into the Trenta valley, as the upper Soča valley, an area of mountain farms and game reserves, is also known. It almost seems as though time has stood still here – but not the road, which now goes up for 1.5km over a series of hairpin bends with a gradient of 11 per cent.

At the end of the climb a descent down into the valley awaits, from which we ascend again at gradients of up to 12 per cent interspersed with flatter sections, almost like a flight of stairs. At

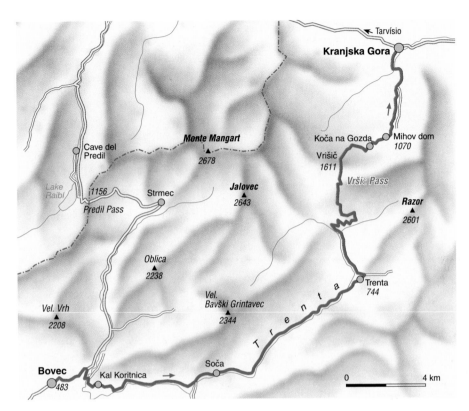

the turning to Vršič the gradient increases to 14 per cent, and for the rest of the route up to the top of the pass (32.5km) it remains at a constant 10 per cent to 14 per cent.

We cross the watershed between the Adriatic and the Black Sea, then careful riding is required on the hairpin bends, which are cobbled in places with a downhill slope of up to 14 per cent, down to Kranjska Gors, 11.5km away. This village at the foot of the Julian Alps hasn't figured much in the field of cycling up to now, but has made an impact in other kinds of sport. The winter sports enthusiasts among us are likely to remember seeing World Cup ski races in the slalom and giant slalom on TV. But even more spectacular is another kind of winter sport practised in nearby Planica (a place you'll look for in vain on the map

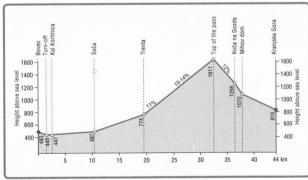

because it's a valley, not a town): ski flying. On 15 March 1936 the Austrian Sepp Bradl was the first man to jump what was at the time an apparently impossible distance of 100m when he touched down after 101m in a perfect Telemark. Today the record, set in 2003 by the Finn Matti Hautamaeki, stands at an unbelievable 231m.

45

ALPINE PASSES
IN ITALY

19 STALLER SADDLE
South Tyrol/East Tyrol

TOUR PROFILE <<

Staller Saddle: 2052m

WESTERN SIDE – Start: Niederrasen, 1005m, turning near Olang in the Puster valley, SS49, about 11km east of Brunico

Directions: Lienz – Sillian – Dobbiaco – Welsberg – Olang – Niederrasen or Brenner Autobahn, exit Bressanone/ Brixen – Mühlbach – Brunneck – Olang – Niederrasen

Level of Difficulty/Maximum gradient: Medium, with a maximum gradient of 13 per cent over about 1.5km

Length: 24.0km

Total ascent: 1050m

Time: 1¾–2½ hrs

Suggested gearing: 39/26

Route: Niederrasen (0.0km) – Overrasen (1.5km) – Antholz-Niedertal (7.0km) – Antholzer See (17.0km) – Enzian mountain lodge (18.5km) – Top of the pass (24.0km)

The Staller saddle is the shortest connection from the South Tyrol Puster valley over into the Isel valley to the Felbertauern route. It should perhaps be said that it's the shortest distance-wise, because the 52km run from Niederrasen, east of Brunneck, to Huben is a few kilometres shorter than the valley route through Lienz. But timewise, for the cyclist at least, it doesn't save anything, because from Niederrasen up to the top of the pass there's a total vertical climb of just over 1000m. If this is making you hesitate, factor in that the road leads through the wonderful and extensive untouched natural landscape of the Defregger mountains, also called the Villgratner mountains, and so gains a number of plus points when set against the heavy goods traffic that awaits you on the valley floor.

The starting point of Niederrasen lies about 11km east of Brunico. Turn onto the South Tyrol L44, which forks off from the Puster valley SS49, into the Antholzer valley. It starts off fairly wide, with mountain slopes edged with green meadows and a 10 per cent gradient up to Oberrasen (15km). Then it's completely flat over the next few kilometres to Antholz-Niedertal (7.0km) and you have the leisure to marvel at the impressive mountains of the Riesenferner range as you cruise along. But past Antholz-Mittertal and Antholz-Obertal progress becomes a little more difficult, although the 10 per cent climbs are repeatedly interspersed with flatter sections.

The relatively pleasant ascent is interrupted by a sign indicating a gradient of 13 per cent (16.0km). You'll pass the Antholzer See

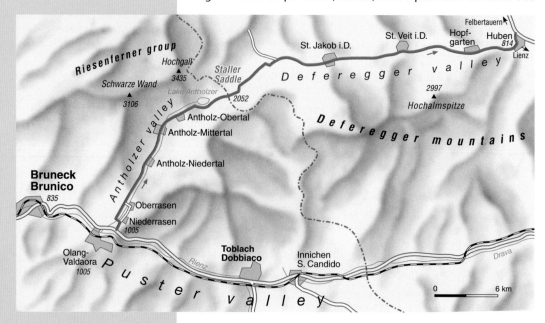

On the Western side of the Staller saddle, high over the Antholzer See at the foot of the precipitous south-eastern slopes of the Hochgall and the Wildgall.

lake, hidden away a little in tall woods next to the road, whose surrounds are used by Italians training for the biathlon, a combination of cross-country skiing and rifle shooting that was introduced in the Winter Olympics in Chamonix in 1924 as a demonstration sport by the name of 'military patrol'. On the south-eastern edge of the lake you can pick up the pace on a level stretch, but may then run into a queue of waiting cars. That's because the climb from here to the top is only possible for the 15 minutes between half past the hour and a quarter to.

The reason for this becomes clear when, past the Enzian mountain lodge (18.5km), the road narrows to a maximum width of 3m, which doesn't leave enough space for two cars to pass easily. For us it's not space that's the problem but the slope, which increases again to 13 per cent. After riding through a 50m unlit tunnel (20.0km) the gradient drops to 10 per cent for a while but rises repeatedly to up to 12 per cent over the next hairpin bends. To compensate, the view opens up back to the Antholzer See far below us, while the fissures and cirques in the precipitous south eastern slopes of the Hochgall and the Wildgall, at least 3273m and 3436m high, are snow-capped even in summer.

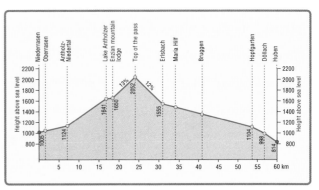

49

TOUR PROFILE <<

EASTERN SIDE – Start: Huben, 814m

Directions: A12 Rosenheim–Innsbruck (Inntalautobahn), exit Kufstein/Süd – Scheffau – Going – St Johann in Tirol – Kitzbühel – Paßthurn – Mittersill – Felbertauern Tunnel – Matrei in Osttirol – Huben

Level of Difficulty/Maximum gradient: Medium, with a maximum gradient of 12 per cent

Length: 36.0km

Total ascent: 1240m

Time: 2–3½ hrs

Suggested gearing: 39/26

Route: Huben (km 0.0) – Döllach (3.5km) – Hopfgarten (6.0km) – Bruggen (19.0km) – Maria Hilf (26.0km) – Erlsbach (29.0km) – Top of the pass (36.0km)

Road conditions: Well-constructed roads on the eastern side apart from a few narrow stretches across bridges. On the western side the narrow, single-lane road from the top of the pass to the Anholzer See has narrow hairpin bends

Pass open: 1 June to 31 October. The border is closed from 8.15pm to 5.30am

Things to see: A short detour on the eastern side towards St Veit with old farm houses and an old parish church; pilgrimage church of St Leonhard and merchant's house in St Jakob

Map: Euro Cart regional map 1:300,000, RV-Verlag, South Tyrol/Veneto sheet

Notes: The descent from the top of the pass over the west side into the Puster valley is only possible for the first 15 minutes of every hour, the climb from the Anholzer See from half past the hour to a quarter to the hour

The sign informs us that the descent from the top of the Staller saddle is limited to certain times.

Opposite: Even though the lack of hairpin bends on the eastern side of the Staller Saddle road allows for a fast style of riding, you should still concentrate.

After 21.5km a sign indicates the last four hairpin bends up to the top of the pass (24.0km), which we reach with a steady 10 per cent climb. The effort required is amply repaid. Before us stretch wonderful mountain pastures covered in spring and summer with a carpet of blue and dark red aquilegias cut through by crystal clear torrents and a small gleaming blue lake. It's a tranquil spot that invites relaxation.

But the descent is waiting for us, which throws up fewer challenges than the ascent. You still have to deal with a drop of 1240m over 28km, but the steepest downhill gradient of 12 per cent is only reached for a short distance near Maria Hilf. Apart from one or two narrow stretches where work is being undertaken to widen it, the road has two lanes throughout and a mere five hairpin bends don't much inhibit a smooth riding style.

A tip: the old wooden houses in the little villages on the upper part of the route, which are often built on extremely steep slopes and are up to five storeys high, are well worth seeing.

20 TRE CIME DI LAVAREDO
Dolomites

TOUR PROFILE <<

Tre Cime di Lavaredo: 2400m

Start: Misurina, 1756m

Directions: A22 Brenner Autobahn, exit Bressanone/Brixen – Brunico – Dobbiaco – Carbonin – Col Sant'Angelo – Misurina

Level of Difficulty/Maximum gradient: Difficult, with a maximum gradient of 16 per cent over about 3.5km

Length: 7.5km

Total ascent: 670m

Time: 1–1½ hrs

Suggested gearing: 39/28

Route: Ristorante Ginzernella, Misurina (0.0km) – Lake Antorno (1.5km) – Tollbooth (3.0km) – Auronzo mountain lodge (7.5km)

Road conditions: Well-constructed roads

Pass open: 1 June to 30 September

Things to see: Lake Misurina: an easy hike with no problems from Auronzo mountain lodge to the Pattern saddle, with a glorious view of the north face of the Tre Cime (about 15–20 minutes)

Map: Euro Cart regional map 1:300,000, RV-Verlag, South Tyrol/Veneto sheet

Notes: There's a lot of traffic on the Tre Cime di Lavaredo mountain road at weekends

The Tre Cime di Lavaredo are the best-known and most impressive mountains in the Dolomites, if not in the whole of the Alps. They owe this attraction to their distinctive shape which early on drew mountaineers from all over to try to scale their slopes. The north face in particular, steep as a wall and overhanging in places, both repelled and attracted mountaineers. The Cima Grande, with its incomparable north face, a good 500m high, smooth as glass from below and apparently impregnable, presented an irresistible challenge to the best climbers. But it wasn't until 12 August 1933 that the famous Italian alpinist Emilio Comici suceeded in conquering it with his two companions, the brothers Angelo and Giuseppe Dimai. After giving up their attempt on the first day, they tried again on the second day, 14 August 1933 and reached the summit at about 10.30am. And so the most difficult rock face in the Alps was conquered and a new frontier established.

This ride offers cyclists looking for a comparable challenge the opportunity to push back their own personal frontiers. That's because a well-constructed toll road leads up to the Tre Cime di Lavaredo to the Auronzo mountain lodge on their southern side, which can lay claim to having one of the highest grades of difficulty for a cyclist. The road doesn't exactly overhang like the north face, but with a maximum gradient of 16 per cent that lasts for a muscle-popping 3.5km it certainly gives riders the impression that it does.

You don't have to be among the best cyclists in the world to conquer this climb, but you need to have done the requisite number of training kilometres and above all have a suitable set-up, in all likelihood a triple chainset. Appropriately equipped, you can set out from Misurina, situated high above Cortina d'Ampezzo on the lake of the same name and then take in the Tre Croce Pass (Tour 21) or, if

A view that causes pain: you need to train hard for a continuous 14–16 per cent climb.

you'd rather do the climb from Dobbiaco in the Puster valley through to the Höhlenstein valley, the Col Sant'Angelo.

Our climb turns off at the northern end of the lake and is very clearly signposted Rifugio Auronzo. On fine summer days, especially at the weekend or in the tourist season, you'll be sharing the blacktop with hordes of motorists, but the traffic is a price worth paying for the awe-inspiring scenic rewards. At the Ristorante Ginzernella (0.0km) the road starts to climb at 10 per cent and keeps up this level of difficulty for the next 1.5km, easing off only when you reach little Lake Antorno. You can rest again along this dark blue, unfortunately rather silted up stretch of water and gaze at the southern side of the Tre Cime di Lavaredo, which rises up from the mass of boulders beneath as a broad, squat, craggy outcrop.

The road goes gently downhill for the next 1.5km to the tollbooth where the going immediately gets tough again. You struggle up over a series of bends on a 16 per cent gradient, which relents briefly for about 1.5km to only 10 per cent, and feels virtually flat in comparison, but the familiar 16 per cent resumes and requires every available ounce of strength you have left. The ascent continues, until after a further 1.5km the start of a stretch of hairpin bends (6.0km) signals the last part of the climb. The gradient now decreases to 14 per cent, which may seem very little in terms of numbers, but in terms of strength is really noticeable, and it only lasts for 1.5km before you reach the long-awaited finish line by the Auronzo mountain lodge (7.5km). There you find considerable hustle and bustle in the large car park at the front, but no view of the north face of the Tre Cime di Lavaredo. For that you have to factor in a walk of almost 20 minutes up to the Pattern saddle.

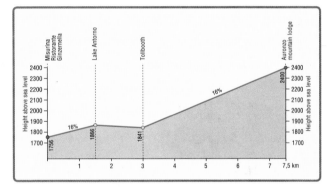

The south face of the Tre Cime di Lavaredo is reflected in the little Lake Antorno, at the lower end of the climb.

TOUR PROFILE <<

Tre Croci Pass: 1809m

WESTERN SIDE – Start: Cortina d'Ampezzo, 1210m

Directions: A22 Brenner Autobahn, exit Bressanone/Brixen – Brunico – Dobbiaco – Carbonin – Gemärkpass – Cortina d'Ampezzo

Level of Difficulty/Maximum gradient: Easy to medium tour with a maximum gradient of 11 per cent on short sections

Length: 8.0km

Total ascent: 600m

Time: 1–1½ hrs

Suggested gearing: 39/26

Route: Cortina d'Ampezzo (0.0km) – Ristorante Lago Scin (3.5km) – chairlift valley station (6.5km) – Top of the pass (8.0km)

EASTERN SIDE – Start: Misurina/Auronzo crossroads, 1509m

Directions: A22 Brenner Autobahn, exit Bressanone/Brixen – Brunico – Dobbiaco – Carbonin – Col Sant'Angelo – Misurina – Misurina/Auronzo crossroads

Level of Difficulty/Maximum gradient: Easy, with a maximum gradient of 12 per cent over short stretches

Length: 4.0km

Total ascent: 300m

Time: ½–1 hr

Suggested gearing: 39/26

Route: Misurina/Auronzo crossroads (0.0km) – Top of the pass (4.0km)

Road conditions: Damaged road surface, particularly on the eastern side.

Pass open: All year

Things to see: Cortina d'Ampezzo: parish church and bell tower, local museum with fossil and mineral collections

Map: Euro Cart regional map 1:300,000, RV-Verlag, South Tyrol/Veneto sheet

The Tre Croci Pass above Cortina d'Ampezzo takes its name from the three crosses erected in memory of a woman from Ampezzo and her two children who froze to death in a snowstorm up here in 1709. The story is a reminder of the dangers of the high mountains and, in the case of cyclists, to pack the right gear and only set out if good weather conditions are forecast. The climb runs along the southern side of the 3216m Cristallo range, one of the most impressive in the Dolomites.

We leave Cortina d'Ampezzo (0.0km) following the signposts for Misurin/Auronzo heading east on an 8 per cent slope. Just as we leave the village the gradient increases to 11 per cent and stays there as far as the Ristorante Lago Scin (3.5km) with only one short noticeable decrease. The next point of reference is the valley terminal of the chairlift to Monte Cristallo after 6.5km, with further gradients of between 9 per cent and 11 per cent en route. Soon after we cross the tree line, we approach the rocky slopes of Monte Cristallo and, looking back, have the most beautiful view of the mountains south-west of the Ampezzo valley with the snowfields of the Marmolada shining out. Then we reach the top of the pass (8.0km) and the Tre Croci Hotel over a gradient that gets no easier.

The road goes down the eastern side for 4km over roads that are bumpy in places and have a downhill slope of up to 12 per cent as far as the Misurina/Auronzo junction (12.0km). If you want you can detour up the 1.5km to Misurina (13.5km) – the 12 per cent gradient soon decreases to 8 per cent – and perhaps follow the climb over the Tre Cime di Lavaredo (Tour 20).

If you really don't want to cope with the Tre Cime's gradient of 16 per cent but don't want to retrace your steps either, there is another alternative. After the turning for Tre Cime di Lavaredo the

road rolls on over the Col Sant'Angelo (16.0km) for about 5km, dropping 300m at a maximum gradient of up to 11 per cent on its way to Carbonin (21.0km).

Above the village, which seems to be just one extended hotel complex, the massive east face of the Monte Cristallo, marked by striking couloirs and ice gullies, soars up almost menacingly. It was climbed first by the famous local mountaineer Sepp Innerkofler, who lost his life in the First World War in a night attack on an Italian mountain post on the nearby Paternkofel. The Austrian and Italian mountain troops confronted each other in grim guerrilla warfare at every gap, jagged rock and summit, sometimes in hand-to-hand combat, risking their lives in the cold, stormy weather and in danger from avalanches. This region in particular, around the Höhlenstein valley, was hotly disputed.

To return to Cortina we take the Passo di Cimabanche, as it's known in Italian. It's not, frankly, much of a pass in any language. The climbs to the foot of the 3139m Hohen Gaisl, easily recognised by its characteristic shape and red shimmering rock faces, is gentle to a fault. There are hardly any bends worth

mentioning and if it weren't for the sign bearing the legend 'Passo di Cimabanche' to alert you to the fact, you might easily ride over the top of the pass (24.5km) without realising. Only when you reach the Ospidale inn, a former hostel dating from the 13th century, are there two hairpin bends, which lead down to the floor of a little valley.

We're in the Ampezzo valley again, which soon turns south and takes us back to Cortina d'Ampezzo between the rocky bank of the Boite on the right-hand side and the long rock wall of the Pomagnonzug on the left-hand side along an easy route that first goes downhill, then flattens out.

Left and opposite: Close-up and long-distance views of the Tre Croce Pass in the mountains of the Cristallo group.

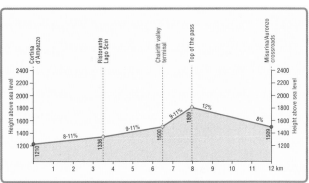

TOUR PROFILE <<

Falzárego Pass: 2117m

EASTERN SIDE – Start: Cortina d'Ampezzo, 1210m

Directions: A22 Brenner Autobahn, exit Bressanone – Brunico – Dobbiaco – Carbonin – Passo di Cimabanche Pass – Cortina d'Ampezzo

Level of Difficulty/Maximum gradient: Medium, with a maximum gradient of 11 per cent

Length: 16.5km

Total ascent: 910m

Time: 1½–2¼ hrs

Suggested gearing: 39/26

Route: Cortina d'Ampezzo (0.0km) – Pocol (5.5km) – Top of the pass (16.5km)

WESTERN SIDE – Start: Andraz, 1428m

Directions: A22 Brenner Autobahn, exit Chiusa/Val Gardena – Ortisei – Santa Cristina Valgardena – Selva di Val Gardena– Sella Pass – Pordoi Pass – Arabba – Andraz

Level of Difficulty/Maximum gradient: Easy, with a maximum gradient of 8 per cent

Length: 11.0km

Total ascent: 690m

Time: 1¼–2 hrs

Suggested gearing: 39/23

Route: Andraz (0.0km) – Turning to Belluno/Selva di Cadore (1.5km) – Top of the pass (11.0km)

Road conditions: 50m unlit hairpin bend tunnel on the western side below the top of the pass and a few cobbled hairpin bends. Extra care needed in wet conditions

Pass open: All year

Things to see: Cortina d'Ampezzo: parish church and bell tower, local museum with fossil and mineral collections, ruins of Andraz Castle on the western side

Map: Euro Cart regional map 1:300,000, RV-Verlag, South Tyrol/Veneto sheet

The Falzárego Pass runs from Cortina d'Ampezzo over into the densely wooded, narrow Cordevole valley, called Livinallongo del Col di Lana in Italian, and on to Andraz. As is widely noted, the road, which winds over the col between the Fanes–Tofana range in the west and the Nuvolaus in the east, has been well used since time immemorial. It hasn't changed much since then, except that it's a bit wider and better constructed and traffic is mainly motorised rather than on foot. Some people also tackle it on a bike, for which you do need to do some training, but the demands are not all that high with a total vertical climb of not even 1000m over 16.5km and a maximum gradient of 11 per cent only on the more difficult eastern side. One more tip: as the eastern side of the Great Dolomites Road goes over the Pordoi Pass (Tour 27) and the Karer Pass (Tour 31) and on to Bolzano the amount of traffic increases in the tourist season and at holiday times.

At these times there's hardly a hotel room to be had at our starting point, Cortina d'Ampezzo, known throughout the world as a winter sports resort and the venue for the 1956 Winter Olympics,

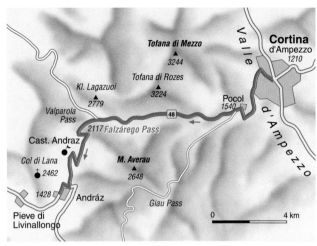

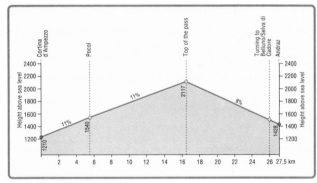

and its centre is packed so full of cars and people that it hardly seems possible to get through even on a bike. At other times you can experience Cortina as a peaceful, almost contemplative little town, one of the region's most worthwhile sights. The Olympic Ice Stadium, for example, or the ski jump in the suburb of Zuel, or the parish church with its massive Byzantine bell tower, beautiful ceiling and wall paintings, or the large block of dolomite bearing a bronze image of Deodat Dolomieu (1750–1801), after whom the mineral was named.

To experience the Dolomites in all their glory head west out of Cortina (0.0km) over hairpin bends with a constant gradient of 11 per cent that start

straightaway. After 3.5km, just before going through a 20m rock tunnel, you can take a last glance back at the scattered villages on the floor of the Boite valley and the mountains of the mighty Cristallo group towering behind them, then a series of numbered, and in some places steep, hairpin bends bring us to Pocol (5.5km). At the turning for the Giau Pass (Tour 23), which is equally worthwhile scenically and has considerably less traffic, we ride upwards at a steady gradient. Suddenly 8km of the route are behind you and the road over the next 2km is almost level. Then the slope goes back up to 11 per cent and as we wind our way up under the south face of the Tofana we can make out on the left the strangely

Opposite: The southern face of the Tofana towers over the forest belt on the eastern side of the Falzárego Pass.

formed rock formation of the Cinque Torri. Hairpin bend 16 (13.0km) is just 3.5km from the top of the pass and at bend 21 you'll see that you're at a height of 2020m. Wind your way up the remaining 100m or so of vertical climb to the pass (16.5km), breathing a little more easily thanks to a decreasing gradient. The tower at the summit doesn't have to be the end. You can add another 75m of vertical climb, with the 1.5km ascent (gradients up to 11 per cent) to the top of the Valparola Pass (Tour 24).

Another way to go a little higher is to take the cable car to the Piccolo Lagazuoi, which opened in 1965 and goes up to 2779m, opening up a 360-degree panorama over the Dolomites. From the top of the pass you can spot the 3342m, glaciated Marmolada, justly called the Queen of the Dolomites, while nearby are the lone peak of Sasso di Stria and the notorious Col di Lana. The latter was blown up by the Italians in the First World War with 5,024 kilogrames of dynamite, and has gone down in history as the Col di Sangue, the Mountain of Blood. This whole area was the site of bitter and deadly conflict during the First World War. Everywhere here you find old, partially restored rock shelters, trenches and emplacements, relics from the time when the Italian alpine soldiers and the Austro-Hungarian forces faced each other as implacable foes.

If you follow the course of the cable car route to the Piccolo Lagazuoi, about halfway up you can make out a reminder of the history of this period. The Cengia Martini is a wide rocky cut in the side of the Piccolo Lagazuoi named after the commanding officer of the Italian battalion that occupied it on 20 October 1915. This gave them a strategic advantage over the Austrian emplacements lower down until the Austrians cut a tunnel into the mountain and, like the Italians at the Col di Lana, blew up the fortified positions.

Hoping that these events are never repeated, we make our way down the 11km descent over the south-west side. Be particularly careful over the first cobbled hairpin bend and a 50m unlit tunnel, but then it's fine to pick up speed on a downhill slope of up to 8 per cent.

You'll notice the rubble of some abandoned youth centres in a hollow in the upper slopes, then the strangely formed horn of the Sasso di Stria rising out of the woods on the western side of the valley. Your arrival in Andraz is heralded by a view of the huge dolomite block of Andraz Castle.

The Falzárego Pass Memorial commemorates fighting here during the First World War.

Opposite: The hairpin bend tunnel in the upper part of the western side of the Falzárego Pass.

On the eastern side of the Falzárego Pass. In the background is the rocky outcrop of Monte Averau.

23 GIAU PASS
Dolomites

TOUR PROFILE <<

Giau Pass: 2236m

NORTHERN SIDE – Start: Cortina d'Ampezzo, 1026m

Directions: A22 Brenner Autobahn, exit Bressanone – Brunico – Dobbiaco – Carbonin – Cortina d'Ampezzo

Level of Difficulty/Maximum gradient: Medium, with a maximum gradient of 12 per cent on long sections

Length: 16.0km

Total ascent: 1030m

Time: 1½–2½ hrs

Suggested gearing: 39/26

Route: Cortina d'Ampezzo (0.0km) – Pocol (5.5km) – Top of the pass (16.0km)

SOUTHERN SIDE – Start: Turning just outside Selva di Cadore, 1300m

Directions: Canazei – Pordoi Pass – Arabba – Andraz – Selva di Cadore

Level of Difficulty/Maximum gradient: Medium, with a maximum gradient of 14 per cent over a 4km stretch at the start

Length: 10.0km

Total ascent: 940m

Time: 1½–2½ hrs

Suggested gearing: 39/26

Route: Turning just outside Selva di Cadore (0.0km) – Fedare mountain lodge (7.0km) – Top of the pass (10.0km)

Road conditions: Well-constructed roads. Great care must be taken on the hairpin bend section on the descent

Pass open: 1 May to 31 October

Things to see: Murogna di Giau, legendary wall of stones on the northern side of the pass road. Cortina d'Ampezzo: parish church with bell tower and fossil and mineral museum in the town centre

Map: Euro Cart regional map 1:300,000, RV-Verlag, South Tyrol/Veneto sheet

The Giau Pass, here from the northern side, is well worth experiencing for its scenery and lack of traffic.

The Giau Pass is the shortest connecting road from the Ampezzo valley over to the Fiorentina, the area at the northern foot of the Civetta and further on into Livinallongo del Col di Lana, and it runs up to the Pordoi Pass as a connecting route. It's neither a significant tourist link nor an important traffic link in the Dolomites but I recommend it highly to anyone who likes riding the Dolomites. For one thing, it's relatively new. It only became passable for motor vehicles in 1968 and has only been fully tarmacked for a few years. No expense was spared on its construction and it's in outstanding structural condition given its limited importance to traffic. The Giau lies immediately south of the Falzárego Pass (Tour 22) and can be considered a worthwhile alternative if you want a longer but much less busy way over into Livinallongo del Col di Lana.

The total length of the road between Cortina d'Ampezzo in the north and Selva di Cadore in the south is 26km, with a total vertical climb of 1026m. On the northern side, in addition to a large number of bends, there are 24 hairpin bends, with 22 to tackle on the southern side. On the northern side the maximum gradient is 12 per cent, and on the southern side 14 per cent. Those are the bare stats, but they don't convey how stunningly beautiful the pass is.

Setting out from Cortina d'Ampezzo (0.0km) the first few kilometres to Pocol (5.5km) are as described in Tour 22 to the Falzárego Pass. In the little hotel complex at the foot of the high rock faces of the Tofana take care not to miss the left-hand turning signposted Pso. d. Giau. The next 2km are an enjoyable run down into the meadows of the Costeanabaches valley, before the road starts to climb through thick larch forests over a series of hairpin bends with a gradient of 12 per cent. Now and then the forbidding smooth rock walls of the Tofana to the north on the other side of the Falzárego Pass appear over the tops of the trees. Anyone who has ever ridden their bike in the tourist season will really appreciate the peace and quiet here.

Between the 10 and 11km mark the gradient decreases noticeably and long flat sections allow you to progress more quickly for a time, but with the start of the hairpin bend section the gradient increases again to 12 per cent. At kilometre 12 you've already reached 1800m, a height that also marks the tree line.

We ride into a high valley whose green alpine meadows are framed by the bizarrely formed Cinque Torri to the north-west and the wall-like Croda da Lago to the south-west, while the first outlines of the jagged rock structures of the Nuvolau mountains can be seen over the top of the pass.

If you look carefully you can make out next to the road a wall made of rough stones which seems to run across the whole of the valley. This is the Murogna di Giau, which has marked the Austrian–Italian border since 1918. Legend has it that in 1752 the inhabitants of the commune of San Vito built it in a single day, to emphatically settle a territorial dispute.

It might be a valley, but it isn't flat: the 12 per cent gradient only slackens every now and then. It doesn't drop signficantly until kilometre 15 and then you soon reach the top of the pass (16.0km) and the mountain lodge in a steep-sided valley between Ra Gusela and Col Piombin. Here, over a cappuccino, you can enjoy the view back to the far-distant Ampezzo mountains while admiring the splendour of the western summits, notably the Marmolada, over 3000m high, with its glaciers gleaming in the sunlight (we hope). And then you can look forward to the descent down the southern slope behind you to Selva di Cadore.

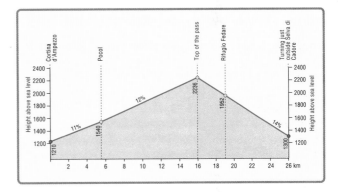

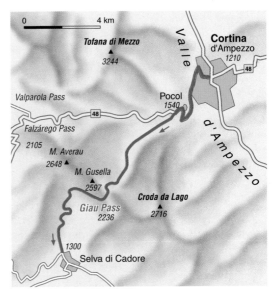

24 VALPAROLA PASS
Dolomites

TOUR PROFILE <<

Valparola Pass: 2192m

NORTHERN SIDE – Start: La Villa, 1387m, about 3km north of Corvara

Directions: The best way is over the Gardena Pass (Tour 25) to Corvara and the Val Badia out to La Villa or the Brenner Autobahn, exit Bressanone, through the Puster valley to San Lorenzo di Sebato near Brunico and through the Val Badia through Longega and Pedraces to La Villa

Level of Difficulty/Maximum gradient: Easy to medium with a maximum gradient of 10 per cent on long sections

Length: 14.0km

Total ascent: 805m

Time: 1½–2½ hrs

Suggested gearing: 39/26

Route: La Villa (0.0km) – San Cassiano (2.5km) – Armentarola (5.5km) – Valparola mountain lodge (13.5km) – Top of the pass (14.0km)

SOUTHERN SIDE: On the southern side the road goes down for 1.5km at a gradient of 10 per cent to link to the top of the Falzárego Pass (Tour 22), 70m lower down

Road conditions: Well-constructed roads

Pass open: All year

Things to see: Tre Sassi ('between the rocks') fort museum at the top of the pass; rockfall area on the Piccolo Lagazuoi just south of the top

Map: Euro Cart regional map 1:300,000, RV-Verlag, South Tyrol/Veneto sheet

Like the Giau Pass the Valparola Pass is one of the Dolomites' lesser known passes, even though it links the Gardena and Falzárego passes. It's a pleasure to ride: despite its very good condition very little traffic passes over it, and it maintains an even gradient of a maximum of 10 per cent. The beautiful countryside here in the central part of the Dolomites speaks for itself, with hills rising to meet the foot of the 2500m Settsass peak at the edge of the Gruppo di Fanis range.

The point of departure is the village of La Villa in Val Badia, about 3km north of Corvara, where, following the signposts to San Cassiano/Passo di Valparola, you should use the the short downhill in the village to attack the next 10 per cent gradient at speed. This should allow you to reach the settlement of San Cassiano (2.5km) easily; high above the top of the pass beneath the rockfall of the Piccolo Lagazuoi is already visible.

After Cassiano the 10 per cent gradient lets up for a while as the road runs almost on the flat to the hotel complex at Armentarola (5.5km). It doesn't hit 10 per cent again until you've crossed the bridge over the Gran Ega (7.0km). The route now winds over a series of hairpin bends first through larch and pine forests and then through bare, rocky countryside at the foot of the rugged rock faces of the Cima Cunturines up to the top of the pass. This is marked by the Valparola mountain lodge (13.5km), in the middle of a wild landscape of rubble and boulders from a rockfall on the Piccolo

On the lower part of the climb over the northern side of the Valparola Pass with the Gruppo del Puez over the Val Badia.

Here you can see almost the whole of the southern side of the Valparola Pass, which is barely 1.5km long.

Lagazuoi, little Lake Valparola and an old ruined fort from the First World War. This was erected in 1897 to defend the southern borders of the Austro-Hungarian empire, despite the fact that Austria-Hungary, together with Germany, had been allies of the Italians since 1882. Its massive walls did not protect it for long. Just a few weeks after the beginning of First World War hostilities it was damaged so extensively by an artillery shell fired from the Cinque Torri that it was evacuated – though the Austrians kept up the pretence that the fort was occupied to encourage the Italians to keep shelling it and waste their ammunition. The fort now houses a war museum.

If you were all set for a long descent you'll be disappointed, because the pass ends after only 1.5km at a 10 per cent gradient, 70m lower down, at the top of the Falzárego Pass (Tour 22). Thus the Valparola Pass is comparable to the Majola Pass (Tour 44) and the Umbrail Pass (Tour 51), both in Graubünden (Switzerland), in that it only really boasts an ascent.

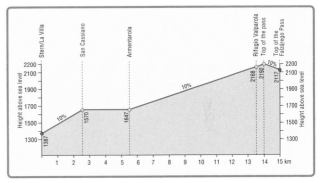

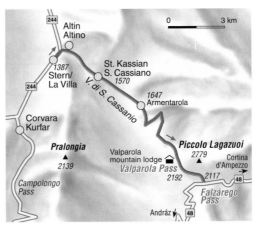

25 GARDENA PASS
Dolomites

TOUR PROFILE <<

Gardena Pass: 2137m

WESTERN SIDE – Start: Selva di Val Gardena, 1563m

Directions: A22 Brenner Autobahn, exit Chiusa/Val Gardena – Ortisei – Santa Cristina Valgardena – Selva di Val Gardena

Level of Difficulty/Maximum gradient: Easy, with a maximum gradient of 10 per cent over about 3km from Selva di Val Gardena to the turning to the Gardena Pass

Length: 9.5km

Total ascent: 575m

Time: 1–1½ hrs

Suggested gearing: 39/26

Route: Selva di Val Gardena (0.0km) – Turning to Gardena Pass (3.5km) – Top of the pass (9.5km)

EASTERN SIDE – Start: Corvara, 1568m

Directions: A22 Brenner Autobahn, exit Bressanone – Rio di Pusteria – San Lorenzo di Sebato – Longega – Pedraces – Corvara

Level of Difficulty/Maximum gradient: Easy, with a maximum gradient of 12 per cent

Length: 9.5km

Total ascent: 570m

Time: 1–1½ hrs

Suggested gearing: 39/26

Route: Corvara (0.0km) – Colfosco (2.5km) – Top of the pass (9.5km)

Road conditions: Well-constructed roads apart from some slight surface damage in the area at the top of the pass. However, on the descent on the eastern side caution is needed in places on tight bends

Pass open: All year

Things to see: Selva di Val Gardena: ruins of Selva di Val Gardena Castle

Map: Euro Cart regional map 1:300,000, RV-Verlag, South Tyrol/Veneto sheet

The eastern side of the Gardena Pass is classified as an easy tour with short climbs peaking at 12 per cent.

The Gardena valley, Val Gardena in Italian, is surely the best known of the many valleys in the Dolomites. This is primarily because it's the most conveniently situated access road from the Isarco valley into the most beautiful part of the Dolomites, the picture-book landscapes of the Sassolungo and Sella ranges.

The Gardena Pass, which connects the Gardena valley in the west with the Val Badia in the east, is perhaps not so well known among cyclists, presumably because it offers vertical climbs of only 574m on the western side and 569m on the eastern side and so doesn't have much of a reputation. It's not worth the effort as a stand-alone tour for a cyclist who has trained hard and is therefore usually mentioned along with the Campolongo Pass (Tour 26), the Pordoi Pass (Tour 27) and the Sella Pass (Tour 28), which when linked in the famous Sellaronda circuit can boast a substantial vertical climb of 2000m over a 57km route.

But for now we'll confine ourselves to the Gardena Pass, which has its western starting point, as does the Sellaronda, in Selva di Val Gardena, the highest village in the Gardena valley. If the vertical climb to the top of the pass is too little for you, you could of course cycle up here from the Isarco valley. But that might be too much of a good thing because whichever route you choose, either from Chiusa to the junction with the Brenner Autobahn or from Ponte Gardena a little way down the valley, you would have to add a vertical climb of 1000m plus. On the Chiusa–Gardena road the maximum gradient is 11 per cent, while on the Ponte Gardena–Gardena road it's as much as 14 per cent on long sections.

For the more leisurely approach, drive up to Selva di Val Gardena (0.0km) with your bike on the roof-rack. The village is attractively spread out among meadows, surrounded by a garland of mountain giants stretching from the Gruppo delle Odle range over the Sella massif to the Sassolungo. Warm up with a gentle tour of the village and note the shops selling wood carvings, a main source of income in the valley. There is a long tradition of carvers and sculptors in wood in the Gardena valley going back to the 17th century and their work enjoys an international reputation. Take a look at the pricetags and you'll probably discover that the bigger and more beautiful pieces are way beyond your budget – but you won't have room for them in your jersey pocket anyway.

Coming out of the village you'll need to build some momentum because the route climbs at 10 per cent round a hairpin bend. At first the view is obscured by forests, but then the Sassolungo massif moves into your field of vision, one of the biggest of all the high walls of the Dolomites, more than 2km long and nearly 1000m high.

At the junction below a stone bridge (3.5km) the road divides. One road goes straight to the Sella Pass, but we turn left. The gradient goes back down to 8 per cent and several hairpin bends over a grassy slope lead up to the Hotel Gerard (5.5km). If the route hasn't been too demanding so far, now it's positively easy, because over the next couple of kilometres you ride on a perfectly flat road directly under the northern slopes of the Sella range.

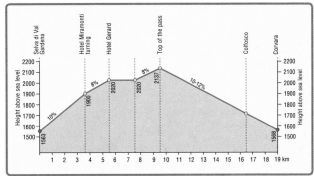

This presents itself as a predominantly grey, smooth wall but a couple of rocky summits can be picked out such as the Murfreittürme, the Murfreitspitze and the Rodelheilspitze ('Sledge of salvation peak'), named, tongue in cheek, after the Rodelklub, the tobogganing club in Ortisei.

The hairpin bends that start at the end of the flat section at 7.5km take us without too much trouble up an 8 per cent gradient to the top of the pass (9.5km) with the impressive Gardena Pass hostel and wonderful views of the Sassolungo and the Massiccio dello Sciliar in the west, the Tschierspitzen in the north and parts of the Sella mountain range in the west.

TOUR PROFILE <<

Campolongo Pass: 1875m

NORTHERN SIDE – Start: Corvara, 1568m

Directions: The best way is over the Gardena Pass to Corvara (Tour 25) or alternatively the A22 Brenner Autobahn, exit Bressanone – Rio di Pusteria – San Lorenzo – Longega – Pedraces – Corvara

Level of Difficulty/Maximum gradient: Easy, with a maximum gradient of 10 per cent

Length: 6.5km

Total ascent: 310m

Time: ¾–1¼ hrs

Suggested gearing: 39/26

Route: Corvara (0.0km) – Gasthof Boè (6.0km) – Top of the pass (6.5km)

SOUTHERN SIDE – Start: Arabba, 1580m

Directions: Through the Val di Fassa to Canazei and over the Pordoi Pass (Tour 27) to Arabba or Cortina d'Ampezzo – Falzárego Pass (Tour 22) – Andraz – Arabba

Level of Difficulty/Maximum gradient: Easy, with a maximum gradient of 10 per cent

Length: 4.0km

Total ascent: 295m

Time: ½–1 hr

Suggested gearing: 39/23

Route: Arabba (0.0km) – Albergo Monte Cherz (3.5km) – Top of the pass (4.0km)

Road conditions: Considerable surface damage along the whole of the route

Pass open: All year

Things to see: Cable railway from Corvara to Piz-Boè mountain station

Map: Euro Cart regional map 1:300,000, RV-Verlag, South Tyrol/Veneto sheet

The Campolongo Pass is easy for cyclists who have trained well and is usually linked with the Gardena Pass (Tour 25), the Pordoi Pass (Tour 27) and the Sella Pass (Tour 28), to form the famous Sellaronda.

The Compolongo Pass, Passo di Campolongo in Italian, connects the Val di Badia and Gader valleys with the upper Cordevole valley, also known as Livinallongo del Col di Lana. On the Sellaronda circuit it's the link between the Gardena Pass and the Pordoi Pass along the eastern side of the Sella between the valley villages of Corvara and Arabba. If you do the circuit clockwise from Selva di Val Gardena, it's the second pass after the Gardena Pass (Tour 25), followed by the Pordoi Pass (Tour 27) and the Sella Pass (Tour 28).

Our departure point, the little village of Corvara (0.0km), known primarily as a winter sports resort, lies in a wide valley at the foot of the indomitable rock tower of the Sassongher. As you leave the village the road climbs at 10 per cent and twists its way up a grassy hillside over 10 hairpin bends, opening up a view back down the valley to the village and the impressive rock formation of the Sassongher behind it.

After 2km you reach the end of the hairpin bend section and ride up a decreasing gradient on a road with few bends, without having to put too much effort in, as we head for the top of the pass. A sign (5.0km) tells us that we're crossing the provincial border between Bolzano and Belluno, also the border between the German-speaking and Italian-speaking parts of Italy, and a little further on we reach the top of the pass (5.5km). It's another grassy

The descent over the southern side of the Campolongo Pass down to Arabba, in the Italian-speaking part of the South Tyrol.

saddle on which stands the Gasthof Boè inn, open all year, from where the road goes down for just 4km, with a downhill slope of up to 10 per cent over five hairpin bends, to Arabba. The poor state of the road means that you need to take care on the descent, especially near the top.

Once in Arabba, you will have realised that the Campolongo Pass isn't much of a tour and may have decided to add on the Pordoi Pass (Tour 27).

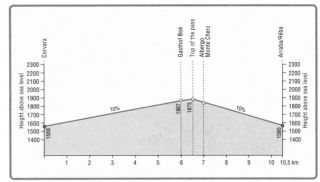

The Dolomites, known universally as one of the world's most beautiful mountain landscapes, can also be explored in the Dolomites cycle marathon, the Maratona dles Dolomites, which was first held on 12 July 1987 and takes in seven passes, including the Campolongo Pass. In 1987 166 riders set out from Pedraces in the Val Badia; the ride has proved so successful that now the number of participants is capped at 8,000. In order to cater for all physical capabilities four routes are offered, the shortest of which is 57km long and has a total vertical climb of 1747m, the longest 175km with a total vertical climb of approximately 5000m. More detailed information can be found at www.maratona.it.

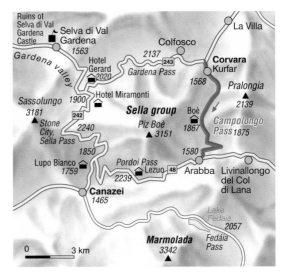

TOUR PROFILE <<

Pordoi Pass: 2239m

EASTERN SIDE – Start: Arabba, 1602m

Directions: A22 Brenner Autobahn, exit Bressanone – Rio di Pusteria – San Lorenzo – Longega – Pedraces – Corvara – Campolongo Pass – Arabba or Cortina d'Ampezzo – Falzárego Pass – Andraz – Arabba

Level of Difficulty/Maximum gradient: Easy to medium tour with an almost continuous maximum gradient of 8 per cent

Length: 9.0km

Total ascent: 640m

Time: 1¼–1¾ hrs

Suggested gearing: 39/23

Route: Arabba (0.0km) – Lezuo inn (8.0km) – Top of the pass (9.0km)

WESTERN SIDE – Start: Canazei, 1465m

Directions: The best way would be over the Sella Pass to Canazei (Tour 28) or alternatively A22 Brenner Autobahn, exit Bolzano/North – Cardano – Passo di Costalunga – Pozza di Fassa – Canazei

Level of Difficulty/Maximum gradient: Medium, with a maximum gradient of 11 per cent

Length: 11.0km

Total ascent: 775m

Time: 1¼–1¾ hrs

Suggested gearing: 39/26

Route: Canazei (0.0km) – Albergo Lupo Bianco (4.5km) – Turn-off to the Sella Pass (6.0km) – Top of the pass (11.0km)

Road conditions: Well-constructed roads. Take care on the descent as there are a lot of hairpin bends

Pass open: All year

Things to see: Cable car from the top of the pass to Sasso Pordoi (2950m)

Map: Euro Cart regional map 1:300,000, RV-Verlag, South Tyrol/Veneto sheet

This cyclist's easy riding style shows that he's in really good shape.

The Pordoi Pass is the connection between the upper Cordevole valley, known as the Livinallongo del Col di Lana, and the Fassa valley between the valley village of Arabba, Rèba in Ladin, and Canzei. The route over the pass runs along the southern side of the Sella mountain and so is also the connecting link of the Sellaronda (Tours 25–28). Of the four pass roads, this is the one with the most hairpin bends: 60 altogether, 33 on the eastern side and 27 on the western side.

Eastern side

Starting the climb in Arabba (0.0km) we hit the first hairpin before we've even left the village, where an altitude marker shows that we are 1609m above sea level. The next milestone shows that there's 8.7km to go to the top of the pass; now hairpin bends follow one after another at a constant gradient of 8 per cent, which allows you to ride smoothly a speed that matches your fitness level. To the right rises the rocky face of the Sella mountain, whose summit is the Piz Boè, 3152m high, while on the left the dark volcanic rock of the Monte Padon is reminiscent of a moonscape. By hairpin bend 20 you can already start to make out the top of the pass, but it's still a long way up there; by hairpin bend 27 the distance between bends is getting considerably longer. You can take a break at the Gasthof Lezuo (8.0km) at hairpin bend 32, though, and from there there's just one more hairpin and one more kilometre to go to the top (9.0km). A monument to the fallen in the First and Second World Wars, made from a block of dark porphyry, errected a little higher up reminds us that this area was hard fought over at one time. If you want an aerial view, you can take a cable car ride on a dizzying journey up to the Pordoi Pass.

Western side

The climb from the western side starts at the well-known tourist resort of Canazei. This main village of the upper Fassa valley spreads out over the valley floor with a magnificent backdrop of mountains. It's the departure point for hiking and mountain climbing in the Marmolada, Sassolungo and Sella mountain ranges. For cyclists it's where three passes meet, because as well as the Pordoi Pass you can also go from here up to the Sella Pass (Tour 28) over the southern side and the Fedáia Pass (Tour 32) to the east. If you ride a few kilometres through the Fassa valley out towards San Giovanni it also leads to the eastern approach to the Costalunga Pass (Tour 31).

For the Pordoi Pass we set off from Canzaei (0.0km) in a sweeping loop with a gradient of 10 per cent. Just as we're leaving the village we encounter the first hairpin bend at a height of 1480m, which is followed in quick succession by five more through a shady fir wood on the western side of the valley. This first section of hairpins ends at the Albergo Lupo Bianco (4.5km) and after another bend the southwest face of the Piz Ciavázes appears in front of us. The gradient remains steady all the way to the turning for the Sella Pass (6.0km), which we soon reach at hairpin 11, where there is a commemorative plaque to the famous Campionissimo, road race legend Fausto Coppi. Just over half of the climb is behind us now, but the most scenically beautiful part still lies ahead. On a gradient now down to 8 per cent we ride up a smooth series of hairpin bends. At hairpin bend 18 a heart-stopping view mandates a stop. The vista from the edge of a small lake sweeps over green alpine meadows to the Sassolungo massif, including the Sassolungo itself, the Punta delle Cinque Dita and the Punta Grohmann, and is one of almost unique beauty.

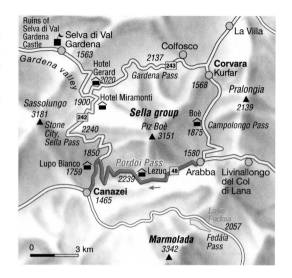

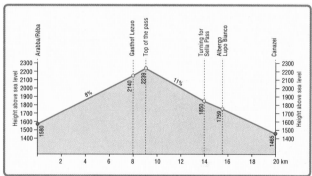

On a gradient that remains constant the road now goes higher without requiring too much effort and the view widens magnificently to take in the table-shaped Sella mountain with its rock banding separating the Schlern dolomite, while to the south gleam the snow fields of the Marmolada. The hairpin bends are numbered and the signs give the height above sea level, so we know that hairpin 23 is at 2171m. The top of the pass (11.0km), now four hairpin bends and a 68m vertical climb away, is soon reached.

The Sassolungo range dominates the view on the southern side of the Pordoi Pass.

TOUR PROFILE <<

Sella Pass: 2240m

SOUTHERN SIDE – Start: Canazei, 1463m

Directions: A22 Brenner Autobahn, exit Bolzano/North – Passo di Costalunga – Pozza di Fassa – Canazei or Cortina d'Ampezzo – Falzárego Pass – Arabba – Pordoi Pass – Canazei

Level of Difficulty/Maximum gradient: Medium, with a maximum gradient of 11 per cent over long stretches

Length: 12.0km

Total ascent: 780m

Time: 1¼–2 hrs

Suggested gearing: 39/26

Route: Canazei (0.0km) – Albergo Lupo Bianco (4.5km) – turn-off for the Pordoi Pass (6.0km) – top of the pass (12.0km)

NORTHERN SIDE – Start: Selva di Val Gardena, 1563m

Directions: A22 Brenner Autobahn, exit Chiusa/Val Gardena – Ortisei – Selva di Val Gardena

Level of Difficulty/Maximum gradient: Easy to medium tour with a maximum gradient of 10 per cent over about 3km between Selva di Val Gardena and the turning to the Gardena Pass

Length: 9.0km

Total ascent: 680m

Time: 1¼–1¾ hrs

Suggested gearing: 39/26

Route: Selva di Val Gardena (0.0km) – turning to the Gardena Pass (3.5km) – Top of the pass (9.0km)

Road conditions: Damage to the road surface, especially in the area at the top of the pass. On the southern side there are some cobbled hairpin bends. Take more care here on the descent in wet conditions

Pass open: All year

Things to see: Selva di Val Gardena: Ruined castle; rockslide area 'Stone City' on the northern side

Map: Euro Cart regional map 1:300,000, RV-Verlag, South Tyrol/Veneto sheet

The Sella Pass, which runs from Canazei in the Fassa valley between the Sella mountain in the east and the Sassolungo range in the west over to Selva di Val Gardena in the upper Gardena valley, is frequently described as an extremely beautiful Dolomites pass. Within the context of the Sellaronda it's the fourth and last mountain test after the Gardena Pass (Tour 25), the Campolongo Pass (Tour 26) and the Pordoi Pass (Tour 27), or at least it is if you've started it in a clockwise direction from Selva di Val Vardena. Then you only have to follow the turning to the Sella Pass 6km above Canazei, you don't have to go down all the way to Canazei. However, if you're going to the Sella Pass as a stand-alone tour then Canazei is recommended as the starting point, even though the first 6km are identical to the climb up to the Pordoi Pass.

Just after Canazei (0.0km) we get the first hairpin bend at a height of 1480m and the road climbs up to the Albergo Lupo Bianco (4.5km) over the next few hairpin bends with a constant gradient of up to 11 per cent. Round another bend we get a good look at the south-west face of the Piz Ciavázes and then reach the turning to the Pordoi Pass

A cyclist has no time to look at the south-western side of the Piz Civázes on the descent over the southern side of the Sella Pass.

at hairpin bend 14 (6.0km) over a gradient which remains constant. Here you find a memorial plaque commemorating the Italian cycling legend, Fausto Coppi. We follow the SS242 over two hairpin bends with a gradient of 10 per cent to the albergo Pian Ciavaneis, where the gradient decreases a little. But not for very long; it increases again to 11 per cent at the beginning of a partially cobbled stretch of hairpin bends.

A sign saying 2000m (10.0km) indicates the last 240m of vertical climb to the top of the pass (12.0km) which we reach 2km later with no decrease in the gradient. The view from up there can really be described as the most impressive that the Dolomites can offer, and they aren't exactly short of scenic beauty. To our right the faces of the Sella mountains rise up like a wall, streaked with black, as well as a soft band of rock in their upper regions and looking not unlike a massive threatening rock castle.

The east face of the Sassolungo is its counterpart on the left-hand side of the valley, one of the most enormous faces of the Dolomites, more than 2km wide and 1000m high. Looking back you can see the firn fields of the Marmolada, at 3342m the highest mountain in the Dolomites and the only one with major glaciers, while in the foreground beyond the green meadows of the valley is the Odle range.

The descent over the northern side also offers us some sights worth seeing, as we will see just after the first hairpin bends with a downhill slope of 9 per cent. By the side of the road innumerable gigantic boulders are piled up from a rockfall on the Sassolungo, called the 'Stone City' by the inhabitants of the Gardena valley. Then we can make out the cable car which goes up to the exposed side of the Sassolungo, but we

must also keep our attention on the road. Even though the downhill slope is more often under 9 per cent than over, the surface is in a very bumpy state. After a downhill slope of almost exactly 5.5km we reach the turning to the Gardena Pass (Tour 25).

It's another 3km downhill from here to Selva di Val Gardena, the main town in the Gardena valley and perhaps one of the best-known tourist resorts in the Dolomites. Incidentally, its name commemorates the the site of the former Selva di Val Gardena Castle, whose ruins you can make out on closer inspection under the yellowish-red rockslide of the face of the Steviola north-west of the town.

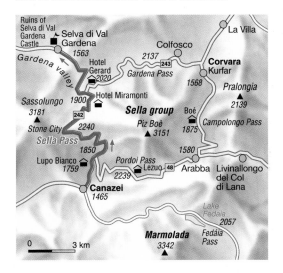

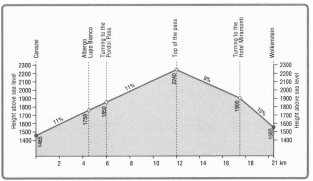

TOUR PROFILE <<

Seiser Alm Pass: 1900m

Start: Ponte Gardena, 468m

Directions: A22 Brenner Autobahn, exit Chiusa – Ponte Gardena

Level of Difficulty/Maximum gradient: Medium to difficult tour with a maximum gradient of 15 per cent for 1km and 13 per cent for another 1km

Length: 20.5km

Total ascent: 1435m

Time: 2–2¾ hrs

Suggested gearing: 39/26

Route: Ponte Gardena (0.0km) – Castelrotto (6.5km) – Castelrotto/Seiser Alm crossroads (8.0km) – Frommer Restaurant (15.5km) – Seiser Alm hotel complex (17.5km) – Summit (20.5km)

Road conditions: Well-constructed roads

Pass open: All year

Map: Euro Cart regional map 1:300,000, RV-Verlag, South Tyrol/Veneto sheet

Notes: Lights are advisable because of the 90m tunnel in the lower part of the climb. In the summer months the Seiser Alm road from San Valentino is closed to traffic from 9am to 5pm. Information about the cost of a daily permit and authorisation for continuing on to Compaccio, about 2km below the Seiser Alm, are available from the information bureau in San Valentino

With an area of 60 square kilometres the Seiser Alm is not only the largest high pasture in the Dolomites, but one of the largest in the whole of the Alps. Above Bolzano, in a uniquely beautiful location at the foot of the 2564m Massiccio dello Sciliar, the Alm, as it's known by the locals, is in season all year round. From spring until autumn there are mountain climbers and hikers here and in winter downhill and cross-country skiers come. Cyclists too can enjoy the outdoor paradise, riding up here from the Isarco valley on well-constructed roads.

In Ponte Gardena (0.0km) we follow the signs for Castelrotto/Seiser Alm and start to climb in the shadow of the Trostburg along an initially narrow route with a gradient of up to 11 per cent. The road soon widens out and a sign (3.5km) indicates the first of two hairpin bends where the gradient increases to 13 per cent. After a 90m unlit tunnel that leads into a deep, gorge-like valley it becomes even steeper. The route snakes up for almost 1km at up to 15 per cent before the climb decreases first to 13 per cent at the end of the gorge (5.5km) and then to 10 per cent on a stretch offering views over the Massiccio dello Sciliar as far as the Castelrotto/Seiser Alm crossroads (8.0km).

On to the wooded hilltops at the foot of the Massiccio dello Sciliar, which end here in mighty rock faces looking south, and we follow the road, signposted to the Seiser Alm, branching off from San Valentino. Among green meadows dotted here and there with houses and old farmsteads gradients of up to 10 per cent alternate with flatter sections until you are past San Valentino (11.0km), when the climb increases to 11 per cent. We're into the woods now, through which the route snakes its way up over several groups of hairpin bends at a gradient that hardly decreases at all.

At the Frommer restaurant (15.5km) the woods thin out and there are three hairpin bends to wind your way up before the gradient eases and you ride onto the wide plateau of the Seiser Alm. The rippling meadows stretch almost as far as the eye can see,

The Seiser Alm, here with the Sassolungo, is hard to surpass for scenic beauty and variety.

bounded to the south by the Massiccio dello Sciliar; as you ride on, the jagged rocks of the peaks of the Sassolungo come into view in the near distance. A hotel complex (17.5km) marks the end of the journey for cars, and we can now follow the gently climbing path in the Sciliar nature park undisturbed. In spring and summer the flowers are abundant, and when you get a view of the Sassolungo at its best angle you'll hardly find a more beautiful spot in all the Alps.

The path goes gently up for 3km to the highest point of the climb (20.5km), which is your turning point – though there is an alternative. You can make this into a circular tour, but it involves cycling over a 4km section of unmade road. This shouldn't really be a serious problem even on road tyres if you adapt the way you ride, except on short sections with a gradient of up to 15 per cent, where you may find you skid a little on the uneven surface.

If you've weighed the pros and cons and decided to ride on, go down to the

Saltner Schwaige guesthouses (23.0km) on a winding and sometimes bumpy road. Follow signposts to Brunelle/ Gardena Valley along an unmade road and ride along at snail's pace beside the stream which you cross at the next wooden bridge, then struggle up a gradient of 12 per cent for about 200m, where it might be better to push your bike. Descend carefully, too; the road is tarmacked once more when you reach the houses of Oltretorrente (27.0km), but don't be carried away by this because it's also narrow and winding. We stop at a junction with a signpost for Streda Minert which takes us towards Ortisei (31.0km).

Follow the tunnel out of Ortisei (32.0km) then the road off to Castelrotto, which immediately welcomes us with a gradient of 14 per cent for 2km. After a flat section the gradient increases to 15 per cent. This only lasts a while before dipping, just briefly, to under 12 per cent. Finally we reach the highest point, the Pinei Pass (37.0km), and a long, gentle descent brings us to Castelrotto (42.5km) where an uphill stretch quickly leads us back, in the other direction this time, to our starting point (52.5km).

Here you can cruise along at a leisurely pace, but the lower end of the climb to the Seiser Alm has gradients of up to 15 per cent.

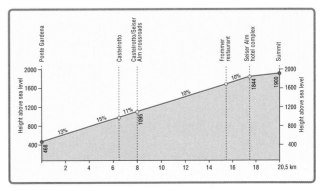

TOUR PROFILE <<

Nigerpass: 1774m

NORTHERN SIDE – Start: Prato all'Isarco, 305m

Directions: A22 Brenner Autobahn, exit Bolzano/North – Prato all'Isarco

Level of Difficulty/Maximum gradient: Very difficult tour with a maximum gradient of 24 per cent over about 1.5km. Short stretches with a gradient of 20 per cent before the Gasthaus Halbweg and through Tiers

Length: 25.0km

Total ascent: 1470m

Time: 2¾–4 hrs

Suggested gearing: 39/28 or a triple chainset

Route: Prato all'Isarco (0.0km) – Gasthaus Halbweg (6.5km) – Tiers (8.0km) – Niger mountain lodge (18.0km) – Tscheiner mountain lodge (23.0km) – entry to the Costalunga Pass (25.0km)

SOUTHERN SIDE: The Nigerpass road comes out about 1km beneath the top of the pass on the western climb up to the Costalunga Pass (Tour 31)

Road conditions: From Prato all'Isarco to Tiers the roads are narrow in places with passing places. There are blind corners, some with traffic mirrors. From Tiers the road is good

Pass open: All year

Notes: You can bypass the difficult section in the lower part of the climb if you follow the signposts to Tiers from Prato all'Isarco

Things to see: Chapel of St Cyprian in Tiers

Map: Euro Cart regional map 1:300,000, RV-Verlag, South Tyrol/Veneto sheet

As a cyclist you can take the easy way out or make things hard for yourself. The Alps offer plenty of tours at all difficulty levels; you can make easy tours easier still by shortening them, or pile on the difficulty by linking challenging rides – or attempting the Nigerpass. It's 'only' 25km long and the total vertical climb is 'only' 1470m and on the basis of these figures would be classed as a medium tour, were it not for for the 24 per cent maximum gradient, which lasts for 1.5km. It's hard to know how you will cope with a route like this in advance, but you certainly shouldn't try to tackle it unless you've done a serious amount of training and know that you can withstand suffering. There's no doubt that you will suffer on the Nigerpass. To minimise the pain, you need to get the most out of your set-up. The gradient is just about possible, and this has been tested, with 42/26, but it's not advisable because this stretch would be no fun at all.

The ride starts in Prato all'Isarco in the Isarco valley, not far from Bolzano. In this little one-street village follow signs for Brie, which take us north into the valley. Things are not particularly exciting at

doesn't really convey what's to come: only the reality of the road rearing up higher and higher can do this. At first it seems that it can't really be a 24 per cent gradient, and perhaps it is only 20 per cent for this initial stretch, but it's still enough to force you out of the saddle and struggle, using the whole width of the narrow road as it climbs between rocks on the left and the Brie gorge on the right. Don't make the mistake of thinking it's over when you leave the gorge: you'll need all your mental and physical power when you emerge onto a grassy hillside – because the route now

The Catenaccio group with the striking Torri del Vajolet forms the mountain backdrop to the Nigerpass.

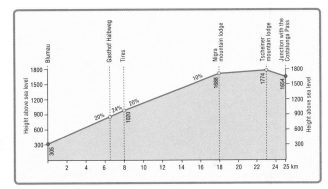

first. We ride the first 3km on a gradient of 10 per cent, nothing out of the ordinary for regular alpine riders, until a sign marked 20 per cent appears. You change into your lowest gear, stand up on the pedals, push hard a few times and soon you've got this steep section under your belt. But don't relax yet. This stretch was just a harbinger of things to come and you're soon back riding up relatively mellow 10 per cent gradients to the Gasthaus Halbweg inn (6.5km).

Another sign: '24 per cent', and this is it. The number alone

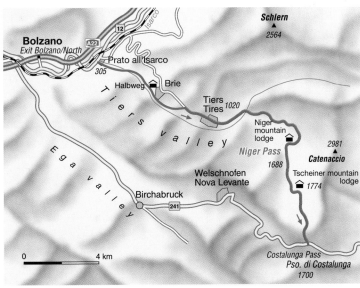

really does climb at 24 per cent. Make it from here up the 1.5km or so to the junction with the Siusi allo Sciliar road and you will have overcome the most notorious climb in the whole of the Alps. As a reward there follows a stretch of awe-inspiring beauty. The pretty little village of Tiers (8.0km) spreads out at the foot of the striking Torri del Vajolet peak and the rocky ramparts of the Catinaccio mountains, the red onion tower of the village church gleaming among green mountain meadows.

The short 20 per cent gradient up through Tiers is hardly worth mentioning, given what's already behind you, and nor are the hairpin bends with a maximum gradient of 10 per cent taking you up to the Niger mountain lodge (18.0km), where you finally touch the top of the pass. The road now runs along at the foot of the Catinaccios past the Tscheiner mountain lodge (23.0km) on a flatter stretch and is no longer a chore but a pleasure. It then rises gently to the junction with the Costalunga Pass road (25.0km), which has just a kilometre to go to its highest point.

As an extra there is also a wonderful view of the main ridge of the Catenaccios, which now moves into our field of vision. In Italian, a catenaccio is a bolt on a door, and borrowed for the mountain range it refers to its impregnability. This is evident from this vantage point: it shows itself as a lengthy series of peaks, towers and wide reddish-coloured rock faces of Wetterstein limestone. Local legend has it that Laurin, the king of the dwarves, lived in the Catenaccios before being defeated in battle by Dietrich von Bern, in spite of a magic hat and a belt that bestowed on him the strength of 12 men. Once you've seen the massif by the red glow of the setting sun you can understand how such stories might arise.

In the upper part of the Nigerpass, just before you reach the Costalunga Pass (Tour 31), you can see the Latemar group.

Opposite: The dramatic Torri del Viajolet.

TOUR PROFILE <<

Costalunga Pass: 1752m

WESTERN SIDE – Start: Cardano, 290m

Directions: A22 Brenner Autobahn, exit Bolzano/North

Level of Difficulty/Maximum gradient: Difficult, with a maximum gradient of 18 per cent over about 1.5km at the start. Longer stretches with a gradient of up to 12 per cent

Length: 24.5km

Total ascent: 1465m

Time: 2¾–4 hrs

Suggested gearing: 39/28

Route: Cardano (0.0km) – Nova Levante (13.5km) – Lake Costalunga (20.5km) – turning to the Nigerpass (23.5km) – Top of the pass (24.5km)

EASTERN SIDE – Start: San Giovanni in Val di Fassa, 1323m

Directions: A22 Brenner Autobahn, exit Egna/Ora – Ora – Cavalese – Predazzo – Moena – San Giovanni

Level of Difficulty/Maximum gradient: Easy, with a maximum gradient of 10 per cent

Length: 10.0km

Total ascent: 370m

Time: 1–1½ hrs

Suggested gearing: 39/26

Route: San Giovanni (0.0km) – Vigo di Fassa (1.5km) – Vallonga (3.0km) – Top of the pass (10.0km)

Road conditions: Well-constructed roads. Bottlenecks in Vigo di Fassa and Cardano

Pass open: All year

Things to see: Vigo di Fassa: church of St John, church of St Juliana and valley museum; Lake Costalunga and Val d'Ega gorge on the western side

Map: Euro Cart regional map 1:300,000, RV-Verlag, South Tyrol/Veneto sheet

Lake Costalunga on the western side of the Costalunga Pass is a jewel among lakes in the Dolomites.

Coming from Bolzano the Costalunga Pass is the easiest introduction to the high mountain world of the Dolomites. That's if you're in a car. With a bike it's rather more difficult, as you have to conquer a total vertical climb of nearly 1500m over gradients of up to 16 per cent in just under 25km.

The small village of Cardano (0.0km), situated a little to the east of Bolzano in the Isarco valley, is the starting point, and the road immediately takes you up a 16 per cent slope into the narrow Ega valley. The reddish porphyry cliffs crowd together, leaving hardly any room for the road, which had to be blasted out of the rock above the wildly foaming waters of the Ega. After 1.5km the gradient finally decreases a little to 10 per cent, interspersed with longer, flatter sections, and reaches Ponte Nova (10.5km).

The oppressive narrowness of the valley is now behind us, but on the way to Nova Levante (13.5km) there are several unlit tunnels and galleries to be tackled over gradients of between 8 per cent and 10 per cent. It's said that giants once came down here from the Latemar to fight the Dirlinger clan who once lived here. We won't

come across any Dirlingers or giants here, just a gradient increasing to 12 per cent that brings us to Lake Costalunga (20.5km). It's undoubtedly one of the most beautiful lakes in the Dolomites, in whose blue waters the towers and crags of the Latemar massif are mirrored. The road winds its way up over further hairpin bends with gradients of up to 12 per cent, decreasing to 10 per cent, and near the enormous stone structure of Latemar Castle (23.5km) we reach the junction with the Nigerpass road (Tour 30). The magnificent mountain peaks of the Catenaccio spread before us to the left and of the Latemar to the right, to whose saddle the road ascends for another kilometre. The top of the pass (24.5km) marks the German-Italian language border, which means that in San Giovanni, less than 400m lower down in the Fassa valley, which we'll reach after a 10km winding descent (gradients up to 10 per cent), Italian is spoken.

If you want to add on additional passes then Canazei makes a good starting point

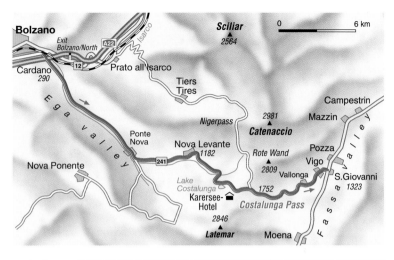

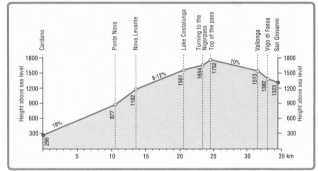

for the Fedáia Pass (Tour 32), the Pordoi Pass (Tour 27) and the Sella Pass (Tour 28): it's just under 16km away and 170m up.

The top of the Costalunga Pass also represents the German-Italian language border in the Dolomites.

TOUR PROFILE <<

Fedáia Pass: 2056m

WESTERN SIDE – Start: Canazei, 1465m

Directions: A22 Brenner Autobahn, exit Bolzano/North – Costalunga Pass – Pozza di Fassa – Canazei or Cortina d'Ampezzo – Falzárego Pass – Arabba – Pordoi Pass – Canazei

Level of Difficulty/Maximum gradient: Easy, with a maximum gradient of 10 per cent

Length: 14.5km

Total ascent: 595m

Time: 1¼–1¾ hrs

Suggested gearing: 39/26

Route: Canazei (0.0km) – Penia (3.0km) – Fedáia reservoir (12.0km) – Top of the pass (14.5km)

EASTERN SIDE – Start: Caprile, 1023m; Cortina d'Ampezzo – Giau Pass – Selva di Cadore – Caprile

Level of Difficulty/Maximum gradient: Medium, with a maximum gradient of 16 per cent

Length: 14.5km

Total ascent: 1035m

Time: 1¾–2½ hrs

Suggested gearing: 39/28

Route: Caprile (0.0km) – Saviner di Laste (1.5km) – Pian (6.0km) – Sottoguda (8.0km) – Malga Ciapéla (10.5km) – Top of the pass (14.5km)

Road conditions: Several sections are narrow on the eastern side. On the western side there are many badly-lit galleries and a 300m unlit tunnel. Slight damage to the road surface throughout

Pass open: 15 April to 15 October

Things to see: The Sottoguda gorge and the cable car ride, in three sections, from Malga Ciapéla to the summit ridge of the Marmolada at a height of 3250m with a wonderful view

Map: Euro Cart regional map 1:300,000, RV-Verlag, South Tyrol/Veneto sheet

Notes: Lights are necessary because of the galleries and the 300m unlit tunnel on the western side

We could join these two by taking the cable car from the Fedáia Pass up to the Marmolada glacier.

The Fedáia Pass takes us up to the highest point of the Dolomites, to the northern foot of the Marmolada. At a height of 3342m this is not only the highest mountain in the Dolomites but also the most heavily glaciated, and it undoubtedly deserves its appellation of 'queen of the Dolomites'. But as high and as magnificent as the Marmolada may be, the cycling tour to the Fedáia Pass is only graded as easy, at least when tackled, as we are doing, from the west.

We leave Canazei (0.0km) in a south-easterly direction along the side of the valley and ride along a route that climbs only moderately to the villages of Alba and Penia (3.0km) towards the end of the valley. Penia in particular is a picturesque maze of old farmhouses clustered round a little Gothic church. The gradient increases and coniferous forest slowly retreats to reveal the rock walls and protective boards of the Vernel, the cornerstone of the Marmolada.

We arrive at the first of four numbered hairpin bends (7.0km), which wind up the side of the valley at a steady gradient of 10 per cent and after 2km lead to the long Pian Trevisan valley. The winding road climbs on at a constant grade up the slopes of the southern side of the valley through a total of 10 galleries, but the only unpleasant part to ride is the last 300m tunnel, which brings us out onto the Fedáia plateau. Then you ride straight to the Fedáia reservoir (12.0km), which collects the meltwater from the Marmolada, and you effortlessly reach the top of the pass, the Marmolada mountain lodge, along a level road following the wall on the southern side of the reservoir.

If you park your bike here and look up at the cirques and icefields of the Marmolada as it slopes down to the north, you'll understand why this summit is known as the Queen of the Dolomites. The whole mountain range is known in Italian as the Marmolada, with the Punta Penia as its highest point at 3342m, the 3259m Punta di Rocca, considered to be the most beautiful peak in the Dolomites for skiing, and the 3218m Monte Serauta. The Punta di Rocca was the first of them to be climbed, by the Englishmen Ball and Birbeck in 1860, while the Punta Penia was finally conquered in 1864 after several attempts, by the famous Austrian alpinist Paul Grohmann, with the aid of guides Angelo and Fulgentio Dimai from Ampezzo.

Now we go over to the eastern side down several valley slopes at a gradient of up to 16 per cent. Get over the dizziness

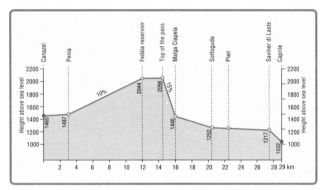

brought on by the deep Sottoguda gorge and finish the tour 14.5km further on and 1000m lower down in Caprile.

Snow lies at the top of the Fedaia Pass until late in May. Behind it towers the vast Monte Civetta.

TOUR PROFILE <<

San Pellegrino Pass: 1918m

EASTERN SIDE – Start: Cencenighe, 774m

Directions: A27 Venice–Belluno, exit Belluno – Agordo – Cencenighe

Level of Difficulty/Maximum gradient: Medium, with a maximum gradient of 18 per cent over 600m and a gradient of 14 per cent over about 2.5km

Length: 20.5km

Total ascent: 1145m

Time: 1¾–2½ hrs

Suggested gearing: 39/28

Route: Cencenighe (0.0km) – Mas (2.5km) – Canale d'Agordo (5.0km) – Falcade (7.5km) – Falcade Alto (12.5km) – Bar Fior di Roccia (18.0km) – Top of the pass (20.5km)

WESTERN SIDE – Start: Moena, 1184m

Directions: A22 Brenner Autobahn, exit Bolzano/North – Cardano – Costalunga Pass – San Giovanni – Moena

Level of Difficulty/Maximum gradient: Medium, with a maximum gradient of 14 per cent

Length: 12.0km

Total ascent: 735m

Time: 1½–2 hrs

Suggested gearing: 39/26

Route: Moena (0.0km) – top of the pass (12.0km)

Road conditions: Well-constructed roads

Pass open: All year

Map: Euro Cart regional map 1:300,000, RV-Verlag, South Tyrol/Veneto sheet

Notes: Lights are advisable because of the 400m dimly lit tunnel on the eastern side

The Catenaccio group shows us its eastern side from the San Pellegrino Pass.

At one time the San Pellegrino Pass, which joins the Cencenighe and Fassa valleys, was an important trade route between Venice and Bolzano and bore the name Monte Alloch. These days the crossing is really only important for tourism, and then mainly in the winter when skiers target the wide, treeless grassy slopes around the top of the pass. But it's also of interest to cyclists, mainly when the skiing stops, because the eastern side offers gradients of up to 18 per cent. When you look for it on the map, you'll find it more or less in the middle between the Marmolada range in the north and the Pala range in the south.

The focal point is the village of Moena in the west, but we start our tour in Cencenighe, situated towards the east. In the middle of the village (0.0km) the signpost saying Canale d'Agordo/San Pellegrino Pass shows us the way and we arrive in a narrow, gorge-like valley on a road with a 10 per cent gradient. On the way to Mas (2.5km) there's a dimly lit 400m tunnel, then the valley broadens out and meadows replace the rocks. Below the eastern foothills of the Marmolada the gradient increases to 12 per cent between Canale d'Agordo (5.0km) and Falcade (7.5km). Further to the south you can make out the peaks of the Pala group, while ahead the road makes its way up over hairpin bends with a gradient of up to 12 per cent to Falcade Alto (12.5km).

Then there's a sign noting a 14 per cent gradient, and the route winds its exhausting way past the turning to the Valles Pass (14.5km) through thick conifer forests, reaching an agonising 18 per cent for almost a kilometre. On the next stretch the incline goes down to 10 per cent, which feels almost pleasant, and at Bar Fior di Roccia (18.0km) you can pause to gear yourself up for the

final 2.5km to the top of the pass (20.5km), still at 10 per cent. There isn't much of a view up here, but there is on the straightish 12km downhill (gradients up to 14 per cent) just before you reach Moena, almost 750m lower down, with the peaks of the Catenaccio group visible in the west.

From Moena you can extend your ride with a choice of two interesting passes. It's about 5km and a vertical climb of 100m or so up the Fassa valley in the direction of Canazei to San Giovanni near Vigo di Fassa, the starting point for the Costalunga Pass (Tour 31). Or you can

ride out of the valley to Predazzo, the starting point for the Rolle Pass (Tour 34), descending 150m over a 9km stretch.

Rapid descent at the San Pellegrino Pass.

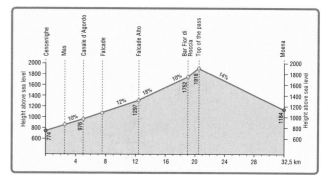

34 ROLLE PASS
Dolomites/Trentino

TOUR PROFILE <<

Rolle Pass: 1980m

WESTERN SIDE – Start: Predazzo, 1018m

Directions: A22 Brenner Autobahn, exit Egna/Ora – Cavalese – Predazzo

Level of Difficulty/Maximum gradient: Medium, with a maximum gradient of 9 per cent

Length: 19.5km

Total ascent: 965m

Time: 1¾–2¼ hrs

Suggested gearing: 39/23

Route: Predazzo (0.0km) – Gasthof Saluna (2.5km) – Bellamonte (4.5km) – Panéveggio (12.0km) – turning to the Valles Pass (13.0km) – Top of the pass (19.5km)

SOUTHERN SIDE – Start: Fiera di Primiero, 717m

Directions: Feltre – Artén – Fonzaso – Imer – Mezzano – Fiera di Primiero

Level of Difficulty/Maximum gradient: Medium, with a maximum gradient of 11 per cent

Length: 21.0km

Total ascent: 1265m

Time: 1¾-2¾ hrs

Suggested gearing: 39/26

Route: Fiera di Primiero (0.0km) – Siror (1.0km) – San Martino di Castrozza (12.5km) – Top of the pass (21.0km)

Road conditions: Well-constructed roads, apart from slight surface damage in the area of the summit and narrow stretches on the lower part of the western side

Pass open: All year

Things to see: Predazzo: Geological Museum; Bellamonte: Chapel of Mary of the Snows; Panéveggio: Nature Reserve Visitors' Museum

Map: Euro Cart regional map 1:300,000, RV-Verlag, South Tyrol/Veneto sheet

The Pala mountains soar up in the south-eastern Dolomites, their most impressive and wildest region. The Rolle Pass connects the Fiemme valley with the Cismon valley, passing through an area of such scenic beauty that part of it has been designated as the Panéveggio nature reserve.

Western side

The starting point for the western route up to the pass is the market town of Predazzo, reached most easily from the Adige valley. The total vertical climb on the 38km route is just under 800m, and the maximum gradient 9 per cent.

In Predazzo (0.0km) follow the signposts to the Rolle Pass and ride up a road with a gradient of 9 per cent through the narrow Travignola valley. At the Gasthof Saluna inn (2.5km) there are four hairpin bends to tackle up a grassy hillside, bringing you to Bellamonte (4.5km). As you leave the village the gradient decreases and you ride past the long, narrow Panéveggio reservoir on an almost flat road to a little clearing in the woods across which the Panéveggio hotel complex (12.0km) spreads itself out.

Past the turning for the Valles Pass, which leads to the San Pellegrino Pass (Tour 33) to the north of here, the gradient increases again to 9 per cent and stays there all the way to the top of the pass. Nothing much happens at first: the road winds its way up over a series of hairpin bends through thick, unspoiled forest, which is reckoned to be one of the most beautiful woodlands in Italy, then suddenly a view of the vast rocky crags of the Pala group opens up. At the top of the pass (19.5km) the striking summit of the Cimon della Pala is particularly impressive, displaying the distinctive silhouette that has given it the nickname the 'Matterhorn of the Dolomites'.

Southern side

Of the southern slope of the pass all that needs to be said is that the traffic system makes the starting point of Fiera di Primiero a little difficult to get to. But we have no criticisms of the route or its scenery.

We leave Fiera di Primiero (0.0km), situated in the valley of the confluence of little-known rivers such as the Cismon and the Canali, via the district called Tonadico. In the next village, Siror (1.0km), we cross the Cismon and the road climbs, first over hairpin bends and then in a straighter line. This continues for quite a long time, with a quite easily manageable gradient of around 7 per cent, rising here and there to 9 per cent, up to the thickly wooded slopes of the western side of the valley. The straight course of the road is broken up twice by hairpin bends, and large information boards at the side of the road every half kilometre inform us of how far we've come. As we climb higher the view opens out onto the peaks and towers of the Pala range and form an impressive display near San Martino di Castrozza (2.5km).

We leave this sprawling tourist town below us, climbing up on a series of hairpin bends (gradient 9 per cent), and we are soon swallowed up by a belt of woodland with more hairpins and an unchanged gradient. We cross a stream (19.0km) and leave the woods behind as the gradient increases to 11 per cent. The hairpin bends are a little narrower now, and soon the striking peak of the 3129m Cimon della Pala, the highest summit of the group, moves further into our field of vision.

At the end of the series of hairpin bends (20.0km), there's another wonderful view of the sloping rocky chain, then the road goes round a mountain ridge into a little high valley. We ride the last kilometre up to the top of the pass (21.0km) at the foot of the Cimon della Pala along an almost level road.

The Cima della Pala above the Rolle Pass is also called the Matterhorn of the Dolomites because of its striking shape.

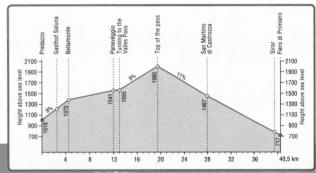

35 JAUFEN PASS
South Tyrol

The Jaufen Pass is a scenically attractive link between Vipiteno in the Isarco valley and San Leonardo in the Passiria valley. It's notable as the birthplace of Andreas Hofer, the famous South Tyrolean freedom fighter, and also as the southern starting point for the Timmelsjoch (Tour 36). If you want to extend the tour, you can bolt on either the Timmelsjoch or ride down the Passiria valley from San Leonardo towards Bolzano and return to Vipiteno by following the southern side of the Penser Joch, as described in Tour 37.

In Vipiteno (0.0km), past the Brenner Autobahn tollbooth, follow the road leading west to the Jaufen Pass to reach Casateia (3.0km) over a flattish route. Not long after the gradient increases to 10 per cent and goes up over a series of bends. The woods thin out to give a view of the Stubai Alps to the north, and then a stretch of hairpin bends, beginning after 5.5km, brings you to Calice (9.0km) at a constant gradient of between 8 per cent and 10 per cent. At the Gasthof Jägerhof inn a plaque notes that Andreas Hofer held a council of war here before defeating the occupying French forces

A reward for the effort of the climb: sunbathing in an alpine meadow.

on 8 May 1808. As the gradient decreases you cross the tree line (16.0km); then the slope is back at 8 per cent-10 per cent up up to the Jaufenhaus hut (17.0km). There are two further generously curved hairpin bends to deal with over an unchanged gradient before you reach the top of the pass (18.5km), where the vantage point gives you a panoramic view of the Tessa group to the west.

On the western side the road now descends steeply to the Wannser valley over six narrow but widely spaced hairpin bends. Further along the narrowness of the road, and in particular the badly frost-damaged road surface, require you to

These cyclists are on the western side of the Jaufen Pass taking part in the Ötztal Cycle Marathon.

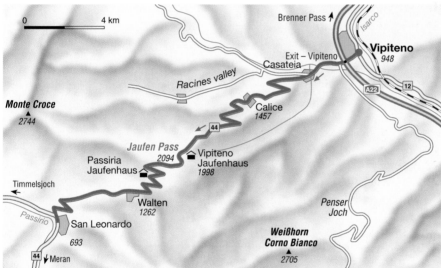

concentrate. In the lowest section there are four narrow hairpin bends following each other in quick succession before you have to brake smartly to a halt in San Leonardo, 21km further on and 1400m lower down. If you're not going on, perhaps to the Timmelsjoch (Tour 36), you can stop for refreshments in the Gasthaus Sandwirt on the southern side of the village, believed to be the house where Andreas Hofer was born.

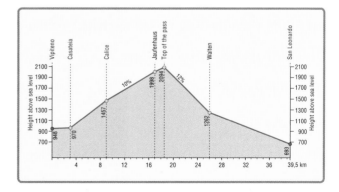

TOUR PROFILE <<

Timmelsjoch (southern side): 2509m

SOUTHERN SIDE – Start: San Leonardo in Passiria, 693m

Directions: Brenner Autobahn, exit Vipiteno – Jaufen Pass – San Leonardo

Level of Difficulty/Maximum gradient: Difficult, with a maximum gradient of 13 per cent over about 3km. Long stretches at a gradient of 10 per cent

Length: 29.5km

Total ascent: 1820m

Time: 3–4 hrs

Suggested gearing: 39/26

Route: San Leonardo (0.0km) – Moso (7.0km) – Gasthof Saltnuss (16.0km) – Gasthof Hoch-First (20.5km) – Top of the pass (29.5km)

NORTHERN SIDE: See Tour 13

Road conditions: Narrow hairpin bends, many unlit tunnels and damage to the road surface

Pass open: 15 June to 15 October. The border crossing is closed from 8pm to 7am

Things to see: San Leonardo: Gasthof Sandwirt, the house where Andreas Hofer was born

Map: Euro Cart regional map 1:300,000, RV-Verlag, South Tyrol/Veneto sheet

Notes: Riders undertake this route at their own risk and must have lights in good working order

The southern side of the Timmelsjoch High Alpine Road, starting from San Leonardo in Passiria, was closed to cyclists for some years, but the ban was lifted in 2000 and cyclists can once more enjoy a route that is extremely attractive, from both a scenic and a technical point of view. One small reservation: the tunnels are unlit in places in the upper part of the route and so lights, both front and rear, are absolutely necessary for reasons of safety.

San Leonardo in Passiria (0.0km) is the birthplace of the best-known freedom fighter in the German-speaking region: Andreas Hofer. He led the Tyrolean farmers in their uprising against Franco–Bavarian rule during the reign of Napoleon, the French emperor. Hofer wanted to restore the Tyrol, which had been transferred to Bavaria in 1805, to Austria and the House of Habsburg. He gained significant victories but couldn't prevent the Tyrol being transferred from the defeated Habsburgs back to Bavaria under the Treaty of Vienna. He lost the last and decisive battle and had to flee, but was betrayed and brought by the French to Mantua, where he was executed by firing squad in 1810.

We leave the village (0.0km) up the valley of the Passirio. As we pass the Hotel Passeierhof the gradient increases to 10 per cent,

The southern side of the Timmelsjoch, with its many bends, hairpins, narrow roads and tunnels is a difficult ride.

but this is interspersed by long, flatter sections until we reach Moso (7.0km), only to increase again to 13 per cent over a 3km series of hairpin bends. Then the gradient falls away, first to 10 per cent and then down further.

We cross the Schneeberg stream and at the Gasthof Saltnuss (16.5km) we can already make out the next clutch of hairpins. At first the slope on the road up to the Gasthof Hoch-First (20.5km) decreases a little, but at the beginning of the series of hairpin bends (22.0km) it goes back up, to 10 per cent, and stays there through the widely spaced hairpin up the barren slopes of the Banker Pass. There's no let-up until 27.0km, when the pain of the climb is replaced by the perils of a gallery and several tunnels in the upper section on the way to the top of the pass (29.5km). The longest tunnel is approximately 600m, and it's pitch black, presenting real danger to anyone foolish enough not to bring bright lights.

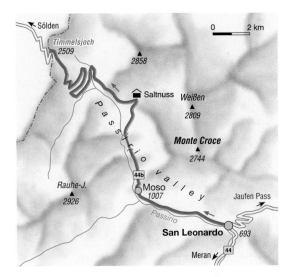

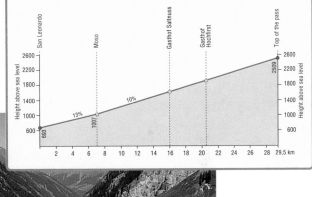

This short stretch on the southern side of the Timmelsjoch clearly shows how many bends there are on the route.

TOUR PROFILE <<

Penser Joch: 2215m

SOUTHERN SIDE – Start: Bolzano, 265m

Directions: A22 Brenner Autobahn, exit Bolzano/North

Level of Difficulty/Maximum gradient: Difficult, with a maximum gradient of 12 per cent

Length: 53.0km

Total ascent: 1950m

Time: 3½–5 hrs

Suggested gearing: 39/26

Route: Bolzano (0.0km) – Gasthof Halbweg (14.0km) – Bundschen (19.5km) – Sarentino (23.0km) – Riobianco (29.5km) – Pens (44.5km) – Top of the pass (53.0km)

Old mountain farms near Pennes on the southern side of the Penser Joch.

The Penser Joch is a scenically attractive and varied link over the Sarntal Alps from the Isarco valley at Vipiteno to Bolzano in the Adige valley. The total length is 69.5km and the highest point at the top of the pass is 2211m above sea level. From the cyclist's point of view it's interesting that the two sides of the pass are quite different. The northern climb from Vipiteno, with its vertical ascent of 1260m and maximum gradients of 13 per cent, is certainly demanding, but it won't demand your last ounce of strength. Not so the southern side. Not only is it 53km long, but it demands a bigger vertical climb, at 1964m, than even the famed Großglockner High Alpine Road (Tour 9) and Stelvio Pass (Tour 40).

Northern side

At the southern edge of Vipiteno (0.0km) follow the signposts for the Penser Joch, cross the Ridnauner stream (fed by the glaciers of the Stubai Alps) and then ride past the customs lorry yard. At first you climb only moderately but a sign (1.5km) soon indicates the beginning of a 13 per cent gradient. This is a long haul, finally reducing to a more manageable 10 per cent only after 5.5km. As the woodlands thin you'll pass through Egg (8.0km), the only village on this side of the pass.

The road winds its way south-west into the Egg valley and takes you up over many curves and hairpin bends, at a gradient of up to 10 per cent, to the southern slopes of the Cima di Stilves. There's no view to speak of, but the top of the pass and the Alpenrose mountain hotel soon move into your field of vision. As you cross the tree line (13.5km) a change comes over the landscape. The road now makes a wide loop up a constant 10 per cent gradient between a carpet of alpine meadows and the rocky slopes below the crest of the Hühnerspiel mountain, and you soon reach the the top of the pass (16.5km) and the hotel.

Southern side

The route over the southern side is a little more laborious, right from the start in Bolzano (0.0km), where you will likely get tied up in traffic. Head out by following the signposts for Sarentino. As you leave town you'll notice Castel Roncolo located spectacularly on a cliff, its walls rising vertically from the bed of the River

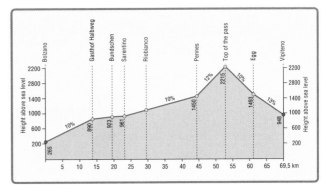

TOUR PROFILE <<

NORTHERN SIDE – Start: Vipiteno, 948m

Directions: A22 Brenner Autobahn, exit Vipiteno

Level of Difficulty/Maximum gradient: Medium, with a maximum gradient of 13 per cent over about 3.5km at the beginning of the climb

Length: 16.5km

Total ascent: 1265m

Time: 1¾–2½ hrs

Suggested gearing: 39/26

Route: Vipiteno (0.0km) – Egg (8.0km) – Top of the pass (16.5km)

Road conditions: 24 partly unlit tunnels between 20m and 500m on the southern side (lights are absolutely essential) and narrow roads with traffic mirrors on blind bends in the Sarentino gorge at the beginning of the climb. Several narrow roads with traffic mirrors on blind bends on the northern side, slight surface damage at the summit

Pass open: 15 May or 1 June to 31 October

Things to see: Vipiteno: Old town, town hall and city tower (Zwölferturm); Reifenstein Castle in Moso near Vipiteno; Sarentino: Church of St Cyprian; Bolzano: Roncolo Castle, cathedral with memorial to Walther von der Vogelweide, administration building of Holy Roman Emperor Maximilian I, Mareccio Castle and town museum

Map: Euro Cart regional map 1:300,000, RV-Verlag, South Tyrol/Veneto sheet

Finally made it: the Alpenrose mountain hotel and the summit of the Penser Joch.

Opposite: On the lower part of the southern side of the Penser Joch road.

Talvera. It's the very epitome of a knight's castle and well worth a visit: enter via a drawbridge to find an inviting castle hostelry in a picturesque castle courtyard. You can see the interior of the castle with its interesting frescoes on a guided tour; they run daily, except for Sundays and bank holidays, from 10am until noon and 3-6pm.

Returning from the Middle Ages, you'll reach the gorge of the Sarentino with its massive rock faces of red-tinged porphyry and bizarrely shaped overhanging projections. Stunning to look at, but less attractive to ride. The gradient is 10 per cent, and there are 24 tunnels, mostly unlit, between 20m and 500m long.

At the Gasthof Halbweg (14.0km), where the horses for the Sarentino stagecoaches used to be changed, you finally put the last of the tunnels behind you. From here to Bundschen (19.5km) 10 per cent gradients alternate with flatter stretches, then you'll arrive at Sarentino (23.0km), charmingly situated between green meadows and wooded hilltops. The route turns off in the direction of Riobianco (29.5km) before the town centre, but if you want you can fortify yourself in the ancient Tyrolean bar of Gasthof Zum Hirschen, diagonally opposite the flamboyant Gothic church of St Cyprian. There's not much traffic, and you should make good progress over gradients mostly well under 8 per cent as far as Pennes (44.5km), where the slope increases, first to 10 per cent, and then, on the last kilometre up to the top of the pass (53.0km), to 12 per cent.

The Penser Joch is a stiff challenge on its own, but if your training has prepared you for something even harder, you can combine it into a circular tour with the the Jaufen Pass (Tour 35). It's best to start this at Vipiteno with the climb over the northern side of the Jaufen Pass, to San Leonardo, down the Passirio valley to Merano, then on to Bolzano to ride back over the southern side of the Penser Joch. This makes a route 150km long with a total vertical climb of 3150m that will take at least 8½ hours just to ride, with stops on top.

38 PASSO DELLE PALADE
South Tyrol/Trentino

TOUR PROFILE <<

Passo delle Palade: 1518m

NORTHERN SIDE – Start: Merano, 302m

Directions: over the Ötztal and Timmelsjoch (Tours 13 and 36) to Merano or A22 Brenner Autobahn, exit Bolzano/South – Terlano – Postal – Merano

Level of Difficulty/Maximum gradient: Medium, with a maximum gradient of 9 per cent

Length: 24.5km

Total ascent: 1235m

Time: 1¾–2½ hrs

Suggested gearing: 39/23

Route: Merano (0.0km) – Lana (6.5km) – Albergo Gfriller Hof (17.5km) – Gasthof Bad Gfrill (19.5km) – Alpine Hotel Panorama (21.5km) – Top of the pass (24.5km)

SOUTHERN SIDE – Start: Fondo, 987m:

Directions: over the Mendel Pass to Fondo (Tour 39) or A22 Brenner Autobahn, exit San Michele all'Adige/Mezzocorona – Mezzolombardo – Dermulo – Fondo

Level of Difficulty/Maximum gradient: Easy, with a maximum gradient of 8 per cent

Length: 14.0km

Total ascent: 535m

Time: 1¼–2 hrs

Suggested gearing: 39/23

Route: Fondo (0.0km) – San Felice (8.0km) – Top of the pass (14.0km)

Road conditions: Well-constructed roads

Pass open: All year

Things to see: Merano: royal castle, Castel San Zeno, town museum and arcades of shops. Niederlana: altar by Schnatterpeck in the old parish church, Castel Leone on the northern side

Map: Euro Cart regional map 1:300,000, RV-Verlag, South Tyrol/Veneto sheet

Notes: Lights are advisable because of the four unlit tunnels, 20-100m long, on the northern side and a 150m tunnel on the southern side

A panoramic view of the Adige valley from the Passo delle Palade.

High over the slopes of the western side of the Adige valley the Passo delle Palade makes its way from Merano over to Fondo in the Val di Non. It's an attractive route if you want to go from Merano up over into the Val di Sole, the region around the Lago di San Giustino in Trentino, or to avoid the unattractive Adige valley from Fondo over the western side of the Mendel Pass to Bolzano or Caldaro. The Passo delle Palade lies in what is known as a 'burgraviate', a type of administrative area that dates back to the time when Merano was the provincial capital of the Tyrol, which then stretched from Kufstein to Lake Garda and from Graubünden to Carinthia. The burgraviate was run from Tirol Castle, situated high above Merano.

Merano (0.0km), our starting point, is now the second largest town in the South Tyrol after Bolzano. Follow the signposts to the Passo delle Palade along the busy main road to Lana (6.5km), where

94

the traffic falls away but the road starts to climb at a gradient of 9 per cent to the edge of the wide Merano basin. After a short, unlit tunnel the supremely beautiful Castel Leone rises up next to the road. Inclines of up to 9 per cent, though mostly lower, bring us to the hills of the low Tesimo mountain range and after two more 100m unlit tunnels (11.5km) we can see far to the east the first Dolomite summits from the Catenaccio to the Latemar.

The road meanders up the Prissiano valley at a gradient of 9 per cent, where it stays until the Albergo Gfriller Hof (17.5km) on the way to the Gasthof Bad Gfrill (19.5km). Over two hairpin bends up to the Alpine Hotel Panorama (21.5km) the gradient goes back up to 9 per cent; we then wind our way up through an unlit 100m hairpin bend tunnel. With the slope decreasing to 7 per cent, thick mixed woodland accompanies us up to the top of the pass, which unfortunately offers no view whatsoever. And nor does the 8 per cent descent to Fondo, apart from a few glimpses in the Val di Non. The views only appear on the road from Fondo to the top of the Mendel Pass and from there to the difficult dead-end road up to Monte Pénegal.

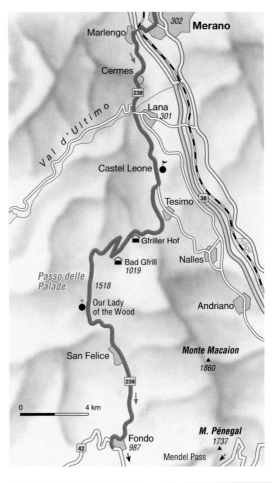

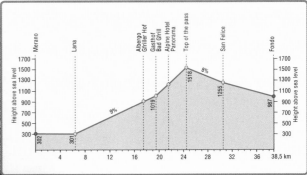

Handlebar bags like these are making a bit of a comeback.

TOUR PROFILE <<

Mendel Pass: 1363m

EASTERN SIDE – Start: Caldaro, 426m on the northern end of Lake Caldaro

Directions: A22 Brenner Autobahn, exit Bolzano/South – Appiano – Caldaro or exit Egna/Ora – Termeno – Caldaro

Level of Difficulty/Maximum gradient: Medium, with a maximum gradient of 10 per cent. On the climb to Monte Pénegal, difficult with a maximum gradient of 18 per cent

Length: 16.0km

Total ascent: 940m

Time: 2–2½ hrs

Suggested gearing: 39/26 (39/28 on the climb to Monte Pénegal)

Route: Caldaro (0.0km) – San Niccolò (5.0km) – Top of the pass (16.0km)

WESTERN SIDE – Start: Fondo, 987m

Directions: A22 Brenner Autobahn, exit San Michele a.A./Mezzocorona – Mezzolombardo – Dermulo – Fondo

Level of Difficulty/Maximum gradient: Easy, with a maximum gradient of 12 per cent on a short section in Fondo, but mostly 8 per cent and under

Length: 9.5km

Total ascent: 376m

Time: 1–1½ hrs

Suggested gearing: 39/23

Route: Fondo (0.0km) – Gasthof Waldheim (2.0km) – Top of the pass (9.5km)

Road conditions: Very narrow roads in the upper part of the eastern side, with occasional passing places. A rather straight road on the western side, with damage to the road surface. On the climb to Monte Pénegal there is considerable damage to the road surface in places

Pass open: All year

Things to see: Caldaro: Museum of Wine; observation tower on Monte Pénegal.

Map: Euro Cart regional map 1:300,000, RV-Verlag, South Tyrol/Veneto sheet

Regular alpine riders sometimes develop a closer relationship with particular passes over the course of the year. Passes that evoke a particular mood, and which you include time and again when planning tours. For me it's the Mendel Pass, from Bolzano or Caldaro over the Mendola ridge into the Val di Non. I can't say exactly why I prefer this pass above all others, but it has something to do with the attractive South Tyrolean scenery and the mild climate around nearby Lake Caldaro, which together conjure up a holiday atmosphere. In spring or autumn, when the weather at home in Bavaria doesn't inspire longer rides, here in the sunshine and mild temperatures you can still enjoy wonderful tours. I think the loveliest times to ride over the Mendel Pass are in April in apple-blossom time and in autumn during the grape harvest, when the leaves on the trees on the Mendola ridge are turning red and gold. It's best avoided in the peak holiday period from August to the beginning of September when day-tripping locals add to the holiday traffic and it can get very congested.

There are two possible starting points. While riders coming from the area around Bolzano will prefer the new and well-constructed stretch of climb that branches off in Appiano, I prefer to start the tour in Caldaro (0.0km). Right from the beginning the road climbs at 10 per cent in this busy town, lying just above Lake Caldaro. You ride up along the narrow town centre roads, which have bumpy cobblestones in places with no let-up in the climb. It remains at 10 per cent as the road heads for the village of San Niccolò (5.0km), and its striking church with a green shingle roof.

Shortly afterwards you reach the road leading up from Appiano and if you look back here you may catch a glimpse of the buildings of Caldaro dotted across the slope, its old manor houses and churches rising out of the vineyards, and the smooth surface of Lake Caldaro with the ruins of Leuchtenburg towering over the eastern bank, a classic upper Adige sight. Then a dense deciduous wood of oaks and chestnuts envelops us and the first hairpin bend also awaits. The road goes up over six hairpin bends with a gradient of 10 per cent. A sign with an altitude reading of 1000m indicates that there's still a good 360m of vertical climb ahead. Immediately after that we reach the beginning of a section of road (11.0km) that was blasted right out the rock. It's almost straight, but the gradient hardly lets up, though you do have a good view of the peaks of well-known Dolomite ranges such as the Sciliar, the Catenaccio and the Latemar.

At the end of this stretch of road (13.5km) a sign at the start of nine hairpin bends indicates that we are nearing the

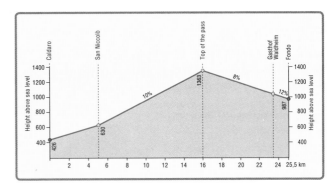

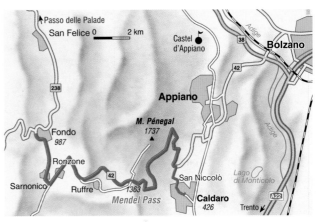

top of the pass (16.0km), riding once more through dense woods and at a gradient that hardly falls below 10 per cent. If it's been too easy for you up till now, here's a new challenge. Some 300m after the top of the pass a dead-end road, badly potholed but tarmacked throughout, turns off to the right to Monte Pénegal. And this has a lot of climbing to offer, as you'll gather right at the start from the 12 per cent gradient.

After about 1.5km the climb increases to 18 per cent over a 300m stretch, decreases briefly to 10 per cent, then shoots back up to 18 per cent for almost 500m. Until the end of the road at the Hotel Facchin, 4km away, gradients of 12 per cent alternate with flatter sections. The last test of strength is the climb up the observation tower teetering next to the hotel.

The new route leading from Appiano up to the Mendel Pass is a well-constructed alternative to the climb from Caldaro.

TOUR PROFILE <<

Stelvio Pass: 2757m

Level of Difficulty/Maximum gradient: Difficult, with a maximum gradient of 12 per cent on long sections

NORTHERN SIDE – Start: Spondigna, 887m

Directions: A12 Innsbruck–Bludenz (Inn Valley Autobahn), exit Zams/Landeck East – Pfunds – Nodrio – Passo di Resia – Malles Venosta – Spondigna

Length: 28.0km

Total ascent: 1870m

Time: 3–4 hrs

Suggested gearing: 39/28

Route: Spondigna (0.0km) – Prato (2.0km) – Gomagoi (8.5km) – Trafoi (12.0km) – Gasthof Weißer Knott (17.5km) – Hotel Franzenshöhe (22.0km) – Top of the pass (28.0km)

SOUTHERN SIDE – Start: Bórmio, 1217m

Directions: from Oberengadin over Pontresina – Bernina Pass – Livigno Pass – Eira Pass – Foscagno Pass to Bórmio or Zernez – in the direction of Passo del Forno – turning for Munt la Schera tunnel – Livigno – Eira Pass – Foscagno Pass to Bórmio

Length: 22.0km

Total ascent: 1540m

Time: 2¾–4 hrs

Suggested gearing: 39/26

Route: Bórmio (0.0km) – Cantoniera IV a (18.5km) – Top of the pass (22.0km)

Road conditions: Roads with tight hairpin bends and considerable damage to the road surface on the descent. Two unlit tunnels (50m and 150m) on the southern side and five unlit gallery tunnels (100–200m)

Pass open: 1 June to 31 October

Things to see: Viewpoint over the Ortler at the Gasthof Weißer Knott; Bórmio: historic town houses and municipal museum

Map: Euro Cart regional map 1:300,000, RV-Verlag, South Tyrol/Veneto sheet

Geographically, the Stelvio Pass links the Val Venosta with the Valtellina or, more broadly, South Tyrol with Lombardy. Scenically, it's one of the most wonderful routes into the still wild and unspoiled Ortler Alps and one of the most worthwhile destinations that a committed cyclist could wish for. In addition it's the third highest pass in the Alps, exceeded only by the 2802m Col de Restefond/Col de la Bonette and the 2770m Col de l'Iseran in the French Alps. (The 2829m Sölden Glacier road [Tour 14] isn't a pass.)

From Spondigna (0.0km) we cross the wide Vinschgau valley on a dead straight, level road to Prato (2.0km) in the Trafoi valley. The houses crowd closely together as we enter Prato and as we leave it the gradient is already increasing to 10 per cent. If you look back at the little village of Ponte Stelvio (7.0km) you can make out, far to the north-east, the snow-covered peak of the Weißkugel, at 3739m the second highest mountain in the Ötztal Alps after the 3772m Wildspitze. After another climb of between 8 per cent and 10 per cent, you reach Gomagoi (8.5km), the first big village of the valley, once an Austrian fortress guarding the route. There's a turning here to Solda, but we want to go higher and so continue up the Trafoi valley to Trafoi (12.0km), the last village before the top of the pass,

A tip: the hairpin bends are banked in places and if you take them really wide on the outside, oncoming traffic permitting, you can ride downhill for a few metres on the radius of the corner and so build up a bit of momentum for the next section of the climb. Eventually you get to the top and are startled at first by the hustle and bustle that prevails here. If you want to ride down the southern side to Bórmio (50.0km), you have not only a descent of 1500m over 22km, but also 31 hairpin bends, seven unlit tunnels and gallery tunnels and countless potholes to negotiate.

Encouraging or disheartening? Information about the route on a kilometre marker.

Opposite: This structure is situated on the southern side of the Stelvio Pass a little below the crossroads at Cantoniera IV a.

where ice floes and hanging glaciers running down from the dark and towering pyramid-shaped Madatschkopf make for dramatic high mountain scenery.

The road progresses upward over a hairpin bend with a gradient of 12 per cent. At the Gasthof Weißer Knott (17.5km) you can admire the majestic glacier crest of the 3905m Ortler, which remains within sight as we go on up to the Hotel Franzenshöhe, named after the Austrian emperor Franz I, that's if you have any attention to spare – the 12 per cent gradient doesn't leave much time for looking around. Mostly your attention will be focused on the road and possibly on the course of the hairpin bends ahead. There are 21 of these between the Hotel Franzenshöhe and the top of the pass (28.0km), which edges closer excruciatingly slowly.

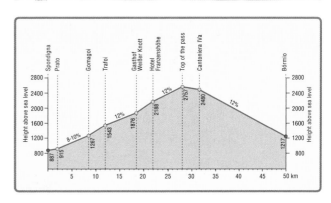

41 GAVIA PASS
Lombardy

TOUR PROFILE <<

Gavia Pass: 2621 m

NORTHERN SIDE – Start: Bórmio, 1217m

Directions: from the north over the Stelvio Pass (Tour 40). Alternatively from Oberengadin to Pontresina and over the Bernina Pass – Livigno Pass – Eira Pass – Foscagno Pass to Bórmio

Level of Difficulty/Maximum gradient: Difficult, with a maximum gradient of 16 per cent on several short sections

Length: 26.5km

Total ascent: 1230m

Time: 2–3 hrs

Suggested gearing: 39/28

Route: Bórmio (0.0km) – Uzzà (2.5km) – San Nicolò (3.0km) – Sant'António (4.0km) – Santa Catarina (11.5km) – Rifugio Plaghera (17.5km) – Rifugio A. Berni (24.0km) – top of the pass (26.5km)

The Gavia Pass, here on the northern side just below the top of the pass, runs through the unspoilt natural landscape of the Stelvio National Park.

It's not all that long since the Gavia Pass was considered to be one of the Alps' most forbidding and dangerous passes. This was because of the state of the road surface, which was littered with potholes and boulders. In places it was so narrow that it was all you could do to keep your balance between cliffs and precipices as vehicles came rushing towards you. I particularly remember a hairy section on the southern side where the narrow, winding road hugged the rock face on one side and plunged several hundred metres into the Valle delle Messi on the other, with only a few token wooden slats protecting the edge.

Cycle sport fans will know this pass well as part of the Giro d'Italia and recall the dramatic events of 5 June 1988 when several participants almost froze to death here in a snowstorm. Spectators waiting at the side of the road were asked to lend the riders warm clothing, and Franco Chioccioli, Urs Zimmermann and Roberto Visentini, who were leading in the overall placings, lost any chance of winning in the raging blizzard. The Dutchman Erik Breukink and the American Andrew Hampsten remained untroubled by the weather conditions. Breukink won the stage with a lead of seven seconds over Hampsten in Bórmio, but Hampsten won the Giro, the first American ever to do so.

Don't let these stories put you off. Times have changed at the Gavia Pass. Nowadays it's tarmacked throughout and has been widened; the dangerous section on the upper part of the southern side in particular has been completely removed with the building

of a new tunnel. The Gavia Pass still isn't a walk in the park – its height and exposed position see to that – but it is an awesome experience in the unspoiled scenery of the Stelvio National Park.

The northern starting point of Bórmio is most easily reached from the Vinschgau valley over the Stelvio Pass (Tour 40) and over the southern slope through the Braulio valley. Riding in this way would be useful training for the Gavia, classified as a difficult tour. The only other access to Bórmio is via a complicated route from the west, for example over the Bernina Pass and the Poschiavo valley to Tirano and from there up the Valtellina to Bórmio or, even more complicated, from the southern side of the Bernina Pass over the Livigno Pass, the Eira Pass and the Foscagno Pass.

Once in Bórmio (0.0km), follow the brown signs for the Gavia Pass to Valfurva, where the gradient increases to 9 per cent just before Uzzà (2.5km). You can conserve your strength a little on the gentle downhill to San Nicolò (3.0km) and the level road to Sant'António (4.0km) before bumpy red cobblestones through the village take us into a gorge-like wooded section of the valley where the gradient rises to 10 per cent. This remains constant almost all the way to an isolated house on the roadside (10.5km), where it increases slightly up to Santa Catarina (11.5km), the last village before the top of the pass.

A short tunnel takes us up to Santa Catarina, then the road becomes narrower and the gradient increases to 12 per cent with short stretches reaching 16 per cent. This section is about 1.5km long, then the gradient falls to a more moderate 9 per cent on the way to the Rifugio Plaghera (17.5km). There's another more difficult stretch waiting here. On the next 5km over the western

side of the Gavia valley there are gradient spikes of up to 16 per cent, which are thankfully interspersed with long flatter stretches. It stays this steep until the last 1.5km before the Rifugio A. Berni (24.0km); from here there are no more difficulties on the way to the top of the

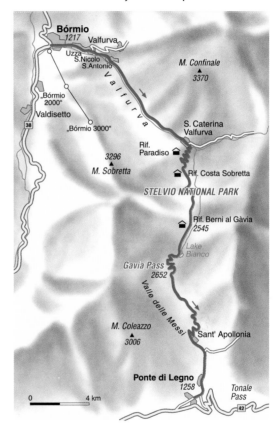

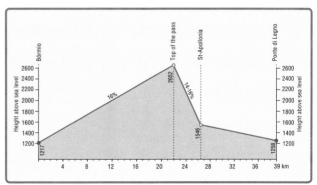

41 Gavia Pass

TOUR PROFILE <<

SOUTHERN SIDE – Start: Ponte di Legno, 1258m

Directions: A22 Brenner Autobahn, exit Bolzano/South – Mendel Pass – Fondo – Male – Dimaro – Tonale Pass – Ponte di Legno or from Switzerland from Lake Como to Sondrio – Aprica Pass – Edolo – Ponte di Legno

Level of Difficulty/Maximum gradient: Difficult, with a maximum gradient of 16 per cent over 800m. 14 per cent gradient on two sections

Length: 17.0km

Total ascent: 1365m

Time: 2–3 hrs

Suggested gearing: 39/28

Route: Ponte di Legno (0.0km) – Sant'Apollónia (4.5km) – Top of the pass (17.0km)

Road conditions: Route tarmacked throughout. Tunnel in the upper region on the southern side. In general, caution on the descents

Pass open: 1 July to 15 October

Map: Euro Cart regional map 1:300,000, RV-Verlag, South Tyrol/Veneto sheet

pass (26.5km) with its two restaurants and little glacial lake, so you can enjoy the wonderful high mountain landscape and look at the monument that commemorates the Alpini soldiers who were victims of a truck accident.

The southern descent of just under 1400m (gradients up to 16 per cent) down to the village of Ponte di Legno is 17km long and offers beautiful views of the Adamello range.

If you want to add on the Tonale Pass don't go into Ponte di Legno but ride round it to get onto the SS42, which goes up from here to the top of the Tonale Pass. As described in Tour 42 this is 11.5km away over a vertical climb of 626m. But then it's another 82km to the Adige valley, which the Noce valley, also known as the Val di Sole or the Val di Non in its upper reaches, joins near Mezzocorona. This is mostly downhill, but you'll still need to be fit for the longer flatter sections and several gradients of up to 8 per cent. If you've had enough you could consider the climb over the northern side of the Campo Carlomagno Pass in Dimaro, 27.5km away from the top of the pass, for a visit to the Brenta group.

The frequently narrow road on the Gavia climbs with a gradient of up to 16 per cent.

Opposite: The panoramic view over the mountains makes the agony of the Gavia a little more bearable.

42 TONALE PASS
Trentino

TOUR PROFILE <<

Tonale Pass: 1884m

EASTERN SIDE – Start: Dimaro, 767m, in the Val di Sole at the turn-off to Madonna di Campiglio

Directions: A22 Brenner Autobahn, exit San Michele a.A./Mezzocorona – Mezzolombardo – Dermulo – Cles – Male – Dimaro

Level of Difficulty/Maximum gradient: Medium, with a maximum gradient of 10 per cent

Length: 27.5km

Total ascent: 1120m

Time: 2¼–3½ hrs

Suggested gearing: 39/26

Route: Dimaro (0.0km) – Piano (4.0km) – Fucine (12.0km) – Vermiglio (16.5km) – Top of the pass (27.5km)

WESTERN SIDE – Start: Ponte di Legno, 1258m

Directions: Either over the Stelvio Pass (Tour 40) to Bórmio – and via Grosio – Tirano – Sondrio – Aprica Pass – Edolo to Ponte di Legno or from the Oberengadin valley from Pontresina – Bernina Pass (Tour 57) – Poschiavo – Sondrio – Aprica Pass – Edolo to Ponte di Legno

Level of Difficulty/Maximum gradient: Easy, with a maximum gradient of 8 per cent

Length: 11.5km

Total ascent: 626m

Time: 1¼–2 hrs

Suggested gearing: 39/23

Route: Ponte di Legno (0.0km) – top of the pass (11.5km)

Road conditions: Well-constructed roads

Pass open: All year

Things to see: Cable car from the top of the Tonale Pass to the Passo Paradiso with a wonderful view of the Presanella group

Map: Euro Cart regional map 1:300,000, RV-Verlag, South Tyrol/Veneto sheet

The Tonale Pass separates the Adamella and Presanella ranges in the south from the Ortler range in the north, linking the residents of the Val di Sole in the east with those in the Oglio valley in the west and on a larger scale the Adige valley near Mezzolombardo and the Valtellina near Tirano. The eastern route over the pass starts in the little village of Dimaro in the Val di Sole, which is also the starting point for the Campo Carlomagno Pass (Tour 43). The western start is the valley village of Ponte di Legno, one end of the Gavia Pass route (Tour 41). The Tonale Pass is of particular interest to us as the link between the two passes, but also makes a worthwhile stand-alone tour.

From Dimaro (0.0km) we ride on the wide, well-constructed road on a moderate gradient up the Val di Sole, with the snow-covered slopes of the Presanella massif and the foothills of the Ortler group in front of us. In Piano (4.0km) the road narrows markedly and through the villages of Mezzana and Pellizano you progress without difficulty up a gentle gradient to Fucine (12.0km). Once again the road narrows and the climb rises to 10 per cent until you reach Vermiglio (16.5km), the last village before the top of the pass. It then loops up the slopes of the northern side of the valley with the Presanella glacier rearing up on the opposite side. A sign announces that we've reached a height of 1600m; to our left is the impressive glaciated north face of the Cima Presanella, at 3556m the highest mountain in the Presanella group. Shortly after, the gradient decreases, the slopes to the summit are conquered with a few hairpin bends before the last 2km, spoiled a little by the ski lifts, climb gently once more to the top of the pass (27.5km).

If you're not satisfied with the view up here you can, if you're suitably dressed, take the cable car up to the Passo Paradiso to enjoy the impressive vista over the Presanella. On the other hand, if you'd rather do more climbing on the bike, first you have to descend 11.5km down the western side over nine hairpin bends, at 8 per cent, to Ponte di Legno. There the climb to the 2612m Gavia Pass (Tour 41) awaits you, one of the most beautiful and interesting passes for cyclists in the eastern Alps.

As indicated in Tour 41 the 17km and almost 1400m vertical climb with maximum gradients of up to 16 per cent on the southern side is no light undertaking. But the Bernina Pass (Tour 57) is the only real alternative to this, and although it's the next pass along, running from Ponte di Legno and the Oglio valley out over Edolo and Trenda into the Adda valley and then up to Tirano, it's still a good 56km away. Plus it's not that easy to get to. With its 1895m vertical climb over a route 34.5km long, the southern side of the Bernina Pass also counts as one of the most difficult tours. The only consolation is that the maximum gradient never exceeds 10 per cent.

War memorial to the fallen of the First World War at the Tonale Pass.

Anyone climbing past this sculpture is free to imagine whatever or whoever might spur them on.

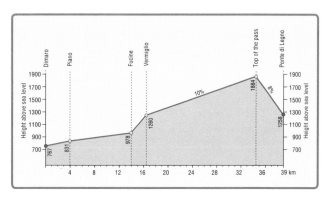

CAMPO CARLOMAGNO PASS
Trentino

The Campo Carlomagno Pass takes its name from the Emperor Charlemagne, who is said to have used this crossing during one of his campaigns in AD 770 to fight the Lombards further south in Italy. Nowadays it's used mainly to access the well-known winter sports resort of Madonna di Campiglio, at the foot of the Brenta Dolomites.

TOUR PROFILE <<

Campo Carlomagno Pass: 1682m

NORTHERN SIDE – Start: Dimaro, 767m

Directions: A22 Brenner Autobahn, exit San Michele a.A./Mezzocorona – Mezzolombardo – Dermulo – Cles – Male – Dimaro

Level of Difficulty/Maximum gradient: Medium, with a maximum gradient of 9 per cent

Length: 15.0km

Total ascent: 915m

Time: 1¼–1¾ hrs

Suggested gearing: 39/23

Route: Dimaro (0.0km) – Folgárida (6.5km) – Genzianella Bar (12.5km) – Top of the pass (15.0km)

SOUTHERN SIDE – Start: Tione di Trento, 600m

Directions: A22 Brenner Autobahn, exit Trento Centro – Ponte Arche – Tione di Trento

Level of Difficulty/Maximum gradient: Medium, with a maximum gradient of 11 per cent on a short stretch in Madonna di Campiglio

Length: 32.5km

Total ascent: 1085m

Time: 2–2¾ hrs

Suggested gearing: 39/26

Route: Tione di Trento (0.0km) – Spiazzo (9.0km) – Pinzolo (15.0km) – Madonna di Campiglio (28.0km) – Top of the pass (32.5km)

Road conditions: Well-constructed roads

Pass open: All year

Things to see: Madonna di Campiglio: wonderful view of the Brenta; Pinzolo: Church of St Vigilius

Map: Euro Cart regional map 1:300,000, RV-Verlag, South Tyrol/Veneto sheet

Northern side

The Val di Sole, the starting point for the northern climb to the pass, is a softly contoured landscape of woods and meadows with extensive orchards and numerous villages, one of which, Dimaro (0.0km), more or less in the middle of the long valley stretching from Mezzolombardo and the Adige valley to the Tonale Pass (Tour 42), is our starting point. You ride into the Meledrio valley following signposts to Folgárida/Madonna di Campiglio on a gradient of 9 per cent. Shortly after the village you hit the first hairpin bend; the road climbs, still at 9 per cent, over further hairpins up open grassy hillsides, then through a thick belt of woodland. Once past the Folgárida hotel complex (6.5km) the incline drops to 7 per cent on the way to the Belvedere restaurant, and over the eastern side of the valley the rock faces of the Brenta group come into view, fissured with deep cirques and gorges. The gradient falls still further and if you're in a hurry you can use the big chainring. Near the Genzianella bar (12.5km) your progress will be slowed when the gradient increases to 5 per cent. The first holiday homes appear at the side of the road and soon after a sign indicates the top of the pass (15.0km), although there are still a few metres to go to the peak. You have the most wonderful view of the Brenta from just below the top of the pass in the village of Madonna di Campiglio, 4.5km down a 7 per cent slope, from where you can then start the tour as described next from the southern side.

Southern side

The small market town of Tione di Trento (0.0km) stretches across a wide, deep valley at the confluence of the Arno and Sarca rivers. Follow signposts to Madonna di Campiglio/Pinzolo north into the wide Rendena valley. At first the route stays almost level along the bottom of the valley and the first gradient, of 8 per cent, doesn't kick in until Spiazzo (9.0km), and takes us up to Mortaso, the next village. There the road levels out again and we ride smoothly into the valley alongside the broad, stony course of the Sarca.

We cross the Sarca (13.0km), then the gradient increases slightly as we go to Vestina (14.5km) before going gently downhill to Pinzolo (16.5km). This village is the real start of the northern route over the pass. The church of St Vigilius, which stands right on our route, is considered to be one of the most important monuments of religious art in Trentino. In the neighbouring village of Carisolo

PASSO
CAMPO CARLO MAGNO
ALT. 1660 s/m

50

Campo Carlomagno Pass

The name of the Campo Carlomagno Pass comes from the Emperor Charlemagne.

we cross the Sarca again and then have to drop to a lower gear because the road now climbs at 9 per cent over the slopes of the western side of the valley. The gradient remains constant as the road winds higher up over another small bridge (20.0km), and in Sant'Antonio di Mavignola (22.5km) we leave the woods behind. Ahead, a fascinating view of the characteristic light-coloured rock faces of the Brenta, whose bizarre peaks are marked with deep cirques, bands of snow and giant pillars, opens up over grassy slopes on the right-hand side of the valley. The road goes up over more hairpin bends, with this magnificent panorama always in view. The well-known tourist resort of Madonna di Campiglio (28.0km) welcomes us with a rather unfriendly gradient increasing to 11 per cent, but it lets up as we leave the village. The road then takes us up to the top of the pass (32.5km), where the only buildings are hotels, but with gradients here of no more than 7 per cent the hard climbing is over.

44 MALOJA PASS
Graubünden/Lombardy

TOUR PROFILE <<

Maloja Pass: 1815m

WESTERN SIDE – Start: Chiavenna, 333m

Directions: Milan – Lecco – Lake Como – Verceia – Chiavenna

Level of Difficulty/Maximum gradient: Difficult, with a maximum gradient of 12 per cent on a short section after Casáccia

Length: 32.5km

Total ascent: 1485m

Time: 2¼–3½ hrs

Suggested gearing: 39/26

Route: Chiavenna (0.0km) – Dogana (10.0km) – Promontogno (13.5km) – Stampa (16.5km) – Borgonovo (17.5km) – Restaurant Albigno (21.0km) – Casáccia (27.0km) – Top of the pass (32.5km)

EASTERN SIDE: The eastern side of the Maloja Pass road between Silvaplana near St Moritz and the top of the pass is 10km long and apart from a short gradient of 6 per cent is completely flat

Road conditions: The roads have been improved and upgraded over the last few years. The narrow roads in the villages, cobbled in places, can usually be bypassed

Pass open: All year

Things to see: Chiavenna: old town, Santa Maria town gate, Paradiso Park and Marmitte dei Gigante Park; top of the pass: Segantini's studio, Belvedere Tower and glacier mills

Map: Euro Cart regional map 1:300,000, RV-Verlag, Italian sheet Piedmont/ Aosta valley

The narrow roads through the villages, like here in Promontagno, can be bypassed.

The Maloja Pass is a topographical peculiarity, because it has only one sloping side, on the west. With a total vertical climb of almost 1500m and gradients up to 12 per cent, this runs from Chiavenna in Italian Ticino for nearly 33km through Bregaglia to the Upper Engadine lake district. The eastern slope from the top of the pass to Silvaplana near St Moritz is just 10km long, but almost completely level. The Maloja Pass, like the Umbrail Pass (Tour 51) and the Valparola Pass (Tour 24), is a Dolomite pass whose two sides are peculiarly imbalanced.

In Chiavenna (0.0km), following the signposts to St Moritz from the bridge over the Meira up a gentle slope towards the Swiss border, there's a wonderful view of the old town and the

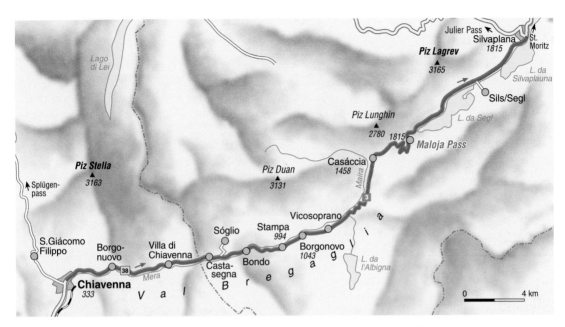

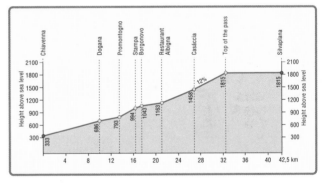

facades of houses that seem to be in danger of falling off the steep bank of the river. At Dogana (10.0km) we cross over into Switzerland and Castasegna is the first village that welcomes us. The road has been constantly upgraded and improved in recent years, and though gradients reach 10 per cent they're mainly well below that, allowing us to make good progress.

The famously beautiful Bregaglia mountains reveal themselves at Promontogno (13.5km), where the razor-sharp north face of the Piz Badile appears above the cleft of the Bondasca valley. You'll get an even more beautiful and extensive view of the unique rock formations of the Sciora group if you turn off just before Spino and follow the 3km long road (gradient 10-12 per cent) leading up to Soglio. The famous painter Giovanni Segantini described this once-seen, never-to-be-forgotten place as being on the threshold of Paradise.

The valley widens out a little and as you approach Stampa (16.5km) two boulders form a natural tunnel, which is called La Porta and separates the southern Bregaglia region from the northern. Then, in a valley, the church of Borgonovo (17.5km) appears. In its cemetery are the graves of several members of the Giacometti family, whose works of art are to be seen in many of the world's most revered museums, and also in the natural history museum in Stampa, the village you've just passed through. If you've missed this, you'll have another opportunity to see Giacometti art further on in St Moritz.

The switchbacks to the west of Lake Sils, fun on the downhill, long on the climb.

Opposite: The eastern side of the Maloja Pass with Lake Sils and Piz Corvatsch in the background.

From Borgonovo to the Albigna Restaurant (21.0km) gentle slopes alternate with flatter sections, then the gradient increases to 10 per cent and stays there over a series of hairpin bends a testing 4km long. You can then recover a little over a more level section to Casáccia (27.5km) before tackling a section with another two hairpins and a gradient of 12 per cent in a little high valley. And it's not over yet. In front lies a vast escarpment leading up to the top of the pass (32.5km), over 4.5km and 13 hairpin bends with an unrelenting gradient of 9 per cent. Once you get there you can visit the observation tower, a little out of the way, from where you have a wonderful view of the steep section behind you.

When you ride on over the pass in the direction of St Moritz on the eastern slope that really isn't a slope, it's as if you're in a different world. No dark, grey granite giants loom here, as they did on the way up. Quite the opposite: emerge into a light and friendly world with dark blue lakes, green pastures and larch woods framed by high mountains that are anything but gloomy. We're in the Upper Engadine lake district, which stretches from the Sils, Silvaplana and Champfer lakes at the foot of the Piz Corvatsch to St Moritz and the lake of the same name, and is rightly considered to be one of the most beautiful landscapes in the Alps.

The rather chic town of St Moritz, now a well-known winter sports resort, began life as a health spa. It's said that there was a healing spring here as far back as the Bronze Age, a good 3000 years ago, and in the Engadine Museum there's a 700–800-year old structure made of larch wood that was used for tapping the spring. Paracelsus praised the waters, and Antonio Perigavano, a doctor, records that in 1674 he prescribed that visitors to the spa should drink spring water, increasing the amount daily by one litre for 10 days and then taking it back down by a litre a day for the next 10 days. We can top up on lost energy instead with an Engadine nut pastry, a delicacy made with caramel and walnuts whose taste is only exceeded by its calorie count. But you can probably work this off again with another climb over the Julier Pass (Tour 55), which starts in nearby Silvaplana.

45 SPLÜGEN PASS

Graubünden/Lombardy

TOUR PROFILE <<

Splügen Pass: 2118m

SOUTHERN SIDE – Start: Chiavenna, 333m

Directions: either over the Maloja Pass to Chiavenna (Tour 44) or Milan – Lecco – Lake Como – Verceia – Chiavenna

Level of Difficulty/Maximum gradient: Difficult, with a maximum gradient of 13 per cent

Length: 33.5km

Total ascent: 1785m

Time: 3¼–4¾ hrs

Suggested gearing: 39/28

Route: Chiavenna (0.0km) – San Giácomo Filippo (4.5km) – Pietra (13.0km) – Pianazzo (18.5km) – Montespluga (26.0km) – Top of the pass (33.5km)

NORTHERN SIDE – Start: Splügen, 1457m

Directions: A13 Chur-Bellinzona (Rhine Valley Autobahn), exit Splügen

Level of Difficulty/Maximum gradient: Easy to medium tour with a maximum gradient of 11 per cent

Length: 9.5km

Total ascent: 681m

Time: 1¼–2 hrs

Suggested gearing: 39/26

Route: Splügen (0.0km) – Swiss customs (8.5km) – Top of the pass (9.5km)

Road conditions: Roads in good condition apart from some slight surface damage on the northern side. On the southern side many blind corners as well as unlit tunnels and galleries with narrow stretches and considerable pothole damage. Increased caution here, lights essential

Pass open: 1 January to 31 October. The border crossing is closed from 8pm until 5am

Map: Euro Cart regional map 1:300,000, RV-Verlag, Italy sheet Piedmont/Aosta valley

Hairpin bends on the upper part of the northern side of the Splügen Pass with the Swiss customs post.

The Splügen Pass is the shortest connecting road from Lake Como in Lombardy, Italy, over to the Swiss Rhine valley, but it's not the easiest nor the fastest. The seriously mountainous terrain that the road builders had to master sees to that, and in the upper reaches they only managed to do so by building a whole series of tunnels and galleries which in places are both narrow and unlit.

Southern side

Our starting point is Chiavenna (0.0km). In Italian, *chiave* means key, and the name Chiavenna alludes to the town's strategically advantageous position at the foot of the Maloja Pass (Tour 44), the Splügen Pass and the Septimer Pass. Follow the signpost for Madesimo and ride into the densely wooded San Giácomo valley. The gradient decreases briefly as you leave town, then rises to 10 per cent over a series of hairpin bends leading to San Giácomo Filippo (4.5km). On the way to Pietra (13.0km) the gradient fluctuates as you go through several little villages on the right-hand slopes of the valley, never falling below 6 per cent and briefly touching 13 per cent. The road zigzags up the escarpment over 20 tight hairpin bends through several tunnels and galleries to Pianazzo (18.5km). These obstacles are extremely unpleasant. The road is narrow in places, with deep potholes and an uneven surface, and things don't much improve until you hit the long flatter section along the lake on the way to the little group of houses that is Montespluga (26km), where the route climbs once more at 10 per cent over another group of hairpins. Suddenly the Italian customs post appears between the rocks at the top of the pass (31.5km) and a little later you pass through the Swiss customs post (33.0km). Now you can put your passport away and make your way down with fewer impediments than there were on the way up.

Northern side

The proud facades of old stone-built noblemen's houses dominate the townscape of Splügen (0.0km), the starting point of the northern approach. Before we even leave the village we cross the Hinter Rhine, then the road goes up between green grassy slopes at a gradient of 10 per cent. We quickly leave behind the dual carriageway to San Bernardino (Tour 75) below us as we climb five hairpin bends, then the dense fir forests close in around us. After 3km the gradient drops and by the side of a bubbling stream we make good progress along a more or less straight road. Over a short climb after a bridge (4.0km) the gradient decreases and doesn't go back up until we cross the treeline. The ride uphill is quite monotonous. There are no real viewpoints, nor any hotels or villages.

On the other hand, the road is in a noticeably better state than on the southern side, which with its many potholes could be used for road-testing suspension forks, and there aren't any tunnels on this side either.

On the eastern slopes of the Surettahorn, where streams gleam like strings of pearls when they catch the light, there's another series of hairpin bends (6.0km), 13 of them, winding their way up to the Swiss customs post (8.5km) over gradients of up to 11 per cent. Then there's just one more hairpin up to the top of the pass (9.5km) and the Italian customs post. The descent down the southern side should be approached with caution for the reasons described. To summarise: three unlit tunnels, two of

them 50m long and one 350m long, six gallery tunnels, 150 to 650m long, and seven galleries, 20 to 250m long.

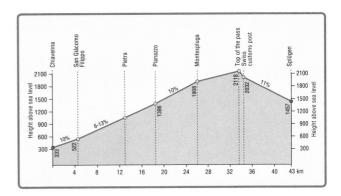

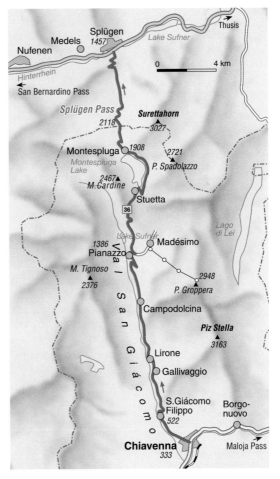

TOUR PROFILE <<

Gressoney High Valley Road :1825m

Start: Pont-St-Martin in the Aosta valley, 300m

Directions: A5 Turin–Aosta, exit Pont-St-Martin

Level of Difficulty/Maximum gradient: Difficult, with a maximum gradient of 12 per cent on a short section in the upper part of the route

Length: 38.0km

Total ascent: 1525m

Time: 2¼–3 hrs

Suggested gearing: 39/26

Route: Pont-St-Martin (0.0km) – Lillianes (5.5km) – Fontainemore (9.0km) – Issime (11.5km) – Gaby (17.0km) – Gressoney-St-Jean (25.0km) – Gressoney-La Trinité 33.5km) – turning loop (38.0km)

Road conditions: Well-constructed roads

Pass open: All year

Map: Euro Cart regional map 1:300,000, RV-Verlag, Italy sheet Piedmont/Aosta valley

Notes: Lights are advisable for the three tunnels, 50m to 150m long

The Monte Rosa massif is one of the most impressive and enormous mountain ranges in the Alps. As an almost insurmountable bulwark of snow and ice it forms a rampart between the Swiss canton of Valais and the Italian region of Piedmont, culminating in the 4634m Monte Rosa. Lyskamm, Castor and Pollux are other well-known peaks that won their first mountaineer conquerors a certain

The village church in Fontainemore is right on the bank of the River Lys.

amount of renown. The Gressoney High Alpine Road, over which we approach the massif from the south is perhaps not so well-known to cyclists but should be regarded as a difficult tour.

Pont-St-Martin (0.0km), our starting point, takes its name from an almost completely preserved bridge from the first century AD, which spans the River Lys here. We leave the straggling village at the end of the Aosta valley and enter the Lys valley on the Gressoney Road, which squeezes through between a house and the rock face to climb to a 200m tunnel (3.0km) over hairpin bends with a gradient of 10 per cent. After this initial stretch there is nothing special to report in the way of gradients. Until you get to Lillianes (5.5km) the road is level and then through Fontainemore (9.0km) and Issime (11.5km) inclines of a maximum of 8 per cent alternate with long flatter and level sections. Not until after Gaby (17.0km), after a 100m tunnel with lights, does the gradient reach 10 per cent again, and stays there to ascend a valley over two hairpin bends (21.0km) before it eases down again on the way to Gressoney-St-Jean (25.0km). From here there's a long, level stretch along the valley floor. The glaciers of the Lyskamm finally appear to give a feeling of the high mountains and over two hairpin bends (30.0km) you reach the top at a gradient of 10 per cent.

After a lit, 50m tunnel (32km) the gradient falls again, the view of the glaciers widens and the road is level until you get to Gressoney-La Trinité (33.5km). The car parks on the edge of the village aren't the end of the climb. The road goes on up over two hairpin bends with a gradient of 12 per cent, then follows a decreasing gradient to a turning loop by a bridge over the Lys (38.0km), which finally marks the head of the valley. The total vertical climb of 1500m may have

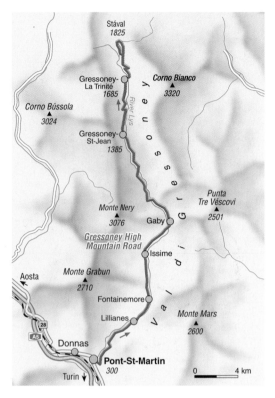

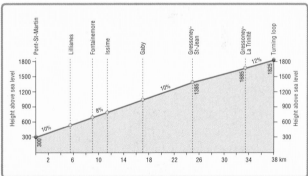

been impressive, but unfortunately the view, with its quite restricted glimpse of the Lyskamm, isn't.

If you're interested in local history you can ride 5km or so from the starting point at Pont-St Martin into the Aosta valley to Bard, where a fortress from the 11th century is still preserved, at which travellers in the Middle Ages had to pay a toll.

TOUR PROFILE <<

Savarenche High Valley Road: 1960m

Start: Villeneuve, 300m on the SS26 in the Aosta valley

Directions: A5 Turin–Aosta (Aosta autostrada), exit Sarre/Aosta West

Level of Difficulty/Maximum gradient: Medium to difficult tour with a maximum gradient of 12 per cent

Length: 27.0km

Total ascent: 1310m

Time: 2¼–3½ hrs

Suggested gearing: 39/26

Route: Villeneuve (0.0km) – Villa Dessous (2.5km) – Introd (3.5km) – turning to Val di Rhèmes (5.0km) – Molère (11.5km) – Eau Rousse (22.0km) – Pont (27.0km)

Road conditions: Well-constructed roads apart from a few narrow roads in the villages

Pass open: 15 June to 31 October

Map: Euro Cart regional map 1:300,000, RV-Verlag, Italy, Piedmont/Aosta valley sheet

Notes: Lights are advisable because of the 250m unlit tunnel

Unfortunately on our trip we don't get to see the 4061m Gran Paradiso, the highest mountain of the Gran Paradiso group.

The Savarenche High Valley Road is well-known to mountaineers as the main approach to the 4061m Gran Paradiso peak. It leads from the Aosta valley to Pont, a little mountaineering village that is the starting point for the Gran Paradiso ascent. With a bike we can get nearly 2000m up – just under halfway.

Start by crossing an old wooden bridge over the Savàra in Villeneuve (0.0km), follow the signposts to Val Savarenche and ride over gradients of up to 12 per cent to Villa Dessous (2.5km) and then on to Introd (3.5km). Passing the turning into the Val di Rhèmes (5.0km) you keep going up over hairpin bends at 12 per cent again. Only after about 7km do you get to a long section with a more moderate gradient, 8 per cent, which takes you into Molère (11.5km) where the slate roofs of the village are striking.

The next stretch of hairpin bends, with gradients of 10 to 12 per cent, leads into a dark gorge. You have to ride through a 250m, unlit tunnel, then the valley becomes a little wider again. The snow-covered peaks of the Gran Paradiso are now in sight and as you follow the Savàra gradients of up to 10 per cent alternate with flatter stretches and even short downhills until you reach Eau Rousse (22km). Once you leave the village the gradient increases to a fairly stiff 12 per cent, and you have to climb several bends as the valley narrows, before an attractive high valley opens up at the foot of the Gran Paradiso range. At the end of the valley (25.0km) you have another 10 per cent gradient to tackle up to the end of the road in Pont (27.0km).

If you arrive in Pont on a summer weekend you may find the village overrun and the car park hopelessly overcrowded with climbers making the ascent of the Gran Paradiso. Were your cycling shoes to allow you to walk into the landscapes at the foot of the Gran Paradiso you would discover that they are among the most beautiful in the Alps. If you are thinking about making the ascent, you should know that it's considered by mountaineers to be one of the easier 4000m climbs, but easy is a relative term: a novice mountain cyclist would likely be defeated by an 'easy' alpine pass. Nevertheless, if you happen to have hiking kit in your support car,

then the next day you should quietly hike up the easy climb to the Emanuele II mountain lodge, 700m up. The name commemorates the founder of the Italian national park system and saviour of the alpine ibex; if you're lucky you may even see one of these shy animals whose numbers have increased to around 6,000.

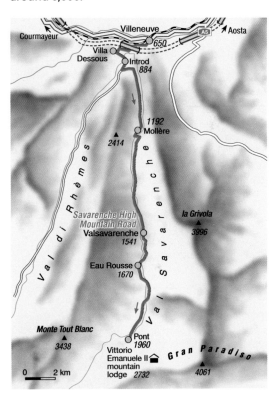

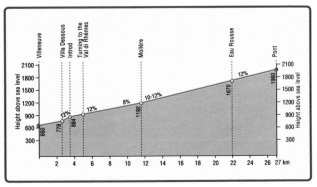

TOUR PROFILE <<

Little St Bernard Pass: 2188m

NORTHERN SIDE – Start: Pré-Saint-Didier, 1004m

Directions: A5 Turin–Chamonix (Aosta valley autostrada), exit Morges

Level of Difficulty/Maximum gradient: Medium, with a maximum gradient of 9 per cent

Length: 23.5km

Total ascent: 1185m

Time: 1¾–2½ hrs

Suggested gearing: 39/23

Route: Pré-Saint-Didier (0.0km) – La Balme (7.0km) – La Thuile (9.5km) – Pesca all Trota Restaurant (16.5km) – Top of the pass (23.5km)

SOUTHERN SIDE – Start: Séez, 904m

Directions: A43 Chambéry–Moûtiers – Séez

Level of Difficulty/Maximum gradient: Medium, with a maximum gradient of 12 per cent

Length: 27.5km

Total ascent: 1285m

Time: 2¼–3½ hrs

Suggested gearing: 39/26

Route: Séez (0.0km) – Villard (3.0km) – La Rosière (23km) – Top of the pass (27.5km)

Road conditions: Well-constructed roads apart from slight damage to the surface in the area at the summit

Pass open: 15 June to 31 October

Things to see: Botanical garden by the ruined hostel and statue of Saint Bernard at the top of the pass

Map: Euro Cart regional map 1:300,000, RV-Verlag, Italy, Piedmont/Aosta valley sheet

As you can see from this picture, the Little St Bernard Pass has a great many hairpin bends on the southern side – 20 altogether.

The only thing that's little about the Little St Bernard Pass is its name. Apart from that from a cyclist's point of view it's a fully-grown pass which, with a vertical climb of almost 1200m, might not exactly put the fear of God into you but does inspire respect. In Pré-St-Didier (0.0km), the starting point on the northern side, you'll be glad to be able to leave behind the very busy dual carriageway through the Aosta valley, even on a gradient of 9 per cent. Hairpin bends allow a glimpse of the impressive southern side of the Mont Blanc massif with Mont Brouillard and the Aiguille Blanche de Peuteray, before it disappears as you ride through a lit tunnel 100m long (3.5km).

The gradient decreases briefly, but after going through a gallery it goes back up then, after another 150m unlit tunnel, you reach the village of La Balme (7.0km) up another moderate slope. The road goes up past the village over bends and hairpins with a constant gradient of 9 per cent and then through the last tunnel on the route you come to La Thuile (9.5km). The gorge-like section of the valley now lies behind us and over more hairpins with a gradient of

9 per cent the road climbs up initially treeless slopes. The first pine forests and rowan trees appear, and then suddenly the Pesca alla Trota restaurant (16.5km). As the name implies it specialises in fish dishes and if your efforts so far have given you an appetite do make a stop: it's the last refreshment opportunity before the top of the pass. The environs are now noticeably more high mountain-like. On the road which climbs again up a gradient of 9 per cent you have a good view of the snow-covered peaks of Mont Bério Blanc to the north-west in a cleft in the valley. After 18.5km a series of hairpin bends begins, leading past ruined stone huts into an increasingly barren landscape. The gradient doesn't ease off until you've passed the remains of a ruined A.N.A.S. (Azienda Nazionale Autonoma delle Strade/Italian Highways Agency) post (19.5km) and then rises all the way to the little Lake Verney (23.0km). Past the lake several more hairpin bends climb a gradient of 8 per cent up to the top of the pass (23.5km), where you can't fail to notice a larger than life statue of Saint Bernard of Aosta and the ruins of some hostel buildings.

If we'd come here a century ago we would have been welcomed with a bite to eat. At the hostel, monks would offer poor travellers two glasses of wine and half a pound of bread. At the turn of the century, as thousands of Italians migrated over the pass in search of work, they would have been fed, put up overnight and given provisions for their journey. Horace-Bénédict de Saussure – a name familiar to many as an early Mont Blanc climber – wrote that nothing was demanded in return, even from well-to-do travellers.

These days the restaurant at the top of the pass charges for its food, and it's best if you go without wine. The descent

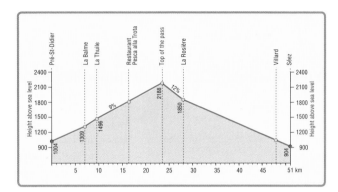

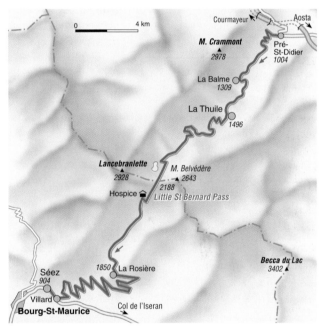

down to Séez (51.0km) in the Val d'Isère is dizzying enough without it: innumerable bends and a total of 20 hairpins seem to go on forever. Once you're down you'll be glad to find a level road beneath your wheels. That won't last long here in the Tarentaise, as this valley in the upper reaches of the River Isère is known, because Séez is just a transit station for another pass, the Col de l'Iseran. At 2770m this is the second highest pass in the Alps. If you'd like to try it, read the description of Tour 80.

49 COL DE MONTGENÈVRE PASS
Piedmont/Dauphiné

*As the figures on this board reveal, the
surroundings of the Montgenèvre Pass
are used for skiing in winter.*

The Montgenèvre Pass is the gateway from Turin in Italy to the
French Alps of the *départments* of Dauphiné, Savoy and Provence.
It leads out of the Susa valley in the direction of the Fréjus tunnel,
past Oulx to the south in the Dora Riparia valley and from there
over the Col de Montgenèvre to Briançon. Here you can access
passes such as the Col du Lautaret (Tour 87), the Col du Galibier
(Tour 83), the Col d'Izoard (Tour 89) and the Col de Vars (Tour 92).
However, these are all bigger and also more difficult than the
Montgenèvre, neither of whose slopes can in any way be classed as
anything other than easy for cyclists who have trained well.

The starting point for the eastern approach, the village of
Cesena–Torinese, lies at the turning into the Chisone valley, which
stretches up to the well-known Italian winter sports resort of
Sestrière, at a height of 2030m. It lies at the foot of the 3130m Mont
Chaberton, also known as the 'King of the Susa Valley' because of
its exposed position. This is well known to mountain bikers for the
track that leads to the fort on the summit, the highest point
accessible by bike in the Alps. That's mountain bike only: the track
is unsurfaced and in a state of disrepair.

Leave the little border town of Cesena–Torinese (0.0km)
heading west on a tarmacked road that climbs at 8-10 per cent

The village of Cesena-Torinese is the starting point for the climb over the eastern side up to the Montgenèvre Pass.

over several hairpin bends. The route follows a wide curve leading into a gallery almost 400m long, and then immediately into a second one. On the southern slope of Mont Chaberton, which closes off the right side of the valley completely, the road goes up again at an 8 per cent gradient and after a short unlit hairpin tunnel reaches Claviere (5.5km).

The Italian border post is to be found right on the edge of the village (6.0km), but, following the implementation of the Schengen Agreement is unoccupied, as is the French border post 200m further on.

The road goes through the village which, legally speaking, is still in Italian sovereign territory, at a gradient of 5 per cent, before entering France at a sign that says France/Les Hautes Alpes. The holiday homes of Montgenèvre can already be seen in the distance and the top of the pass (7.5km) is soon reached.

After a short descent the road goes upwards again a little, then you bowl along down over the western side, where the downhill slope never exceeds 10 per cent and is mostly well below it. Having arrived at the bottom of the Clarée valley there are even several kilometres of a gentle counter climb to be dealt with, ending right by the old fort which guards the entry to the valley. This stronghold was established under Louis XIV in the middle of the 17th century and has not only withstood the test of time almost unscathed but was able to resist capture, in 1815, by an Austro-Savoyard army almost 20 times superior in strength.

If you want to ride straight down past the fort into the centre of Briançon there's a 700m descent with a gradient of 18 per cent, but it's better to use the ring road which has a downhill gradient of 8 per cent and doesn't put such a strain on the brakes.

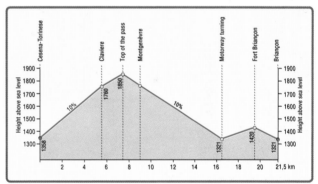

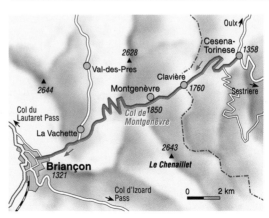

TOUR PROFILE <<

Col de la Lombarde: 2351m

NORTHERN SIDE – Start: Vinádio, 898m, about 35km south-west of Cuneo

Directions: A6 Turin–Savona, exit Fossano – Cuneo – Borgo San Dalmazzo – Vinádio

Level of Difficulty/Maximum gradient: Difficult, with a maximum gradient of 13 per cent

Length: 21.5km

Total ascent: 1455m

Time: 2–3 hrs

Suggested gearing: 39/26

Route: Vinádio (0.0km) – Pratolungo (0.5km) – Alm Baraccone (8.km) – Chapel (10.0km) – Top of the pass (21.5km)

SOUTHERN SIDE – Start: Isola, 873m; Nice – Plan-du-Var – St-Sauveur-sur-Tinée – Isola

Level of Difficulty/Maximum gradient: Medium to difficult tour with a maximum gradient of 11 per cent on long sections

Length: 21.0km

Total ascent: 1480m

Time: 2–3 hrs

Suggested gearing: 39/26

Route: Isola (0.0km) – Ski lift valley station (13.5km) – Isola 2000 (16.5km) – Top of the pass (21.0km)

Road conditions: The southern side between Isola and the winter sports resort of Isola 2000 is well constructed. On the northern side, particularly in the upper region, there is considerable surface damage in places. Caution is necessary on the descent

Pass open: 15 June to 31 October

Map: Euro Cart regional map 1:300,000, RV-Verlag, Italy, Piedmont/Aosta Valley sheet

Notes: The border post at the top of the pass is officially closed from 10pm to 7am

The Col de la Lombarde is a high alpine crossing from Cuneo in the Stura valley over to the French Tinée valley, which comes up from Nice to the Col de Restefond/Col de la Bonette (Tour 94). It takes us through the middle of the Mercantour National Park, an unspoiled natural landscape where the twists and turns of the road, which is narrow in places, deters motorists. Cyclists who aren't afraid of a 13 per cent gradient can therefore expect an enjoyable run with very little traffic, at least on the Italian side, the French side has been better constructed and has more vehicles.

Northern side

It's about 30km from Borgo-San-Dalmazzo, near Cuneo, to Vinadio, our starting point (0.0km). Just outside the village we follow the signposts to Colle della Lombardoand in Pratolungo (0.5km). The narrow road makes its way up over hairpin bends with a gradient of 11 per cent. At a junction continue to follow the signs for Sant'Anna. The gradient increases to 13 per cent over another group of hairpin bends (5.5km), then the road crosses to the other side of the valley

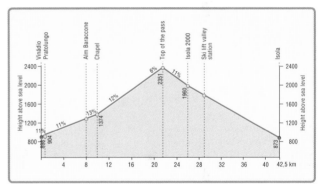

where further hairpin bends climb a gradient of 10-12 per cent that ends at the Baraccone alpine hut (8.0km).

You'll quickly cross a little valley opening and ride over hairpin bends with a gradient of 13 per cent up to the bleak slopes of the western side of the valley. A small chapel (12.0km) marks the halfway point of the climb, and is followed by an almost level section about 2km long, breathing space before the next group of hairpin bends takes the gradient back up to 12 per cent, before it finally decreases. On the last few kilometres up to the top of the pass (23.0km) it hardly gets above 6 per cent.

Up here the landscape is barren and littered with boulders and there's not a single restaurant to be seen. After a descent of 1km, when the poor state of the road first becomes obvious, the road goes past the former French border post and after the new ski resort of Isola 2000 the surface improves again. Two lanes, wide and well constructed, descend rapidly down a slope of up to 11 per cent. Nevertheless, five 50- to 150m galleries, no fewer than 37 hairpin bends and narrow stretches in the valley village of Isola require continual application of the brakes.

Southern side

The easiest way to get to the village of Isola, our starting point on the southern side, is by climbing the northern side as just described. Otherwise you have to ride

Opposite: If you like hairpin bends, you'll love the Col de la Lombarde. The road snakes its way up the mountain as though it's part of the landscape.

a good 80km into the Tinée valley from Nice or take the difficult way over the Col de Restefond/Col de la Bonette pass.

When you get to Isola (0.0km) the climb begins with a gradient of 11 per cent right from the start. The road goes up the narrow valley, without any views, over several groups of hairpin bends with a gradient of not less than 10 per cent. You cross from side to side of the valley several times and after 6.5km reach a junction in the road. This is the first of several and it doesn't matter which road you decide to take, because they all come together again a little further on.

After two avalanche galleries (8.5km) the gradient decreases to 9 per cent, and then to 8 per cent after a short tunnel (9.5km). It soon rises to 10 per cent, relenting briefly at the valley station of the little ski lift (13.5km), before stiffening again on the long haul to the outskirts of Isola 2000 (16.5km). During the 1993 edition of the Tour de France Miguel Indurain and his rival Toni Rominger completed this section a little faster than us. Rominger won the 12th stage which started in Serre Chevalier and ended here 179km later, having the advantage of wide tyres, but Miguel Indurain won the Tour for the third time.

The climb isn't over yet. We ride up around the northern side of the village on several hairpin bends and meet the road that goes through the village by the closed customs post (18.0km). This is now noticeably narrower, the road surface is considerably worse and it climbs on up over hairpin bends with a gradient of 8 per cent. Just below the top of the pass (21.0km) there's one last 11 per cent gradient, then we've conquered the Col de la Lombarde on its southern side.

If talk of the Tour de France has whetted your appetite for racing in this territory, you can try it yourself. Every year in July La Fausto Coppi race takes place in Piedmont, starting from Cuneo, and in the adjoining French Maritime Alps. The race commemorates Fausto Coppi (1919–1960), the most famous Italian cyclist whose battles with Italian rival Gino Bartali – the stuff of legend. Both men were known as mountain specialists and anyone considering competing in the Coppi should be too. In addition to the Col de la Lombarde, the Col du Restefond/Col de la Bonette (Tour 94) at 2802m is still the highest alpine pass and is regularly included in the programme. Further details are available on www.faustocoppi.net.

Opposite: The northern side of the Col de la Lombarde can boast a total of 35 hairpin bends.

The area at the top of the Col de la Lombarde doesn't seem to be suitable for a very long visit.

ALPINE PASSES IN SWITZERLAND

51 UMBRAIL PASS
Graubünden

TOUR PROFILE <<

Umbrail Pass: 2503m

NORTHERN SIDE –

Start: Santa Maria Val Müstair, 1375m

Directions: A12 Innsbruck-Landeck (Inn Valley Autobahn), exit Landeck/ East – Landeck – Pfunds – Nauders – Reschenpass – Mals – Glurns – Taufers – Santa Maria

Level of Difficulty/Maximum gradient: Medium, with a maximum gradient of 11 per cent on long sections

Length: 14.0km

Total ascent: 1130m

Time: 1¾–2½ hrs

Suggested gearing: 39/26

Route: Santa Maria (0.0km) – Gasthaus Alpenrose (6.0km) – Gasthaus Muraunza (11.5km) – Top of the pass (14.0km)

SOUTHERN SIDE: On the southern side the pass road goes down an 8 per cent downhill slope for 0.5km to Cantoniera IV a, about 3km below the top of the pass on the southern side of the climb up to the Stelvio Pass (see Tour 40)

Road conditions: Almost half of the climb is on unmade roads. The hard dirt road is however also suitable for racing tyres

Pass open: 15 May to 15 November; Swiss customs are closed from 10pm to 6am from 1 July to 30 September and from 8pm to 8am the rest of the year

Map: Euro Cart regional map 1:300,000, RV-Verlag, Switzerland sheet

Although it's unmade in places, you can ride over the northern side of the Umbrail Pass if you're careful.

The Umbrail Pass offers an alternative for those who would like to cycle the Stelvio Pass but not the difficult climb out of the Vinschgau valley over the Stelvio Pass road (Tour 40). The Umbrail Pass provides a link to the Stelvio from Santa Maria, situated in the Swiss Münstertal. Because this valley village is considerably higher at 1370m than the 887m Spondigna in the Vinschgau valley it makes for an easier climb. But there's still a total ascent of nearly 1400m to tackle, at least if you want to get up to the Stelvio Pass, since the Umbrail Pass ends some 250m lower down. Note that the road is unmade in places, but is relatively easy to cycle even with narrow racing tyres both up- and downhill, if you take care.

As you leave the village of Santa Maria (0.0km) the road climbs at a gradient of 11 per cent and after 2km you reach the first of a

total of 33 hairpin bends. The route winds its way up at a constant 11 per cent until you suddenly have a sandy track beneath your wheels. Beyond the Gasthaus Alpenrose (6.0km) the valley is narrower, a kilometre further on the gradient decreases, but rises again to 10 per cent once you've crossed the Muraunza. After 9.5km the road crosses the river again and is once more tarmacked, with gradients of 11 per cent alternating with flatter sections to the former Gasthaus Muraunza (11.5km).

Now we go up a narrow road with poor surface in places, up tight hairpin bends with a constant gradient of 10 per cent, in the final part of the ascent to the top of the pass and the Swiss border post (14.0km).

If you can show them your passport you can pass through and continue down to a crossroads marked by some ruined shelters, known as Cantoniera IV a, for about half a kilometre on a downhill slope of up to 8 per cent. Then down to Bórmio there's a further descent of 19km with a gradient of 12 per cent, but the condition of the road is poor and there are two unlit tunnels and five unlit tunnel galleries through the impressive scenery of the Braulio valley.

Most people won't want to miss the climb to the Stelvio Pass, at 2757m the highest point in the eastern Alps and the third highest alpine pass overall. There's a vertical climb here of exactly 277m to tackle over 3km with a quite regular gradient of 10 per cent. The Stelvio is a popular destination for tourists in cars and on motorbikes, most of whom come up the eastern side from the Vinschgau valley, and the top is busy with crowds and souvenir shops.

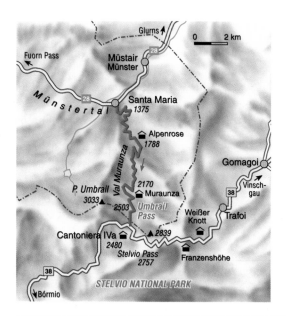

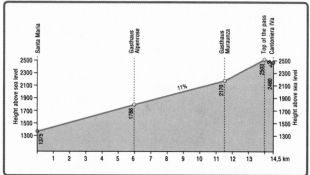

The customs post at the top of the Umbrail Pass.

52 FUORN PASS
Graubünden

TOUR PROFILE <<

Fuorn Pass: 2149m

WESTERN SIDE – Start: Zernez, 1472m, in Upper Engadin

Directions: A12 Innsbruck–Bludenz (Inn Valley Autobahn), exit Zams/Landeck East – Pfunds – Martina – Scuol – Susch – Zernez

Level of Difficulty/Maximum gradient: Medium, with a maximum gradient of 10 per cent

Length: 22.0km

Total ascent: 855m

Time: 1½–2½ hrs

Suggested gearing: 39/26

Route: Zernez (0.0km) – Ova Spin (8.0km) – Punt la Drossa (13.0km) – Parc Naziunal il Fuorn Hotel (15.5km) – Buffalora Restaurant (20.0km) – Top of the pass (22.0km)

EASTERN SIDE – Start: Santa Maria Val Müstair, 1375m

Directions: A12 Innsbruck–Bludenz (Inn Valley Autobahn), exit Zams/Landeck East – Pfunds – Nauders – Reschenpass – Burgeis – Schluderns – Taufers – Santa Maria Val Müstair

Level of Difficulty/Maximum gradient: Easy to medium tour with a maximum gradient of 10 per cent

Length: 16.0km

Total ascent: 775m

Time: 1¼–2 hrs

Suggested gearing: 39/26

Route: Santa Maria (0.0km) – Valchava (1.5km) – Tschierv (7.5km) – Top of the pass (16.0km)

Road conditions: Well-constructed roads

Pass open: All year

Things to see: Zernez: National Park Museum

Map: Euro Cart regional map 1:300,000, RV-Verlag, Switzerland sheet

The Swiss National Park lies to the east of the valley where the Upper Engadin and the Lower Engadin rivers meet. A single road crosses this otherwise unspoiled natural landscape, running from Zernez in the Inn valley in the west to Santa Maria in the Val Müstair in the east, familiar if you've done the climb to the Umbrail Pass (Tour 51). It leads over the Fuorn Pass, also known as the Pass dal Fuorn.

Before you start, you could visit the National Park Museum in Zernez (0.0km) to learn about the flora and fauna along the route. It's situated at the side of the road in the park, which we find by following the signposts for Ofenpass/Meran. Level at first, the road climbs after about 2km at 10 per cent and quickly leaves the valley floor behind, passing through three galleries. The climb eases off at 5.5km.

The gradient soon increases to 10 per cent again. Far below us lies the Spöls gorge, then we ride to Ova Spin (8.0km) in the national park. There we have a long descent to the border post at Punt la Drossa (13.0km). A tunnel leads from here to the Italian customs-free area of Livigno, which attracts motorists for the cheap petrol, hence the high volume of traffic.

We follow the signposts for Müstair/Ofenpass on a gradient of 10 per cent up to the Parc Naziunal il Fuorn Hotel (15.5km). The valley finally widens out and the first karst peak towers above the woods as they thin out. The 10 per cent gradient is now frequently relieved by flatter sections, until you find yourself at the Buffalora restaurant (22.0km) in the middle of a little plateau and surrounded by meadows and woods again. Two more kilometres with a

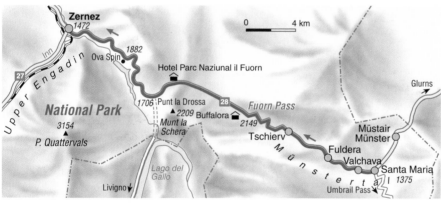

The Fuorn Pass leads us through the completely unspoilt natural landscape of the Swiss National Park.

Opposite: This cyclist is really relaxed and at ease on the road to the Fuorn Pass, even with an older style of bike.

constant gradient of 10 per cent, then you're at the top of the pass (22.0km). The name, Ofenpass/Pass dal Fuorn, commemorates a former iron-smelting plant that has now been replaced by a restaurant. We can make out in front of us the peaks of the Ortler, quite small from up here, but at 3899m the highest mountain in the South Tyrol; then the route rolls away down a 14km descent with a gradient of 10 per cent to Santa Maria in the Val Müstair.

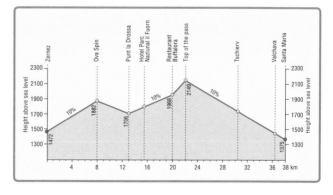

TOUR PROFILE <<

Flüela Pass: 2383m

WESTERN SIDE – Start: Davos, 1560m

Directions: A13 Bregenz–Chur (Rhine Valley Autobahn), exit Landquart – Schiers –Klosters – Davos

Level of Difficulty/Maximum gradient: Medium, with a maximum gradient of 10 per cent

Length: 13.0km

Total ascent: 825m

Time: 1¼–2 hrs

Suggested gearing: 39/26

Route: Davos (0.0km) – Pischa cable car valley station (4.0km) – Gasthaus Alpenrose (5.0km) – Gasthaus Tschuggen (7.0km) – Top of the pass (13.0km)

EASTERN SIDE – Start: Susch, 1426m, in the Lower Engadin

Directions: A12 Innsbruck–Bludenz (Inn Valley Autobahn), exit Zams/Landeck East – Pfunds – Martina – Scuol – Ardez – Larin – Susch

Level of Difficulty/Maximum gradient: Medium, with a maximum gradient of 11 per cent

Length: 13.5km

Total ascent: 825m

Time: 1¼–2 hrs

Suggested gearing: 39/26

Route: Susch (0.0km) – Top of the pass (13.5km)

Road conditions: Well-constructed roads

Pass open: All year

Things to see: Davos-Dorf: local history museum in the former presbytery. Davos-Platz: Ernst Ludwig Kirchner Museum

Map: Euro Cart regional map 1:300,000, RV-Verlag, Switzerland sheet

The Flüela Pass is on the road that runs from Davos through the Flüela valley up to the top of the pass and from there through the Susasca valley down into Lower Engadin and little village of Susch. In the Middle Ages it was an important trade route transporting ore from Graubünden to the North Tyrol and bringing salt back in return. The Flüela maintained an advantage over the other two crossings in the Rhaetian Alps, the Albula Pass (Tour 54) and the Julier Pass (Tour 55), since it provided the easiest and shortest connection, which is still true today.

The starting point for our tour is one of the best-known tourist resorts in Switzerland: Davos. Once a peaceful Walser village, it is now a model of metropolitan efficiency and prestige. It owes the upturn in its fortunes to a doctor, Alexander Spengler, who set up a sanatorium here for people with lung diseases and thus initiated the town's rise as a health resort. Its present-day appearance, with its modern concrete buildings, isn't particularly attractive. However, St Johann's in Davos-Platz with its odd pointed corkscrew spire and the little 15th-century mountain church in Davos-Frauenkirch, with the wall facing the mountain built to withstand avalanches, are worth a look.

We leave the town via the Dorf district (0.0km) and ride into the Flüela valley on gradients of between 8 per cent and 10 per cent. Past an old original farmhouse we reach the head of the valley and the Pischa cable car valley station (4.0km), then the well-constructed road winds its way up a constant gradient and at the Gasthaus Alpenrose (5.0km) we cross the treeline. Past the Gasthaus Tschuggen (5.0km) the surroundings are noticeably more mountainous and over three hairpin bends with a now quite regular climb of 10 per cent you make it to the top, accompanied only by stones and boulders. Past a little mountain hut we cross the Flüela stream, then comes the fourth and last hairpin bend (12.0km) and only one more bend separates us from the top of the pass by the Flüela Pass Hotel (13.0km). This is situated in the middle of a barren, stony high mountain landscape between the 3085m Flüela-Weißhorn to the north and the

3147m Schwarzhorn to the south where two little lakes aren't able to make the surroundings any more attractive. Ten hairpin bends with a downhill gradient of up to 11 per cent lie in front of us on the way down over 13km of well-constructed roads to Susch. Here we are welcomed by cobbled streets, an old fortified medieval tower and a view of Castle Rohan on the Chaschins Hill. Also worth a look are the Evangelical Church built in 1515 in the late Gothic style and its impressive organ, the La Tuor and La Praschun towers and the old Engadin farmhouses and artisans' houses.

Opposite: There are only ten of these hairpin bends on the eastern side of the Flüela Pass.

This picture gives all the information you need apart from the time it'll take you to complete the climb.

TOUR PROFILE <<

Albula Pass: 2315m

WESTERN SIDE – Start: Tiefencastel, 851m

Directions: Bregenz–Chur (Rhine Valley Autobahn), exit Zillis – Thusis – Sils – Tiefencastel

Level of Difficulty/Maximum gradient: Medium to difficult tour with a maximum gradient of 12 per cent over long sections

Length: 31.5km

Total ascent: 1465m

Time: 2¼–3½ hrs

Suggested gearing: 39/26

Route: Tiefencastel (0.0km) – Surava (2.5km) – Alvaneu-Bad (5.5km) – Filisur (9.5km) – Bergün (17.0km) – Preda (23.5km) – Lake Palpuogna (25.0km) – Alm Weißenstein (27.5km) – Top of the pass (31.5km)

EASTERN SIDE – Start: La Punt, 1687m

Directions: A12 Innsbruck–Bludenz (Inn Valley Autobahn), exit Zams/Landeck East - Pfunds – Martina – Scuol – Zernez – Brail – Zuoz – La Punt

Level of Difficulty/Maximum gradient: Easy to medium tour with a maximum gradient of 12 per cent

Length: 9.5km

Total ascent: 630m

Time: 1¼–1¾ hrs

Suggested gearing: 39/26

Route: La Punt (0.0km) – Top of the pass (9.5km)

Road conditions: Good roads on the eastern side, however on the descent watch out for the railway tracks just before La Punt. On the western side the road is narrow in places. Slight damage to the road surface at the top

Pass open: 1 June to 31 October

Things to see: Preda: historic railway trail from the station in Preda to Bergün (8km). Bergün: village street with houses built in the Engadin style.

Map: Euro Cart regional map 1:300,000, RV-Verlag, Switzerland sheet

Of the three access roads going into the Engadin in central Switzerland, the Flüela Pass (Tour 53), the Albula Pass (Tour 54) and the Julier Pass (Tour 55), the Albula goes through the most beautiful landscapes. It's also the most varied and most interesting, though that isn't immediately apparent in our starting point of Tiefencastel. The name of the village, meaning 'the castle in the depths', is the only clue that a fortified settlement with a royal court stood here in Carolingian times. A fire in 1890 razed the last few traces to the ground. Only the village's Baroque parish church remains.

We leave Tiefencastel (0.0km) and ride through Surava (2.5km) and Alvaneu-Bad (5.5km) on a moderate gradient that only increases to 10 per cent here and there in the villages. The narrow road through Filisur (9.5km) offers a close-up view of the massive house facades with their wall paintings and deeply inset windows, picturesque oriels and wide round-arched doorways that are characteristic of the Engadin style. The route stays at the bottom of the valley until you've completed 13.5km, and then the gradient increases to 10 per cent. Suddenly you find yourself in the Bergün gorge, a tight, forbiddingly narrow cleft in the rock through which the foaming and roaring Albula 150m below has cut its way. We wind our way up this section beneath overhanging rock walls and over two hairpin bends with a gradient of 12 per cent, which relents slightly as we reach Bergün (17.0km). If you suddenly hear a loud wheezing over the next stretch of hairpin bends (10-12 per cent), it's not a rival coming up on your heels, but a train on the Rhaetian railway between Thusis and Samedan, negotiating its own tricky course of bends and tunnels.

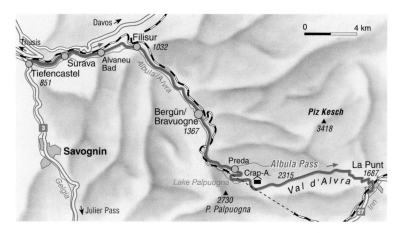

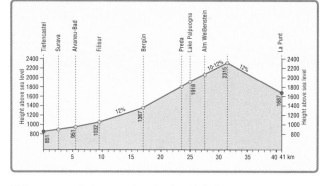

In Preda (23.5km), the railway disappears into a 5865m tunnel, while we have to ride up a 10 per cent gradient. The atmospheric Lake Palpuogna, gleaming dark green, enhances the landscape a little, but check the notices before you take a dip as swimming isn't always allowed. We ride past the Versuchsalp für Tierproduktion Weißenstein (The Weißenstein animal breeding trial farm) (27.5km) into an increasingly bleak and barren mountain landscape and suddenly find ourselves in the midst of countless gigantic boulders.

This scene of destruction is the Val di Diavel, Devil's valley, the result of a huge rockslide on the slopes of the Piz de las Blais to the south. Here a road, narrow in places, has been created leading to the top of the pass (31.5km) over a steady gradient of between 10 per cent and 12 per cent. There waiting for us is not just a restaurant, but also green alpine meadows and grazing cows.

The descent goes rather faster than the ascent, nine hairpin bends with downhill gradients of up to 12 per cent spread out over nearly 10km down to La Punt. Here I'd like to give you a piece of advice: the level crossing just before you enter the village presents a hazard in the form of a ramp which inevitably catapults any rider whose speed is faster than walking pace into orbit.

Opposite: The descent on the eastern side of the Albula Pass takes us into Engadin, the valley of the Inn.

TOUR PROFILE <<

Julier Pass: 2284m

NORTHERN SIDE – Start: Tiefencastel, 851m

Directions: A13 Bregenz–Chur (Rhine Valley Autobahn), exit Zillis – Thusis – Sils – Tiefencastel

Level of Difficulty/Maximum gradient: Medium to difficult tour with a maximum gradient of 10 per cent

Length: 37.0km

Total ascent: 1435m

Time: 2½–4 hrs

Suggested gearing: 39/26

Route: Tiefencastel (0.0km) – Oberhalbstein (6.0km) – Cunter (8.5km) – Savognin (9.5km) – Tinizong (12.0km) – Rona (15.0km) – Sur (20.5km) – Marmorera reservoir (22.5km) – Bivio (27.5km) – Julier hostel (35.5km) – Top of the pass (37.0km)

SOUTHERN SIDE – Start: Silvaplana, 1815m, about 6km west of St Moritz

Directions: A12 Innsbruck–Bludenz (Inn Valley Autobahn), exit Zams/Landeck East – Pfunds – Martina – Scuol – Zernez – St Moritz – Silvaplana

Level of Difficulty/Maximum gradient: Easy, with a maximum gradient of 11 per cent

Length: 7.5km

Total ascent: 470m

Time: 1–1½ hrs

Suggested gearing: 39/26

Route: Silvaplana (0.0km) – Alp Alesch (5.0km) – Top of the pass (7.5km)

Road conditions: Well-constructed roads. Lights are advisable for both the tunnels (150m and 200m) on the northern side

Pass open: All year

Things to see: Roman columns at the top of the pass; detour from Silvaplana to St Moritz and its Segantini museum

Map: Euro Cart regional map 1:300,000, RV-Verlag, Switzerland sheet

In this picture, near the cyclist and the sign, you can just see the two Roman columns.

As described for the Albula Pass Tiefencastel is also the starting point for a tour over the Julier Pass. See Tour 54 for a description.

Leave the village (0.0km) on a road with a gradient of 10 per cent, which climbs first between neat alpine meadows and then through pine woods. After about 4.5km the gradient decreases and after two galleries and two unlit tunnels, 150m and 200m long, we reach Oberhalbstein (6.0km), which is also the name of the valley which goes up from here to the top of the pass in several stages. The road keeps to the valley floor and after the villages of Cunter (8.5km) and Savognin (9.5km) we get to Tinizong (12.0km), only slightly higher up and through a landscape familiar to some from the work of the famous Italian painter Giovanni Segantini (1858–1899), who lived here and later at Maloja. He knew how to interpret the moods of this landscape better than anyone else, and if you want to know more you can see his work in the Segantini museum in St Moritz.

There is still some way to go on this trip. After Tinizong the valley becomes narrower and the gradient up to Rona (15.0km) increases to 10 per cent again. Until you reach the next village, Sur (20.5km), these gradients alternate with long flatter sections. If you need a break you could take a detour to paradise here. Figuratively speaking, that is: the painted dome of St Martin in Sur-Curt, one of the most beautiful Baroque churches in Graubünden, depicts Paradise in seven concentric circles.

Now the gradient increases to a constant 10 per cent over several hairpin bends and suddenly the Marmorera reservoir (22.5km) appears ahead, its 70m grassy earth dam merging into the landscape. We ride without too much effort along the left-hand bank of the reservoir, which owes its name to the village of Marmorera which disappeared beneath its waters, and into the wooded hollow of Bivio (27.5km). Its name is derived from the Latin *bivium*, 'two roads', because the Septimer Pass used to branch off here into the Bregaglia valley. Unfortunately this has long since fallen into disrepair and can now only be used by hikers and mountain bikers who aren't afraid of slipping and sliding at times.

After leaving the narrow centre of the village our route wends its way further east and the road climbs at 10 per cent again into a landscape that is fast becoming alpine. But there are flatter sections which make it relatively quick to cover, until we reach the start of a stretch of hairpin bends (31.0km). This takes us, with considerably more effort and a wonderful view of the mountains of the Piz d'Err group to the north, to the Julier hostel (35.5km), whose surroundings can really be described as high alpine. There's just another 1.5km to cover, at a gradient that stays at a more or less constant 10 per cent up to the top of the pass (37.0km). This is littered with a mass of boulders that look like the Cyclops scattered them up here, among which two ancient columns clearly stand out, erected here by the Romans as an offering to their gods.

The road now descends for a noticeably shorter distance on the

eastern side to Silvaplana in the Upper Engadin. There are only three hairpin bends to deal with on it's 7.5km length and once you've reached the short, steep 11 per cent downhill the descent is soon behind us. From here to St Moritz and the Segantini Museum there's only 6km of flatter road to cover.

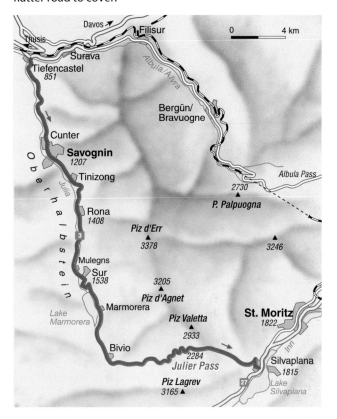

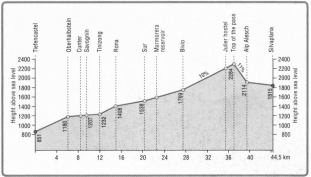

TOUR PROFILE <<

Livigno, Foscagno and Eira Passes: 2315m

Start: Turn-off to Livigno, 2054m, about 2km below the top of the pass on the western side of the Bernina Pass

Directions: The best way is over the northern side of the Bernina Pass (Tour 57)

Level of Difficulty/Maximum gradient: Medium, with a maximum gradient of 12 per cent on short sections on the Livigno and Eira Passes

Length: 50.0km

Total ascent: 720m

Time: 2½–4 hrs

Suggested gearing: 39/26

Route: Turning to Livigno (0.0km) – Top of the Livigno Pass (4.0km) – Livigno (18.5km) – Eira Pass (25.0km) – Trepalle (27.5km) – Top of the Foscagno Pass (31.5km) – Hairpin bend 3 north of Bórmio (50.0km)

Road conditions: Considerable surface damage in place especially on the Foscagno and Eira Passes

Pass open: Livigno Pass, 15 June to 6 November or 10 May to 15 December. Foscagno and Eira Passes open all year

Things to see: Zernez: Museum in the National Park Building

Map: Euro Cart regional map 1:300,000, RV-Verlag, Switzerland sheet

Notes: There is a great deal of traffic on the route at the weekends in particular because of shopping trips to the duty-free zone of Livigno

The Livigno Pass, or Forcola di Livigno in Italian, is perhaps best known locally for traffic bulletins reporting its closure. It leads from the southern side of the Bernina Pass (Tour 57) over into the Italian duty-free zone of Livigno and from there over the Eira and Foscagno Passes into Italy's Valdidentro valley and on to Bórmio, where you can extend your ride with a trip over the Stelvio Pass (Tour 40) or the Gavia Pass (Tour 41).

After a descent of around 3.5km down the southern side of the Bernina Pass, look out for the left turn to Livigno (0.0km). The road goes through the Swiss La Motta border post, staying more or less level, and then climbs several hairpin bends with gradients of up to 12 per cent to reach the top of the Livigno Pass (4.0km), the watershed between the Adda and Inn rivers. A last look back at the southern foothills of the Bernina range, and a long descent begins, ending at the bottom of the Spöl valley in the duty-free zone of Livigno. Here you can stock up on cheap confectionery and spirits; if you have a support vehicle your crew will love the low petrol prices.

Lake Livigno is more than 8km long and up to 119m deep.

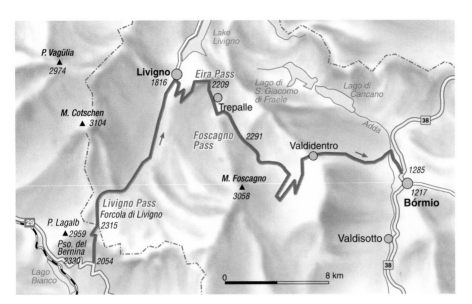

In the centre of Livigno (18.5km) follow the signposts for Bórmio and leave the town over hairpin bends with a gradient of up to 12 per cent. After a short stretch of pinewoods the road starts to flatten out and soon reaches the top of the unsigned Eira Pass (25.0km). Now a 2.5km descent begins down a wooded slope dotted with the houses of Trepalle village and into the Foscagno valley (27.5km). This is the start of the climb to the top of the Foscagno Pass. It's easily described: the road begins to climb the right-hand side of the valley at a gradient of 10 per cent and doesn't let up until the Italian border post at the top of the pass (31.5km) 4km later. That's the hard stuff over, and you're rewarded with a long descent down into densely populated Valdidentro. The road joins the southern side of the Stelvio Pass a little way above Bórmio at Hairpin Bend 3 (50.0km).

If you want to continue from here over the south-western side and through the romantic landscape of the Braulio valley to the Stelvio Pass (Tour 40), the short detour down to Bórmio, lying about 70m lower down, is a good idea. Over the last century of its 2000-year history Bórmio has developed into one of the best-known tourist centres in the Lombardy region. The heart of the town, with about 4100 inhabitants, is the old town and Via Roma with its many businesses and frescoes on the walls of the houses, which are well worth seeing. Places of interest include the Torre delle Ore, the Palazzo dei Simoni, the Torre degli Alberti and the San Vitale Church, all clustered around lively Piazza del Kuerc. Of even greater interest to your sore muscles are the town's thermal baths, where the water comes directly out of the rocks at a temperature of between 35ºC and 41ºC.

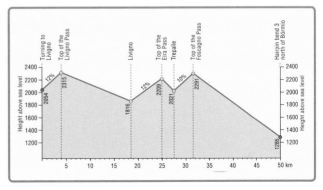

57 BERNINA PASS
Graubünden/Lombardy

TOUR PROFILE <<

Bernina Pass: 2330m

NORTHERN SIDE – Start: Pontresina, 1805m, near St Moritz in the Upper Engadin

Directions: A12 Innsbruck–Bludenz (Inn Valley Autobahn), exit Zams/Landeck East – Pfunds – Martina – Scuol – Zernez – St Moritz – Pontresina

Level of Difficulty/Maximum gradient: Easy, with a maximum gradient of 10 per cent

Length: 15.0km

Total ascent: 525m

Time: 1¼–2 hrs

Suggested gearing: 39/26

Route: Pontresina (0.0km) – Montebello car park (5.0km) – Bernina Häuser (8.0km) – Diavolezza cable car valley station (9.0km) – Lagalp cable car valley station (10.5km) – Lake Bianco (13.5km) – Top of the pass (15.0km)

The Bernina Pass, which connects the Swiss Upper Engadin with the Italian Poschiavo valley, takes us right into the heart of one of the most spectacular glaciated landscapes in the eastern Alps. The Bernina group boasts not only the highest peaks in the region, the 3905m Piz Palü and the Piz Bernina, at 4049m the only summit of over 4000m in the eastern Alps, but also the most beautiful. The Piz Bernina is a difficult and arduous climb for mountaineers, but our wheeled ascent to the top of the pass counts as one of the easier alpine tours, at least if you approach it from the northern side from Pontresina – the southern side from Tirano in the Adda valley through the Poschiavo valley with a vertical climb of almost 1900ms over 39.5km counts as one of the harder routes.

If you've been wondering about place names such as S-chanf or La-Punt-Chamues-ch while exploring the Upper Engadin, they're in Rhaeto-Romance, a language spoken only in parts of the Graubünden and parts of the South Tyrol and Friuli. In the old houses in the Engadin style in Pontresina (0.0km), our starting point, the living space is called 'stüra', the kitchen 'chadato' and the larder 'chaminada'. Cyclists from Bavaria should recognise this dialect, because Rhaeto-Romance originated in the Roman

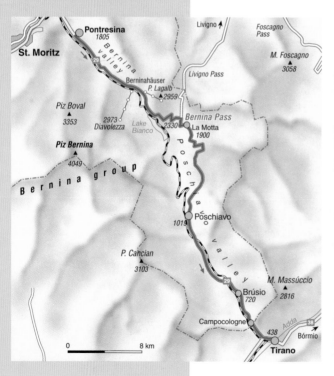

province of Rhaetia (lat. Raetia) which in about 15BC stretched from the Upper Danube in the north to the upper Italian lakes in the south and from the St Gotthard Pass in the west to the Brenner Pass in the east, and therefore also included Bavaria.

From Pontreina a flattish road leads into the Bernina valley, where after a few hundred metres the Rosegg valley soon reveals a view of the mountain peaks of the Bernina group. Past the turning there (3.5km) the road climbs at 8 per cent, and over two hairpin bends you reach a car park whose descriptive name, Montebello, 'beautiful mountain', hardly seems to do it justice. The view that opens up to the south over the wide hollow of the Morteratsch valley, the glaciated landscape towering behind it,

is among the most magnificent in the alpine region. You're looking at the highest mountains of the Bernina group with the Piz Palü, 3900m high, and the Piz Bernina, 4049m, which make their presence felt here in dazzling white above the Swiss stone pine and larch woods of the valley landscape.

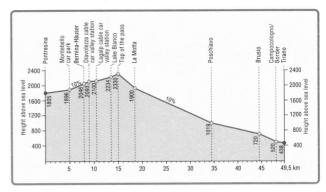

Montebello car park, on the northern side of the Bernina Pass, gives a wonderful view of the Bernina group across the Morteratsch valley.

57 Bernina Pass

TOUR PROFILE <<

SOUTHERN SIDE – Start: Tirano, 438m

Directions: Either over the Gavia Pass (Tour 41) to Bórmio and through Grosio to Tirano or A22 Brenner Autobahn, exit San Michele a. A./Mezzocorona – Mezzolombardo – Cles – Male – Tonale Pass – Edolo – Aprica Pass – Sondrio – Tirano

Level of Difficulty/Maximum gradient: Difficult, with a maximum gradient of 10 per cent

Length: 34.5km

Total ascent: 1895m

Time: 3¼–4¾ hrs

Suggested gearing: 39/26

Route: Tirano (0.0km) – Campocologno/Border (1.5km) – Brusio (5.0km) – Poschiavo (15.0km) – La Motta (31.0km) – Top of the pass (34.5km)

Road conditions: Well-constructed roads

Pass open: All year

Things to see: Pontresina: alpine museum, Spaniola tower. Montebello car park on the northern side with a glorious view of the Bernina group. Poschiavo: Collegiate Church of San Vittore, 13th-century, Baroque Church of Santa Maria Assante, Spaniole quarter

Map: Euro Cart regional map 1:300,000, RV-Verlag, Switzerland sheet

Lake Bianco at the top of the Bernina Pass. In summer you can watch kite-surfers here.

Opposite: The Bernina hostel at the top of the Bernina Pass.

Mountain climbers may perhaps know the famous Biancograt on the Piz Bernina, a razor-sharp curved ridge of firn (old snow) and ice, which in spite of its forbidding contours is reckoned to be one of the easier destinations for competent mountaineers. The Bumiller Pillar on the middle peak of the neighbouring Piz Palü on the other hand was rated an extreme climb in 1887, the year it was first conquered, and is still classified today as very difficult.

No such obstacles await us, because soon the road becomes flatter and following the tracks of the Bernina railway we soon reach Bernina Häuser (8.0km). This is Europe's highest adhesion railway, built between 1906 and 1910 – 'adhesion' is the term used to describe conventional railways, as opposed to cog or funicular systems. The slope, therefore, is gentle. You soon get to the Diavolezza cable car valley station (9.0km), and from there to the Lagalp cable car valley station (10.5km) it stays that way, before rising to 10 per cent up to the little Lake Bianco (13.5km). The lake takes its name from the white colour of the glacier on the Piz Cambrena above which feeds it; its surface is usually a milky-green. Now just a few more hairpin bends separate us from the Bernina hostel (15.0km), which is only 150m away from the top of the pass.

While the northern side of the Bernina Pass is much too beautiful to be taken at racing speed, the same cannot be said of the southern side. So it is here that the local Velo Club Valposchiavo organises occasional amateur races, starting in Poschiavo. The 18km route up to the top of the pass entails a vertical climb of 1330m. For more information see http://www.veloclub-valposchiavo.ch.

58 WILDHAUS PASS
Appenzell Innerrhoden/St Gallen

TOUR PROFILE <<

Wildhaus Pass: 1090m

EASTERN SIDE – Start: Oberriet, 422m

Directions: A1 then A13 Winterthur–Chur, exit Oberriet

Level of Difficulty/Maximum gradient: Easy to medium tour with a maximum gradient of 10 per cent

Length: 25.5km

Total ascent: 670m

Time: 1½–2½ hrs

Suggested gearing: 39/23

Route: Oberriet (0.0km) – Rüthi (4.0km) – Gams (18.5km) – Zollhaus Hotel (21.5km) – Wildhaus/Top of the pass (25.5km)

WESTERN SIDE – Start: Neu St Johann, 759m

Directions: A1 then A13 Winterthur–Chur Autobahn, exit Wil/Thurau – Wil – Wattwil – Neu St Johann

Level of Difficulty/Maximum gradient: Easy, with a maximum gradient of 10 per cent

Length: 18.0km

Total ascent: 335m

Time: ¾–1½ hrs

Suggested gearing: 39/23

Route: Neu St Johann (0.0km) – Stein (5.0km) – Alt St Johann (10.5km) – Unterwasser (12.5km) – Wildhaus/Top of the pass (18.0km)

Road conditions: Well-constructed roads

Pass open: All year

Map: Euro Cart regional map 1:300,000, RV-Verlag, Switzerland sheet

As you can clearly see from this picture of the eastern side of the Wildhaus Pass, there are all sorts of obstacles to contend with on the descent from the pass.

If you want to explore the mountains in eastern Switzerland in the region where Austria, Liechtenstein and Switzerland meet, there is an easy, but scenically beautiful, tour over the Wildhaus Pass, coming from the Rhine valley. It lies on the southern edge of the Alpstein region in north-eastern Switzerland, in the canton of Appenzell, where three distinct chains dominate the view over the low-lying area of the Rhine and Lake Constance. The highest peak, the 2501m Säntis, is easily identifiable, not so much because of its height or shape but because of the huge transmitter that can be seen for miles around – though not from our starting point in Oberriet (0.0km), some 30km south of Bregenz on Lake Constance in the Rhine valley.

As we leave the village two enormous boulders stand close to the road, which briefly slopes downhill at 10 per cent, but then undulates gently without incident, until just before Rüthi (4.0km). The character of the route remains the same through to Gams (16.5km). You need to be alert for pedestrians in the smaller villages that sprawl among the foothills of the Alpstein region, an area wooded in some places and covered with green meadows in others. As you progress, you have an increasingly uninterrupted view of the mountains of the Bregenz forest to the north-east, while to the south and the south-east the rocky peaks of the Rätikon are visible over the duchy of Liechtenstein.

In the centre of Gams (18.5km) you have to be careful not to miss the signpost to Zurich/Wildhaus. You also have to change to a lower gear because we're now leaving the Rhine valley. The road starts to climb immediately at a 10 per cent gradient and the valley is soon left behind. At one point the climb increases to a stiff 15 per cent, but only for a very short section. After about 3km, at the Zollhaus Hotel

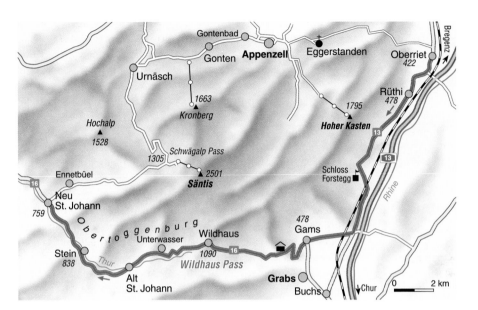

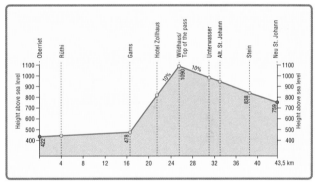

(21.5km), we ride into a dense mixed wood and the gradient drops back to a very pleasant 6-8 per cent. On a winding but well-constructed road we soon reach the first houses of Wildhaus (25.5km), where the gradient goes up again, to 10 per cent. This is only a temporary aberration before it eases off, as a panoramic view opens up to the surrounding mountains. In particular, to the west our attention is attracted by the dramatically serrated peaks of the Churfirsten range, 13 of them, dropping down to Lake Walen. To the north you can see the rock walls of the Schafberg rising immediately behind the village church, their channels and rocky gorges covered in snow well into spring. The Säntis is not visible, however.

We can take our time now and enjoy the scenery, because the hardest part of the route is behind us. On a wider and well-constructed road we swoop down a long 10 per cent descent to Unterwasser (31.0km) on the valley floor of the Wildhuser Thur. The freewheeling ends at the next village of Alt St Johann (33.0km); from here the road to Stein

(38.5km) is level, apart from a short stretch with a gradient of 8 per cent. This is the Obertoggenburg, and on a fine day you'll be enchanted by its scenic charm, with its grassy hills, low-lying valleys, isolated groups of trees and farmhouses dotted here and there.

In Nesslau, the first larger town in the valley, the road starts to go more steeply downhill again and soon we reach Neu St Johann (43.5km), the end point of our tour over the Wildhaus Pass. And still not a glimpse of the Säntis: for that you'll have to do the Schwägalp Pass tour (Tour 59), which is described next.

59 SCHWÄGALP PASS
St Gallen/Appenzell Innerrhoden

TOUR PROFILE <<

Schwägalp Pass: 1305m

WESTERN SIDE – Start: Neu St Johann, 759m

Directions: A1 then A13 Winterthur–Chur Autobahn, exit Withurau – Wil – Wattwil – Neu St Johann

Level of Difficulty/Maximum gradient: Easy, with a maximum gradient of 10 per cent

Length: 10.5km

Total ascent: 550m

Time: 1–2 hrs

Suggested gearing: 39/23

Route: Neu St Johann (0.0km) – Top of the pass (10.5km)

EASTERN SIDE – Start: Appenzell, 775m

Directions: A1 then A13 Winterthur–Chur Autobahn, exit St Gallen – St Gallen – Teufen – Gais – Appenzell

Level of Difficulty/Maximum gradient: Easy, with a maximum gradient of 12 per cent on short sections

Length: 20.0km

Total ascent: 530m

Time: 1½–2¼ hrs

Suggested gearing: 39/26

Route: Appenzell (0.0km) – Gontenbad (2.0km) – Rossfall (11.0km) – Hotel Rossfall (14.0km) – Top of the pass (20.0km)

Road conditions: Well-constructed roads

Pass open: All year

Map: Euro Cart regional map 1:300,000, RV-Verlag, Switzerland sheet

The best way to describe the Obertoggenburg, this wonderful landscape of hills at the foot of the western side of the Säntis, is with the help of a local myth. The story goes that here in the Alpstein region way back in the mists of time there lived a giant who had the idea of building a little town in Obertoggenburg. He went to nearby Montafon, picked up the houses that the dwarves had built there and put them in a big sack. On his way back, the sack tore on a rock and the houses swirled like snowflakes onto the slopes, hills and valleys, where they remain standing to this day. Anyone looking from our starting point in Neu St Johann (0.0km) to the houses and farmsteads scattered widely on the green slopes of the mountain with the limestone massif of the Alpstein and the Churfirsten as a magnificent background would almost believe this story.

No serious difficulties await on the way to the Schwägalp Pass, but you'll need to select a low gear because the 10 per cent gradient out of the town lasts for almost 2km. It then becomes a gentle descent and on the right-hand side past the houses in Ennetbühl is the first glimpse of the highest mountain in the Alpstein region, the 2501m Säntis. We can enjoy the view on long downhill stretches that alternate with climbs of up to 6 per cent on the next section of the route along the Luterenbach. But then, after about 6.5km, the gradient increases again to 10 per cent and stays there until the top of the pass (10.5km).

This runs right beneath the dark, smooth rock wall of the west face of the Säntis, a very alpine backdrop. It also forms the border between the cantons of St Gallen and Appenzell, and now we ride over several hairpin bends with downhill slopes of up to 12 per cent into the canton of Appenzell. A wide valley at the foot of the Hochalp welcomes us, then we cross the Urnäsch by the Hotel Rossfall (16.5km). We cruise gently downhill along by the

The Obertoggenburg, as the region on the western side of the Schwägalp Pass is called, is a Swiss picture-book landscape.

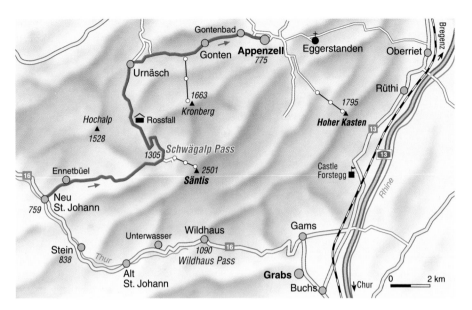

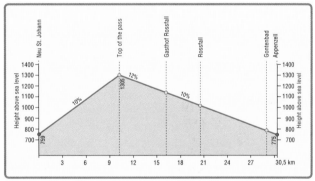

side of the river to the town of Rossfall (19.5km), where we reach the end of the Schwägalp Pass.

For most of us the tour doesn't end here. The route links nicely with the Wildhaus Pass (Tour 58) via the Schwägalp Pass, and you can easily ride back over Appenzell to Oberriet from here.

When we turn off in Urnäsch in the direction of Appenzell/Gais our return route at first remains level or slightly downhill between hills to drop down first past Gontenbad (28.5km) and then more steeply to Appenzell (30.5km). Take care here, because at the time of writing the signposts on the road left a lot to be desired. First follow the signpost 'Alle Richtungen' (All other routes) from the middle of Appenzell. This leads us to signposts for Brülisau/Wasserauen and along the Sitter in the Steinegg (34.0km) district. The last signpost to look out for is to Eggerstauden/Oberriet; you can concentrate a little more on the road and the scenery again. It's a small, narrow road with no hairpin bends, which we follow along the foothills of the Alpstein.

It climbs gently between green meadows and past isolated farmsteads and not until after Eggerstauden (37.5km) do we have to pedal a little harder, before it starts to go downhill over many bends, on a 10 per cent slope, into a wood called the Chräzerenwald. In Hölzlisberg (41.5km) the road widens again and the wood recedes and gives us a first glimpse of the Rhine valley below. Be on the alert for the not very obvious turning to Oberriet in Eichberg. Straight after that you reach the valley floor (44.5km) where only a few kilometres of level road separates you from Oberriet (48.0km).

The Klausen Pass links the Swiss canton of Glarus with the Gotthard route. It's one of the most beautiful Swiss passes, and takes us right into the heart of Switzerland, and the home territory of the folk hero William Tell.

Eastern side

From Glarus (0.0km), the capital of the eponymous canton, we ride into the Linth valley on a wide, well-constructed road. The valley is densely populated, and 8 per cent climbs alternate with long gentle downhill stretches and level sections through a series of small villages, before you arrive in Linthal (15.5km) at the beginning of the actual pass route.

In front of us the glaciers of the Tödi and the Bifertenstock form the head of the valley. We cross the Linth, and over two cobbled hairpin bends with a gradient of 10 per cent the road climbs through mixed woodland on the right-hand side of the valley. Two short, dimly lit tunnels (18.5km) take us to another group of hairpins, with the same 10 per cent gradient, up to the Gasthof Bergli (20.0km). The beautiful view of the glacier to the south is intermittent, with further bends and hairpins going up a gradient that's seldom below 10 per cent.

TOUR PROFILE <<

Klausen Pass: 1952m

EASTERN SIDE - Start: Glarus, 472m

Directions: A3 Zurich–Chur, exit Niederurnen – Glarus

Level of Difficulty/Maximum gradient: Medium to difficult tour with a maximum gradient of 10 per cent

Length: 39.0km

Total ascent: 1480m

Time: 2¾–4 hrs

Suggested gearing: 39/26

Route: Glarus (0.0km) – Linthal (15.5km) – Gasthof Bergli (20.0km) – Urner Boden valley (26.0km) – Hotel Wilhelm Tell (30.0km) – Head of the valley (32.0km) – Vorfrutt alpine meadows (36.5km) – Top of the pass (39.0km)

Clouds get caught on the rugged limestone rock faces of the Jägerstock on the eastern side of the Klausen Pass.

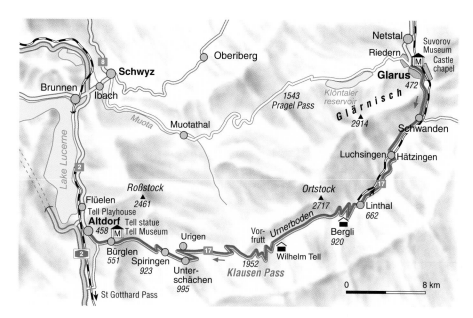

Then, suddenly, after about 6km, a glorious surprise. In front of us a high, wide valley opens up, without exaggeration it is one of the loveliest landscapes in Switzerland. It's the wild, romantic Urner Boden valley, bounded to the north by the rugged limestone rock faces of the Jägerstock and to the south by the Claridenstock glaciers. The road runs on the flat along the valley floor, through green meadows criss-crossed by little streams and scattered with mountain huts and enormous moss-covered boulders, up to the Hotel Wilhelm Tell (30.0km), then up an 8 per cent gradient to the head of the valley (32.0km), where a huge rock face threatens to block the way.

Over a set of hairpin bends with a gradient of 10 per cent the road crosses to the slopes on the right-hand side of the valley. It then takes us into the Chlus valley, from where there's a bird's-eye view of the Urner Boden, the largest alpine meadow in Switzerland. A final group of hairpins over a 10 per cent gradient, past the Vorfrutt alpine

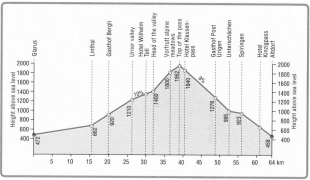

meadows (36.5km), now takes us up to the top of the pass (39.0km), named after St Nicholas.

A little way downhill, by the Hotel Klausenpass, you'll get a really beautiful view of glaciers and rocky mountain peaks, down from the Claridenstock over the Schärhorn and the Gross Ruchen to the Gross Windgällen.

Western side

As well as passing through beautiful scenery, the western side of the pass takes us into the home territory of Switzerland's most famous citizen, the

TOUR PROFILE <<

WESTERN SIDE – Start: Altdorf, 458m

Directions: A2 Lucerne–Bellinzona, exit Amsteg – Erstfeld – Altdorf

Level of Difficulty/Maximum gradient: Medium to difficult tour with a maximum gradient of 9 per cent

Length: 25.0km

Total ascent: 1495m

Time: 2¼–3 hrs

Suggested gearing: 39/26

Route: Altdorf (0.0km) – Hotel Kinizigpass (2.5km) – Spiringen (8.0km) – Unterschächen (11.5km) – Gasthof Posthof Urigen (15.5km) – Hotel Klausenpass (23.5km) – Top of the pass (25.0km)

Road conditions: Well-constructed roads, though there are two cobbled hairpin bends and narrow roads through tunnels on the eastern side

Pass open: 15 May to 31 October

Things to see: Glarus: Castle chapel, Suvorov Museum and art exhibition hall; Urner Boden: the largest alpine meadows in Switzerland; Bürglen: Tell monument, Tell chapel and Tell Museum; Altdorf: Tell monument and historical museum

Map: Euro Cart regional map 1:300,000, RV-Verlag, Switzerland sheet

The western side of the Klausen Pass takes us right into the home territory of the Swiss national hero, William Tell.

Oppoiste: Finally there – 1952m above sea level. Finished – in both senses of the word!

national hero Wilhelm Tell. According to legend, the famous apple-shooting incident took place in Altdorf (0.0km), our starting point. The tale should be taken with a pinch of salt, because neither this incident nor the existence of a Wilhelm Tell are accepted as historical fact, notwithstanding the impressive statue of Tell with his crossbow in his right hand and his left arm around his son in Altdorf's main square. Our route climbs at a gradient of 9 per cent past the statue and through Bürglen, said to be the folk hero's home town, where a conspicuous statue in the village square commemorates him. There is also a Tell Chapel dating from 1582 on Staldengasse and the Tell Museum, housing many paintings and documents, in the Wattigwiler Turm. At the Hotel Kinzigpass (2.5km) the road goes downhill briefly into the Schächen valley, then it takes us along the Schächen on a 7 per cent gradient to the start of a group of hairpin bends (7.0km) that lead up to Spiringen (8.0km) on a 9 per cent gradient. The gradient then decreases, and just before Unterschächen (11.5km) it even goes downhill again. Over widely spaced hairpin bends with a gradient of 9 per cent we climb up to the Gasthof Posthof Urigen (15.5km). There follows a lit, 250m tunnel (18.5km) with the same gradient before the road becomes narrower and snakes up to the rock faces at the foot of the Windgällen in the Schächen valley. Two hairpin bends with a gradient of 9 per cent take us to the Hotel Klausenpass (23.5km). Where you get probably the most beautiful view of the mountain peaks, with glaciers in some places and rocky in others, stretching from the Claridenstock over the Schärhorn and the Gross Ruchen to the Gross Windgällen. Then you only have 1.5km with a 7 per cent gradient in front of you to the top of the pass (25.0km).

61 PRAGEL PASS
Schwyz/Glarus

On this section of the western side of the Pragel Pass the incline is 18 per cent.

The Pragel Pass is probably as little known as the Klausen Pass (Tour 60) is renowned. Situated just a little to the east of the Klausen, it doesn't have the same spectacular scenery, running instead through tranquil countryside, with very little traffic. But the term 'tranquil' refers strictly to the surroundings, not to the pass itself, which incorporates gradients of up to 18 per cent. If you're very fit you can combine the Klausen Pass and the Pragel Pass which have their starting point and end point respectively in Glarus. The total distance is 129.5km and the vertical climb 2760m.

Brunnen (0.0km), on the shore of Lake Lucerne, is our departure point. From here we follow signposts for Schwyz/Muotathal. For the first few kilometres up to Ibach (4.0km) we speed along on a level road, until the gradient increases to 8 per cent through thick forest. Past the Stoos funicular railway station (8.5km) the road becomes flatter again and until you get to Muotathal (15.5km) it hardly climbs at all as it follows the stream of the same name along the valley. In the village of Hinterthal (16.5km) we cross the Muotathal and a short climb with a gradient of 14 per cent gives us a foretaste of what's to come. Soon after the Gasthaus Pragelpass (18.5km), which is the beginning of the actual route over the pass, the road narrows and climbs at 18 per cent, where it stays for 2km. After that the incline drops to a still significant 14 per cent on short

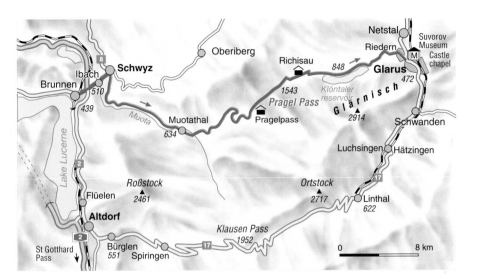

rises, but reaches frequent peaks of 18 per cent. After a further 2km it finally decreases to a bearable 10 per cent and then a flatter section, which at one point goes slightly downhill, brings us to the top of the pass (29.5km), a flower-filled plateau with a wonderful view of the limestone massif around the Bisi valley in the south-west. We continue on a steep 14 per cent downhill to the valley floor from Richisau, with the north faces of the Glärnisch rising ahead, then pass the Gasthaus Richisau (37.0km) on the flat, before descending to the Klöntalersee reservoir (40.5km). After Tiedern (49.5km) only a final gentle climb separates us from Glarus (50.5km), the finishing point of the eastern climb.

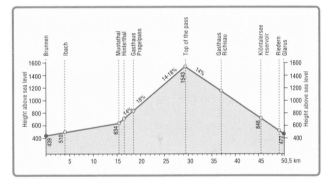

The Pragel Pass played an important role in Swiss history. It's inseparably linked with the name of Suvorov, a name you still come across in the Gotthard and Glarner regions. In the aftermath of the French Revolution almost the whole of Europe was in the grip of war. In spring 1799, Austria, England and Russia formed an alliance to wage war on France, which, under Napoleon had conquered Italy in 1795/96 and Switzerland in 1798. It was the Russian general Alexander Suvorov who managed to take back the Italian region in the spring of 1799. The Austrians won back part of eastern Switzerland, and the allies plotted to expel the French from the whole of the country. While the Austrians and the English attacked, General Suvorov and his army were to come as reinforcements from Italy over the St Gotthard Pass. After furious fighting Suvorov took the Gotthard Pass, but the French stopped him at the Pragel Pass and forced him to retreat. He later managed to reach his allies by a different route, but the war against the French was lost and Switzerland was allowed to remain a republic until the fall of Napoleon.

TOUR PROFILE <<

Oberalp Pass: 2045m

EASTERN SIDE – Start: Disentis/Mustér, 1143m

Directions: A12 Chur–Bellinzona (Rhine Valley Autobahn), exit Reichenau – Flims – Laax – Disentis/Mustér

Level of Difficulty/Maximum gradient: Medium, with a maximum gradient of 10 per cent

Length: 22.0km

Total ascent: 905m

Time: 1½–2½ hrs

Suggested gearing: 39/26

Route: Disentis/Mustér (0.0km) – Sedrun (8.5km) – Rueràs (12.0km) – Tschamut (16.5km) – Top of the pass (22.0km)

WESTERN SIDE – Start: Andermatt, 1447m

Directions: A2 Zurich–Bellinzona (Gotthard Autobahn), exit Göschenen – Andermatt

Level of Difficulty/Maximum gradient: Easy, with a maximum gradient of 10 per cent

Length: 11.5km

Total ascent: 600m

Time: 1¼–2 hrs

Suggested gearing: 39/26

Route: Andermatt (0.0km) – Top of the pass (11.5km)

Road conditions: Well-constructed roads on the western side, surface damage on the eastern side

Pass open: 15 May to 15 October

Things to see: Disentis/Mustér: Benedictine abbey with a Baroque church and monastery museum; Andermatt: Maria Hilf pilgrimage church and Suvorov house

Map: Euro Cart regional map 1:300,000, RV-Verlag, Switzerland sheet

Notes: Lights are advisable because of the 200m hairpin tunnel and the 800m unlit gallery on the western side

Is there room in your jersey pocket for a souvenir like this?

The Oberalp Pass links the Swiss Graubünden with Valais, over the Furka Pass (Tour 65), or with Ticino, over the St Gotthard Pass (Tour 64). It follows a road through the Upper Rhine Valley that has been a well-travelled trade route since early times and is still a major transport artery. There are high volumes of traffic, and the road isn't always wide enough for it, so it's a bit of a trial for cyclists.

But don't let this deter you. The pass does have its attractions. The town of Disentis, called Surselva in Rhaeto-Romanic, is known as the spiritual and cultural centre of the Upper Rhine Valley, which it owes to the monastery founded here in 750, the oldest Benedictine monastery in Switzerland. You can't miss its huge gleaming white walls rising up over the village, and the two domed towers of the monastery church of St Baptist in the Vorarlberg Baroque style are famous landmarks in the valley. The 15th century altar is particularly worth seeing. It was carved by Ivo Strigel, whose Allgäu workshop produced a whole series of famous altars in Graubünden, southern Germany and South Tyrol. The monastery holds interesting collections of medieval ecclesiastical and folk art but they can only be viewed by prior arrangement.

We leave Disentis (0.0km) past the turning for the Lukmanier Pass (Tour 63) on an initially wide road where short climbs of up to 10 per cent alternate with longer, flatter sections. After about 5km the route becomes noticeably narrower, but shortly before Sedrun (8.5km) goes gently downhill. We've arrived in Tavetsch, as the countryside in the Upper Rhine Valley is known, and the mountain peaks we can see above the sides of the valley, with the Oberalpstock to the north and the Piz Gannaratsch to the south, are already over the 3000m mark.

Our road stays on the valley floor then climbs moderately up to Rueràs (12.0km). The valley slowly narrows and on the slopes of the Chrüzlistock we make our way a little more quickly up to Tschamut (16.5km), up gradients of between 8 per cent and 10 per cent. Ahead of us on the slopes of the northern side of the valley we can make out the road up to the top of the pass and the galleries of the Furka-Oberalp-Bahn mountain railway. We reach a section of hairpin bends (18.0km) over which we get closer to the railway tracks on a gradient that doesn't drop below 10 per cent. We meet the line after 21km and then there's another kilometre to go to the top of the pass (22.0km). There are no particular attractions here, apart, perhaps, from the view of the 2.5km long Lake Oberalp, nearly filling the valley basin.

Along the northern side of the lake we are welcomed by an 800m avalanche gallery that we have to share with the railway line. Further on the road over the western slope down to Andermatt is in good condition. There's only a 200m hairpin tunnel to bother us now; apart from this you can tackle the nine hairpin bends, with an even downhill slope of 10 per cent, with ease. Below stretches the wide trough-shaped Urseren valley, and you soon reach the little crossroads village of Andermatt on the valley bottom.

If you want to go further you can now choose between the Furka Pass (Tour 65) and the St Gotthard Pass (Tour 64), but there is also a third option. If you ride down into the valley along the Gotthard road for about 11km to Wassen, from there you can tackle the eastern side of the Susten Pass (Tour 67).

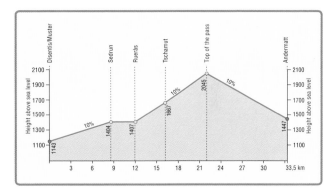

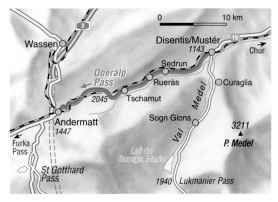

155

63 LUKMANIER PASS
Graubünden/Ticino

TOUR PROFILE <<

Lukmanier Pass: 1940m

NORTHERN SIDE – Start: Disentis/Mustér, 1143m

Directions: A13 Chur-Bellinzona (Rhine Valley Autobahn), exit Reichenau – Flims – Laax – Disentis/Mustér

Level of Difficulty/Maximum gradient: Medium, with a maximum gradient of 10 per cent

Length: 20.5km

Total ascent: 800m

Time: 1½–2¼ hrs

Suggested gearing: 39/26

Route: Disentis/Mustér (0.0km) – Curaglia (5.0km) – Platta (7.0km) – Parde (8.0km) – Acla (10.0km) – Gions (11.5km) – Avalanche gallery (18.0km) – Top of the pass (20.5km)

SOUTHERN SIDE – Start: Biasca, 301m

Directions: A13 then A2 Chur-Bellinzona–Biasca (Rhine Valley Autobahn then Gotthard Autobahn), exit Biasca

Level of Difficulty/Maximum gradient: Difficult, with a maximum gradient of 8 per cent

Length: 43.0km

Total ascent: 1640m

Time: 3–4 hrs

Suggested gearing: 39/23

Route: Biasca (0.0km) – Malvaglia (8.0km) – Acquarossa (14.0km) – Torre (19.5km) – Olivone (23.5km) – Top of the pass (43.0km)

Road conditions: Well-constructed roads apart from surface damage at the summit

Pass open: 15 May to 31 October

Map: Euro Cart regional map 1:300,000, RV-Verlag, Switzerland sheet

Notes: Lights are advisable because of the tunnels (60-100m) and the gallery tunnels (600m to 2km) on the northern side and the 2 tunnels (100m) and the gallery (50m) on the southern side

To go from the Vorderrhein valley into Ticino, you go over the Oberalp Pass (Tour 62) to Andermatt or else over the St Gotthard Pass (Tour 64). But if you are looking for a shorter route, more beautiful scenery and above all less traffic, you can take the route over the Lukmanier Pass. At 1940m above sea level, it's the second lowest pass road in Switzerland, after the Maloja Pass (Tour 44), which is 1810m above sea level, and crosses the main ridge of the Alps. The gradients here are also quite moderate, ranging over long stretches between 4 per cent and 6 per cent, and never exceeding the 10 per cent mark. A 23-tooth sprocket ought to be enough for a very fit cyclist, although a 25- or 26-tooth sprocket is recommended, because over the whole route the ride is classified as being of medium difficulty.

The northern slope is 20.5km long with a vertical climb of just under 800m. The 43km long southern route, with a total vertical climb of some 1600m, requires considerably more stamina, though the gradient never exceeds 8 per cent.

As it is for Tour 62 to the Oberalp Pass, Disentis (0.0km) is our starting point. After a final look at the enormous Benedictine monastery with its impressive 17th-century facade and the two towers of the monastery church, we take the turning to the Lukmanier Pass. For the time being you don't have to pay much attention to what gear you're in, because for the first couple of kilometres to the mouth of the Medel Rhine gorge in Vorderrhein the road goes down an 8 per cent slope. We ride over a bridge into the Höllenschlucht, on the right-hand side of which the road now starts to climb at a gradient of 10 per cent. Once a dangerous and dreaded section of the route, this has now been completely

transformed by three 60- to 100m tunnels and a 600m gallery tunnel, but for safety's sake lights on your bike won't come amiss. Once you're through the tunnels you reach the first village, Curaglia (5.0km), over two hairpin bends with a steady 10 per cent gradient.

After the narrow gorge a wide, high valley opens up in front of us and we've left the initial slog behind us. We quickly make progress through Platta (7.0km) and Parde (8.0km), hardly ascending at all, at least until Acla (10.0km), where the gradient increases to 10 per cent. In spite of the many place names the high valley has only been sparsely populated up to now; the names refer only to little groups of houses.

We pass Gions (11.5km), the last of these hamlets, on our way up to the top of the pass, and the surroundings become considerably more alpine. There is nothing left to remind us that the name of the pass derives from *lucus magnus*, or 'large wood': only a few scattered trees of the previously dense woodland remain.

Above us the enormous 100m high concrete wall of the Lai da Sontga Maria

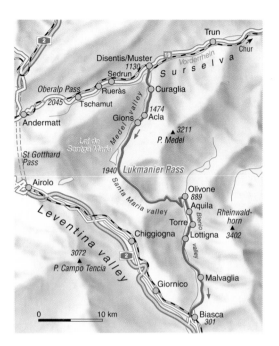

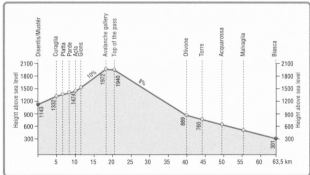

reservoir can be made out. However, before we reach it there are several short tunnels and galleries and two hairpin bends (17.5km) over a gradient of 6 per cent to 8 per cent to contend with. Once we've left these behind we ascend gently through a 2-kilometer gallery on the left-hand bank of the lake, and halfway through we cross the highest point of the climb, at 1972m. We therefore reach the 'top of the pass (20.5km)' and the San Marie hostel on a road with a gentle downhill slope.

The gallery at the top of the Lukmanier Pass is almost 2km long.

157

TOUR PROFILE <<

St Gotthard Pass: 2108m

NORTHERN SIDE – Start: Amsteg, 591m

Directions: A2 Zurich–Bellinzona
(Gotthard Autobahn), exit Amsteg

Level of Difficulty/Maximum gradient:
Difficult, with a maximum gradient of
10 per cent

Length: 34.0km

Total ascent: 1590m

Time: 2¾–4 hrs

Suggested gearing: 39/26

Route: Amsteg (0.0km) – Wassen
(10.5km) – Göschenen (15.0km) – Urner
Loch tunnel (20.5km) – Andermatt
(21.5km) – Hospental (24.5km) – Mätteli
restaurant (29.0km) – Top of the pass
(34.0km)

The St Gotthard Pass is known as the 'Pass of Passes', even though cyclists are more likely to award the Großglockner High Alpine Road or the Stelvio Pass this accolade. Certainly there are higher and more beautiful alpine passes, but none of them can provide the same variety of impressive scenic features. The St Gotthard also scores highly for historic interest.

Schöllenen gorge was an insurmountable obstacle in prehistory, and it wasn't until the first half of the 13th century that it was spanned by a daring bridge. The devil is said to have had a hand in creating it, and it's popularly known as the Devil's Bridge. The crossing created the shortest link between Basle and Milan, and the previously extremely isolated rural communities around Lake Lucerne experienced a sudden upturn in their economic fortunes, which spurred other envious villagers into action. The rural communities of Uri, Schwyz and Unterwalden joined forces at the end of the 13th century in an alliance from which the modern confederation developed.

Now it's time to get on the bike, in Amsteg (0.0km), where the pass begins. We follow the Reuss valley road, which climbs at 10 per cent. Fortunately rush hour traffic uses the autobahn, and some people certainly use the railway too, for which enough space has been found in the narrow valley. While the autobahn and the railway run in a more or less straight line, our country road uses the whole width of the valley. Gradients of up to 10 per cent time and again crop up between flatter sections as far as Wassen (10.5km), whose church tower, visible for miles around, is a famous landmark in the valley.

In Göschenen (15.0km) the autobahn disappears into a 16.3km tunnel, the second longest tunnel in the world after the 24.5km

These days the Devil's Bridge on the northern side of the St Gotthard Pass is bypassed by a modern road.

Laerdal tunnel in Norway on the E6 between Oslo and Bergen, which opened in March 2000. We ride over hairpin bends with a gradient of 10 per cent into the dark and gloomy Schöllenen gorge.

On both sides, steep and forbidding granite walls rise up; between them the road searches out its way, running mostly through tunnels and galleries. With a constant gradient of 10 per cent we quickly gain height, and after leaving the long stretch of galleries another gallery welcomes us, followed by a short tunnel. If you stop at the next car park and take a look into the little gorge you can still make out what remains of the old Devil's Bridge there.

We leave the Schöllenen gorge through the Urner Loch (20.5km), a 64m natural tunnel that is often described as the oldest road tunnel in the world, and we ride into the wide open expanse of the Urseren valley. We reach Andermatt (21.5km), situated at the intersection of three pass roads – the Furka Pass (Tour 65), the Oberalp Pass (Tour 62) and the St Gotthard Pass – on a level road and keep going on the flat until we reach Hospental (24.5km), the turning to the Furka Pass. We ride over another hairpin bend with a 10 per cent gradient into the desolate high valley of the Gotthardreuss. The road maintains this gradient over a long-drawn-out bend on the slopes of the right-hand side of the valley, overgrown with scrub, up to the Mätteli restaurant (29.0km). There is yet another hairpin bend, and then the road follows a more or less straight line over a gradient of between 8 per cent and 10 per cent up to the top of the pass (34.0km). Here you can park your bike in front of the historic buildings of the former hostel.

If you want to find out more about the history of the St Gotthard Pass you should visit the museum in the Alten Sust. There

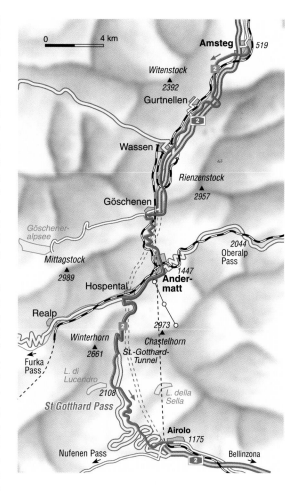

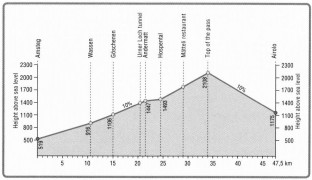

you'll find out that the southern climb through the Val Tremola, the 'shaking valley', down to Airolo was known for a

159

TOUR PROFILE <<

SOUTHERN SIDE – Start: Airolo, 1175m

Directions: A2 Zurich–Bellinzona (Gotthard Autobahn), exit Airolo

Level of Difficulty/Maximum gradient: Medium, with a maximum gradient of 10 per cent

Length: 13.5km

Total ascent: 935m

Suggested gearing: 39/26

Route: Airolo (0.0km) – Top of the pass (13.5km)

Road conditions: Well-constructed roads on the northern side. On the old pass road on the southern side, through the narrow Val Tremola, there are hairpin bends that are cobbled in places. In wet or bad weather conditions this section should be avoided and the new, well-surfaced bypass used instead

Pass open: 15 May to 15 October. The old pass road through the Val Tremola, between the top of the pass and Airolo, is also closed between these dates in bad weather

Things to see: Wassen: Church of St Gallus; Schöllenen gorge near Göschenen; Devil's Bridge; Suvorov monument by the Devil's Bridge car park; Urner Loch (known as the first rock tunnel in the Alps, dating from 1707–1708). Andermatt: pilgrimage church of Maria Hilf and Suvorov House. Top of the pass: museum of the history of the pass in the Alten Sust. Airolo: Airolo Castle (guided tours)

Map: Euro Cart regional map 1:300,000, RV-Verlag, Switzerland sheet

This stagecoach from 1836 still runs on the old St Gotthard Pass road through the Val Tremola today for tourists. The cobblestones can be clearly seen.

Opposite: The old St Gotthard pass road through the Val Tremola, the 'shaking valley', seen from the new bypass opposite.

long time as one of the most dangerous and feared passes in the Alps. The danger came first and foremost from avalanches against which the area is almost completely unprotected. That shouldn't be a problem in summer, although care should be taken when riding over the 24 hairpin bends, narrow and cobbled in places, which were built in 1836 for stagecoach traffic.

In fog or when visibility is poor it's extremely inadvisable to use this road, even if it's open. It's easier, quicker and safer to use the road that runs a little further to the west and bypasses the Val Tremola with six wide hairpin bends.

65 FURKA PASS
Uri/Valais

On the eastern side of the Furka Pass. A first glimpse of the 3631m high Dammastock.

TOUR PROFILE <<

Furka Pass: 2436m

EASTERN SIDE – Start: Hospental, 1480m, about 3km west of Andermatt

Directions: Either over the Oberalp Pass (Tour 62) or A2 Zurich–Bellinzona (Gotthard Autobahn), exit Göschenen – Andermatt

Level of Difficulty/Maximum gradient: Medium, with a maximum gradient of 11 per cent on long sections

Length: 17.5km

Total ascent: 960m

Time: 1¾–2½ hrs

Suggested gearing: 39/26

Route: Hospental (0.0km) – Realp (5.5km) – Hotel Galenstock (10.5km) – Tiefenbach Railway Halt, DFB railway (12.5km) – Furka Hotel (17.0km) – Top of the pass (17.5km)

To get from the St Gotthard route out of the Urseren valley up into Upper Valais, also known as Goms, you can take the easy way out. Just stow your bike in the car and load both of them onto a Furka–Oberalp train. This will complete the journey from Realp station in the canton of Uri to Oberwald in the canton of Valais in just 20 minutes. However, then you'd miss the scenery of a high pass, unique in the whole alpine region, but more about that later.

First we get onto our bikes in Hospental (0.0km), some 2km west of Andermatt, and start off gently downhill for the next few kilometres. Just before you reach Realp (5.5km), the eastern railway depot, the gradient increases considerably to 11 per cent and you make your way up to the top over several hairpin bends. Looking back a wonderful view opens up over the mountains of the Gotthard group to the south, while to the east you can easily follow the course of the hairpin bends working their way up to the Oberalp Pass (Tour 62). Below us we can already see the buildings of the Hotel Galenstock (10.5km), which we reach over a total of seven hairpin bends on a gradient that doesn't fall below 11 per cent. From here you can see the course of the road continuing up to the top of the pass, though it's still a fair way off.

High over the stony bed of the Furkareuss river the road continues on with gradients between 8 per cent and 10 per cent, but dead straight, on the right-hand side of the valley. The already sparse vegetation becomes even sparser, the surroundings become more and more inhospitable and if you're in need of refreshment you'll find this at the Tiefenbach Railway halt (12.5km). Refreshment of another kind is on offer from the streams of water constantly rushing down from the rocky slopes of the wintry heights, to disappear foaming and gurgling in little canals under the road. At the 16km mark there are two more hairpin bends to contend with, which take us up to the Furka hotel (17.0km). Then there's just 500m on a moderate gradient to the rather uninteresting top of the pass (17.5km).

Save stopping until you reach a little car park a few hundred metres further on. This gives a wonderful view of the basin of the Rhone Valley down below with a group of hairpin bends going up to the Grimsel Pass (Tour 66), which seems to lead straight into the glaciated peaks and ridges of the Berner Alps. You can make out the summit of the Eiger between the tops of the Fiescherhörn mountains and the Lauteraarhorn.

This isn't the surprise that I mentioned at the beginning. This comes a little under 2.5km further on and 200m below the Hotel Belvédère (20.0km). The Rhone glacier is right there on the opposite side of the road, almost touching the road. Yes, it's pitifully small compared to the once-gigantic ice mass that, as late as 1818, filled the valley below us and during the last ice age covered the whole of Valais. However, it's still impressive: nowhere else can you climb off your bike and climb straight onto a glacier. If you want to, you can even walk through a tunnel in the glacier, a good 100m long. It's a strange feeling

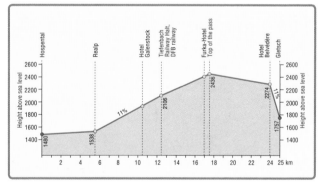

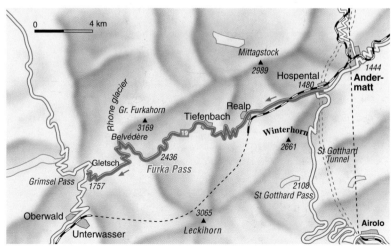

TOUR PROFILE <<

WESTERN SIDE – Start: Gletsch, 1757m

Directions: Either over the Nufenen Pass from Airolo to Ulrichen (Tour 69) and through Oberwald to Gletsch, over the Susten Pass from Innertkirchen to Gletsch (Tour 67), or through the Rhone Valley (Valais) to Gletsch

Level of Difficulty/Maximum gradient: Easy to medium tour with a maximum gradient of 11 per cent

Length: 7.5km

Total ascent: 680m

Time: 1¼–2 hrs

Suggested gearing: 39/26

Route: Gletsch (0.0km) – Hotel Belvédère (1.0km) – Top of the pass (7.5km)

Road conditions: Bottlenecks/constrictions by the Hotel Galenstock on the eastern side and in front of the glacier on the western side. Care needed when crossing the railway lines in front of the glacier. Slight surface damage, especially at the summit

Pass open: 1 June to 31 October

Things to see: Rhone glacier with a glacier grotto opposite the Hotel Belvédère. Gletsch: Hotel Glacier du Rhône from the Belle Époque; glacier nature trail by the English chapel behind the hotel. If you're looking for a room for the night, the Grand Hotel Glacier du Rhône is recommended

Map: Euro Cart regional map 1:300,000, RV-Verlag, Switzerland sheet

to walk into its frozen heart between eerily groaning and cracking ice walls by the weak glow of a lightbulb – and suddenly come face to face with a polar bear. Fortunately it's just a souvenir seller in costume, offering to be photographed next to you.

Out unscathed into the open air again and back on the bike, we go down a long slope with a gradient of 11 per cent. Well maintained to start with, the sometimes risky route appears to be stuck directly onto the moraine on the left-hand side of the valley. Lower down the surface becomes considerably worse and just before Gletsch (25.0km) it's a good idea to slow down to a walking pace for the sake of our narrow tyres as we cross the Furka railway line, a single-track cogwheel steam railway that was officially closed down in 1941 but has since re-opened.

Furka Pass

The Hotel Belvédère on the western side of the Furka Pass situated directly above the Rhone glacier.

A view from the top of the Furka Pass of the western side of the Furka Pass and the southern side of the Grimsel Pass. In the background are the peaks of the Berner Alps.

66 GRIMSEL PASS
Valais/Bern

TOUR PROFILE <<

Grimsel Pass: 2165m

SOUTHERN SIDE – Start: Gletsch, 1759m

Directions: either over the Furka Pass from Hospental to Gletsch (Tour 65) or through the Rhône valley (Valais) to Gletsch

Level of Difficulty/Maximum gradient: Easy, with a maximum gradient of 9 per cent

Length: 6.0km

Total ascent: 406m

Time: ¾–1¼ hrs

Suggested gearing: 39/23

Route: Gletsch (0.0km) – Lake Toten (5.5km) – Top of the pass (6.0km)

NORTHERN SIDE – Start: Innertkirchen, 622m

Directions: A8 Lucerne–Berne link, exit Brienz – Meiringen – Innertkirchen

Level of Difficulty/Maximum gradient: Difficult, with a maximum gradient of 11 per cent

Length: 27.5km

Total ascent: 1545m

Time: 3–4 hrs

Suggested gearing: 39/26

Route: Innertkirchen (0.0km) – Guttanen (8.0km) – Hotel Handegg (14.0km) – Top of the pass (27.5km)

Road conditions: Well-constructed roads

Pass open: 15 June to 15 October

Things to see: Innertkirchen: detour in the direction of Meiringen to the Aare gorge

Map: Euro Cart regional map 1:300,000, RV-Verlag, Switzerland sheet

Notes: Lights are necessary because of tunnels up to 500m long on the northern side

The southern side of the Grimsel Pass boasts six hairpin bends.

The Grimsel Pass is the only link from the upper Rhone Valley into the Bernese Oberland, apart from the car train through the Lötschberg Tunnel. If we do the journey from the south to the north our starting point is the village of Gletsch (0.0km). 'Village' is actually a bit of an exaggeration because it seems to consist of just the large Hotel Glacier du Rhône complex, six storeys built of rough stone blocks. It's worth having a closer look at it. It dates from the turn of the 20th century, the so-called Belle Époque, when rich, enterprising Englishmen set about conquering the Alps. The present owners have tried not to change the style of the hotel and have kept the original furniture and furnishings. Even the wallpaper dates from this time, and when you're inside this venerable old house you really feel as though you've gone back in time to the excitement of those pioneering days, when news that an Englishwoman had been chauffeur-driven over the Grimsel Pass caused a real sensation in newspapers on the continent and in the UK.

Today when we make our way over the Grimsel Pass by bike there's definitely nothing sensational about it in cycling terms. Quite the opposite: at 6km to the top with a vertical climb of 406m its vital statistics are hardly worth mentioning. But the scenery does remain something special. If you want to learn a bit about it in advance, take a walk on the nature trail that starts behind the Hotel Glacier du Rhône by the English chapel and shows you some glacial features and rare alpine plants. It's hard to believe, but the Rhone

glacier, whose meagre remains you may already have admired on the journey over the Furka Pass, reached almost to the hotel less than 100 years ago, and at its height stretched to Lyon in France.

You'll see the first kilometre stone, with the inscription '0km', after just a few turns of the pedals at the beginning of the climb. In fact it's the only kilometre stone: instead there are six uniform hairpin bends whose gradient doesn't exceed 9 per cent but doesn't fall below it either. These open up a view of the Galenstock, the Rhone glacier and the hairpin bends of the Furka Pass. Just below us the Rhone makes its way, still a young river here and known as the Rotten in this part of Valais. The top of the pass is signalled by the little Lake Toten (5.5km), which ostensibly got its macabre name ('toten' means 'dead' in German) in 1799 when it's said that soldiers killed in the war between the Austrians and the French were thrown into it. A little further on we reach the top of the pass (6.0km) on a level road.

The surrounding views are magnificent. This is a landscape of almost gigantic proportions, composed of granite walls covered in ice and peaks topped by firn, from which huge glacier streams run down to flow into reservoirs like fjords, stretching for kilometres. The descent, which is almost 30km long and goes down over several valleys in the canton of Berne, is one of compelling beauty, with ever-changing views. Rock walls of Aare granite polished smooth by glacier ice alternate with reservoirs in dammed valleys that stretch for kilometres. Not even structures such as turbines, dam walls and power lines erected to harness hydroelectric power can spoil this magnificent impression for long. The road has also been upgraded in the last few years, making possible a fast descent

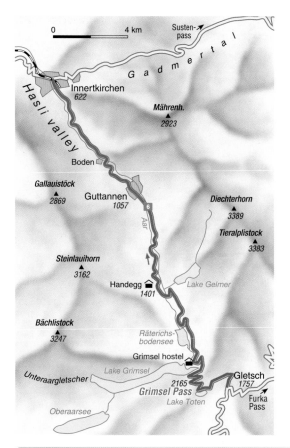

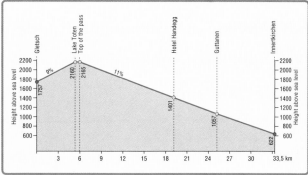

only slowed down now and then by several tunnels up to 500m long. It's actually a pity that the ride down is over so soon, at Innertkirchen (33.5km). On the other hand you now have the climb up to the Susten Pass (tour 67) ahead.

67 SUSTEN PASS
Bern/Uri

TOUR PROFILE <<

Susten Pass: 2224m

WESTERN SIDE – Start: Innertkirchen, 622m

Directions: A8 Lucerne–Bern, exit Brienz – Meiringen – Innertkirchen

Level of Difficulty/Maximum gradient: Difficult, with a maximum gradient of 9 per cent

Length: 28.0km

Total ascent: 1605m

Time: 2¼–3½ hrs

Suggested gearing: 39/26

Route: Innertkirchen (0.0km) – Wiler (1.5km) – Nessental (6.0km) – Furen (10.0km) – Gadmen (12.0km) – Obermad (12.5km) – Hotel Steingletscher (22.5km) – Top of the pass (28.0km)

EASTERN SIDE – Start: Wassen, 916m, on the St Gotthard Pass road

Directions: A2 Zurich–Bellinzona (Gotthard Autobahn), exit Wassen

Level of Difficulty/Maximum gradient: Medium, with a maximum gradient of 9 per cent

Length: 18.0km

Total ascent: 1310m

Time: 2–3 hrs

Suggested gearing: 39/23

Route: Wassen (0.0km) – Färnigen (9.0km) – Top of the pass (18.0km)

Road conditions: Well-constructed roads

Pass open: 15 June to 15 October

Things to see: Wassen: Church of St Gallus; detour from Innertkirchen to the Aare gorge near Meiringen

Map: Euro Cart regional map 1:300,000, RV-Verlag, Switzerland sheet

Notes: Lights are necessary because of the tunnels, unlit in places, on both sides of the pass and a 325m tunnel at the summit

The view of the western climb shows the well-constructed Susten Pass road.

The Susten Pass, which connects the Aare valley at Innertkirchen with the St Gotthard route at Wassen, is one of the most modern pass roads in the Alps. This is primarily because it was built relatively recently, between 1938 and 1945, and planners assumed that traffic volume was going to increase. It was constructed to be wide throughout, with very few hairpin bends and plenty of car parks at beauty spots and viewpoints. With 26 bridges and 14 tunnels, of which only the longest, the 325m tunnel at the summit, is a problem for cyclists, it runs mainly along the slopes on the sunny side of the valley and harmonises well with the impressive scenery. Another plus point for cyclists is that the gradient doesn't exceed the 9 per cent mark on either side.

Before setting off, it's worth a short detour to the Aare gorge, lying a few kilometres out of the valley near Meiringen. Since the last ice age the Aare has worn away a gorge 200m deep and almost 1.5km long, and with its numerous niches, grottoes, arches and bays it has become one of the main attractions in the Bernese Oberland.

Riding out of Innertkirchen (0.0km) you'll hit two hairpin bends with a 9 per cent gradient en route to Wiler (1.5km). The wonderful view of the Engelhörner in the west unfortunately disappears as you go through the first unlit, 100m tunnel (2.5km), which takes you into the wide Gadmer valley. Inclines of up to 9 per cent alternate at first with flatter sections and short descents. If you pay attention you'll see, about halfway to Nessental (6.0km) on the left-hand side, the turning to the Engstlenalp mountain road (Tour 68). If you have enough time and you're fit enough then this climb up an almost 15km long no-through-road is recommended for the impressive scenic panorama it offers. As we continue on, all the panorama we have for the time being is the glaciated peak of the Sustenhorn. Through another tunnel we reach a flatter road to Gadmen (12.0km) and get up some speed alongside the limestone cliffs of the Gadmerflüe to Obermad (12.5km). This is the highest continuously inhabited settlement on this side of the pass. The inhabitants have to evacuate to a bunker for protection when there's the threat of an avalanche.

In summer there's no danger of that for us and so we happily put up with the road climbing at a gradient of 9 per cent. Over several groups of hairpin bends and through the occasional short rock tunnel we wind our way up to Bäregg through the Gschlettersschlagwald on the slopes of the Fünffingerstock and then on to 'Hell', as a region of spruce and stone pines criss-crossed by streams is called. We slowly get closer to the Hotel Steingletscher (22.5km), where a view of the glacier coming down from the Sustenhorn is guaranteed to stop you in your tracks. But the panorama becomes even more breathtaking. The most

impressive view is from a car park (26.0km), reached on another hairpin bend with a gradient of 9 per cent. An information board gives a key to the mountains which stretch from the Sustenhorn over the Bockberg, the Gwächtenhorn and the Vorder Tierberg to the Giglistock. The eye is drawn here again and again to the immense ice stream of the Stein glacier which reaches down almost as far as the Hotel Steingletscher.

From here it's only 2km over a constant gradient to the top of the pass and the 325m tunnel at the summit. Once you emerge from it the Sustenhorn in particular dominates the alpine landscape and you can start on the 18km descent to Wassen on well-constructed roads.

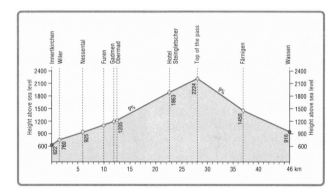

68 ENGSTLENALP MOUNTAIN ROAD
Bern

TOUR PROFILE <<

Engstlenalp Mountain Road: 1837m

Start: Turning to Engstlen on the western side of the Susten Pass between Wiler and Nessental, 847m

Directions: A8 Lucerne–Bern, exit Brienz – Meiringen – Innertkirchen – Wiler – turning to Engstlen

Level of Difficulty/Maximum gradient: Medium, with a maximum gradient of 12 per cent on longer sections

Length: 14.5km

Total ascent: 990m

Time: 1½–2¼ hrs

Suggested gearing: 39/26

Route: Engstlen (0.0km) – Wagenkehr tollbooth (4.0km) – Arvenstüble Restaurant (9.5km) – Hotel Engstlenalp (14.5km)

Road conditions: Well-constructed roads

Pass open: 1 May to 31 October

Things to see: Wonderful viewpoint by Lake Engstlen just above the Hotel Engstlenalp

Map: Euro Cart regional map 1:300,000, RV-Verlag, Switzerland sheet

If you're fit enough and still hungry for more after taking on the Susten Pass (Tour 67), you can extend your stay in this magnificent landscape by tackling the Engstlen mountain road (not a pass, as it has a dead-end). Alternatively, if you only think you have one big climb in you, consider coming up here instead of the Susten. It's shorter, with comparable views, and it has the additional advantage of very little traffic, though it packs in plenty of difficult climbing.

Keep your eyes peeled for the hard-to-spot turning to Engstlen on the western side of the Susten Pass, between Wiler and Nessental. From Engstlen (0.0km) up to the Wagenkehr tollbooth (4.0km) the road climbs up a really steep gradient mostly between 10 and 12 per cent through the dense Mühletal forest. From here you have your first wonderful view of the rugged rocky peaks of the Engelhörner mountains to the south with the glaciated Wetterhorn and Schreckhorn towering over them, while the Gen valley opens up in the foreground. From there you first swoop downhill along the valley floor where, apart from short climbs on a gradient of up to 7 per cent, the road runs more or less on the level beside the Gentalwasser stream. Just before the Arvenstüble restaurant (9.5km) the gradient increases again to 10 per cent, and then still further to 12 per cent at the start of a little valley terrace (10.5km). Two hairpin bends that climb a slightly more merciful gradient higher up the valley are soon behind us and the road goes up again on a gradient of 12 per cent on the right-hand side of the valley, in more or less a straight line.

The road plays this game, a short let-up in the gradient followed by a climb of up to 12 per cent, twice more, maintaining the last steep climb for a good kilometre up to the Hotel Engstlenalp (14.5km). From here there's a hiking trail to Lake Engstlen, which

Fog often rises here from nearby Lake Lucerne.

In contrast to the Susten Pass, the Engstlenalp mountain road has very little traffic. In the background are the Engelhörner mountains with the glaciated Wetterhorn and Schreckhorn.

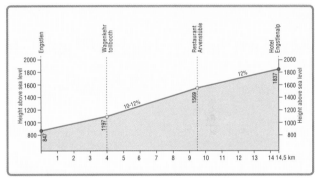

is situated in unspoiled scenery and framed by the Titlis glaciers and the craggy Wendenstöcke. Even though your footwear is probably unsuitable, and even though you may prefer to push your bike than leave it unattended, you should make this trip. Engstlen is the jewel of the alpine lakes. J. Tyndal, an English scholar, described it in 1866 as one of the most delightful places in the Alps, and Johann Wolfgang von Goethe and Albert Einstein are known to have visited. Its flora and fauna are unique and the many alpine roses that surround it are particularly impressive with their blaze of colour. Only the hardiest souls will find the prospect of a swim inviting, but for a charge of €10 an hour you can take a boat out on the lake and give your arm muscles, not generally required to do much when cycling, a workout.

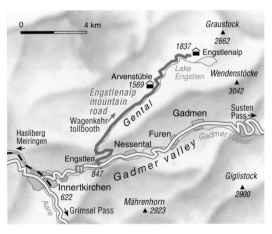

171

69 NUFENEN PASS
Ticino/Valais

TOUR PROFILE <<

Nufenen Pass: 2478m

EASTERN SIDE – Start: Airolo, 1175m

Directions: A2 Zurich-Bellinzona (Gotthard Autobahn), exit Airolo

Level of Difficulty/Maximum gradient: Medium, with a maximum gradient of 10 per cent

Length: 24.0km

Total ascent: 1305m

Time: 1¾–2½ hrs

Suggested gearing: 39/26

Route: Airolo (0.0km) – Fontana (5.0km) – Ossasco (6.5km) – Ronco (10.0km) – All'Acqua (12.5km) – Cantina di Cruina (16.0km) – Top of the pass (24.0km)

WESTERN SIDE – Start: Ulrichen, 1346m

Directions: over the Furka Pass (Tour 65) or the Grimsel Pass (Tour 66) to Gletsch and through Oberwald to Ulrichen or through the Rhone Valley (Valais) to Ulrichen

Level of Difficulty/Maximum gradient: Medium, with a maximum gradient of 13 per cent for about 1km at the start of the climb

Length: 14.5km

Total ascent: 1135m

Time: 1½–2½ hrs

Suggested gearing: 39/26

Route: Ulrichen (0.0km) – Top of the pass (14.5km)

Road conditions: Well-constructed roads apart from slight surface damage in the area of the summit

Pass open: 1 July to 31 October

Things to see: Airolo: castle (guided tours); scenic Ulrichen with old wooden Valais-style houses

Map: Euro Cart regional map 1:300,000, RV-Verlag, Switzerland sheet

On the western side of the Nufenen Pass, just below the top of the pass.

At 2478m the Nufenen Pass is the highest pass in central Switzerland and indeed the whole of Switzerland. It's also the shortest link between Ticino and Valais, and if you would prefer not to take the longer route over the St Gotthard Pass (Tour 64) or the Furka Pass (Tour 65), you should choose the Nufenen. Note, though, that it has one of the shortest opening times in the whole alpine region, from the beginning of July to the end of October. There is a good reason for this, which will be familiar to skiers, snowboarders and ski mountaineers who are well versed in winter mountain safety, namely avalanches. But more on that later.

First we have to look for the turning into the Val Bedretto in Airolo (0.0km), a lively little town best known as the southern end of the busy St Gotthard Pass and tunnel. We, on the other hand, have our climb in a westerly direction almost to ourselves.

At first we make good progress over a gradient of up to 8 per cent, alternating with flatter sections, through the villages of Fontana (5.5km) and Ossasca (6.5km), gaining height slowly. The road, which is in relatively good condition given its lack of importance to traffic, needs getting used to. With expansion joints at frequent intervals that have been filled in again and again with tar, it sometimes reminds you of a runway. When you're climbing this is nothing to worry about, but on the descent it causes an unpleasant jarring.

The main village of the valley is Bedretto, from the Latin *bedra*, meaning a birch wood. But if you scan the mountain slopes nearby you'll see that they're almost barren. In previous centuries the abundant stock of trees here was cut down without a second thought. This removed the only natural protection that exists against avalanches, the biggest danger to human settlement in the high mountains. The humble little villages exposed to this danger, most of them packed closely together on the scree, were left without protection, and many of the churches in the valley

seldom below 8-10 per cent, until we reach a tiny lake (23.0km). We quickly reach the top of the pass (24.0km) and reflect on how the quality restaurant there can pay its way during the short period that it's open.

The road going down over 13 hairpin bends is in good condition and has a magnificent view of the wild landscape of rocks and ice of the upper part of the Bernese Alps to the north-west. Just before Ulrichen (38.5km), a scattered village full of character with many old wooden houses, the downhill increases to 13 per cent for more than 1km – particularly tough if you start the climb from this side.

The Pizzo Gallina massif above the Nufenen Pass is 3063m high.

were built to stop avalanches. These days strong avalanche barriers shelter the villages during the long winters and in some places you can also make out patches of reforestation in which robust larches, particularly well adapted to the altitude, have been planted. That also explains the short opening period of the pass, since there is no danger of avalanches during this time frame.

We ride into the valley on a more or less straight road that doesn't start to climb any more steeply until it gets to Ronco (10.0km). Until All'Acqua (12.5km) the 10 per cent gradient alternates with short flatter sections, but after that it stays pretty much constantly at 10 per cent. In front of the Cantina di Cruina, two stone lodges with slate roofs, we have to tackle the first two hairpin bends of the climb, soon followed by more. We get to the top by the south-west slope of the Mittaghorn, on a gradient

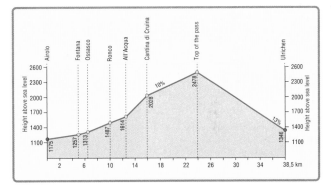

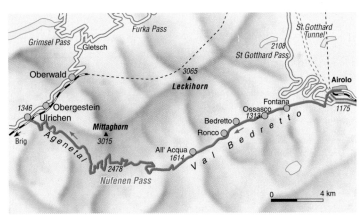

TOUR PROFILE <<

Große Scheidegg Pass: 1962m

WESTERN SIDE – Start: Interlaken, 567m

Directions: A8 Lucerne–Bern, exit Wilderswil–Interlaken

Level of Difficulty/Maximum gradient: Medium to difficult tour with long sections at 12 per cent

Length: 31.0km

Total ascent: 1395m

Time: 2¼–3½ hrs

Suggested gearing: 39/26

Route: Interlaken (0.0km) – Widerswil (1.5km) – Zweilütschinen (8.0km) – Gündlischwand (9.0km) – Lütschental (11.0km) – Burglauenen (15.0km) – Grindelwald (17.0km) – Hotel Wetterhorn (24.0km) – Hotel Lauchenbühel (26.0km) – Top of the pass (31.0km)

EASTERN SIDE – Start: Turning on the main road from Meiringen to Innertkirchen, opposite the Gasthof Zum Lamml, 595m

Directions: A8 Lucerne–Interlaken, exit Brienz–Meiringen. In Meiringen head for Innertkirchen

Level of Difficulty/Maximum gradient: Medium to difficult tour with a maximum gradient of 14 per cent for 500m. Longer gradient up to 11 per cent at the start

Length: 16.5km

Total ascent: 1370m

Time: 2–3 hrs

Suggested gearing: 39/28

Route: Hotel Zum Lammi (0.0km) – Gasthof Zwirgi (2.0km) – Kaltenbrunnen Restaurant (3.0km) – Hotel Rosenlaui (6.0km) – Schwarzwaldalp chalet (8.5km) – Top of the pass (16.5km)

Road conditions: Drainage channels and cattle grids on the eastern side on the downhill slope

Pass open: May to October depending on snow conditions

Map: Euro Cart regional map 1:300,000, RV-Verlag, Switzerland sheet

The Große Scheidegg will be well known to the mountaineers among us. It's a crossing high above Grindelwald at the foot of the 3701m Wetterhorn with an impressive view of the mountains of the Jungfrau region. In contrast to the better-known Kleine Scheidegg, which stretches upwards immediately below such well-known peaks as the Eiger, the Mönch and the Jungfrau, the Große Scheidegg can easily be reached by bike if you're not afraid of long 12 per cent gradients. But there is one small problem. While the western side from Interlaken is tarmacked throughout, with the upper part only open to residents and post buses, the eastern side is unfortunately not fully tarmacked. By riding carefully you can easily manage it on narrow clincher tyres, which will particularly interest those who want to go back to Interlaken by doing the 77km round trip.

For the time being we're in Interlaken (0.0km), situated on a wide alluvial plain between Lake Thun and Lake Brienz, also called the Bödeliby the locals, and our goal is just the Große Scheidegg. We leave the spa town following signposts for Grindelwald/Lauterbrunnen through the Matten district and reach the farming village of Widerswil (1.5km). Thus far, the landscape is hiding its charms. We ride into the thickly wooded Lütschine valley, and as far as the turning for Grindelwald near Zweilütschinen (8.0km) gentle climbs alternate with equally gentle downhills. The valley broadens out, and so does the view of the climbs waiting for us, but for now, apart from a short climb of 6 per cent just before Gündlischwand (9.0km), we can bowl along on an almost level road to Lütschental (11.0km).

Now you'll need the strength that you've conserved so far. The 12 per cent gradient starts here and runs as far as the Burglauenen railway station (15.0km), where it finally decreases a little as you arrive at the first houses in Grindelwald on a level road. You can't quite see why it's called 'Glacier town' when the mighty Eiger towers over the green meadows of the right-hand side of the valley, and the Wetterhorn and the Schreckhorn dominate the skyline in front of you. But it becomes clear when you ride through the village on a gradient of 10 per cent interspersed with short downhill stretches, and suddenly you can see the Lower Grindelwald glacier, which comes perilously close to the village houses. It starts at a height of nearly 4100m on the Schreckhorn and stretches for more than 9km to its lowest point at 1260m.

This isn't the only glacier on this tour, as we'll see when we ride up to the Upper Glacier car park by the Hotel Wetterhorn (24.0km) over a gradient of 12 per cent, which fortunately alternates with flatter sections and short downhill slopes. This glacier also comes down from the Schreckhorn and reaches right to the road. The road is narrower now but is still tarmacked and the 12 per cent gradient keeps up as you ride further on. You battle on past the Hotel Lauchbühel (26.0km) with more or less difficulty, depending on your state of fitness, up to

the top of the pass with its hotel and souvenir stalls (31.0km). More than 200 years ago no less a person than Johann Wolfgang von Goethe stood here when he hiked from Grindelwald over the Große Scheidegg on his second trip to Switzerland in the autumn of 1779. Little is known of the dangers he must have overcome as he made his way up here; we, on the other hand, have to watch out for drainage channels and cattle grids after the Schwarzwaldalp chalet (36.5km) on the almost 17km-long descent, which is untarmacked throughout, down over the eastern side to Willingen (47.5km).

Oppoiste: The Wellhorn and the Wetterhorn with the Rosenlaui glacier seen from the climb over the eastern side of the Große Scheidegg pass road. Unfortunately this road, also known as the Rosenlaui road and the Schwarzwaldalp road, isn't surfaced throughout.

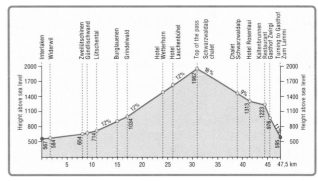

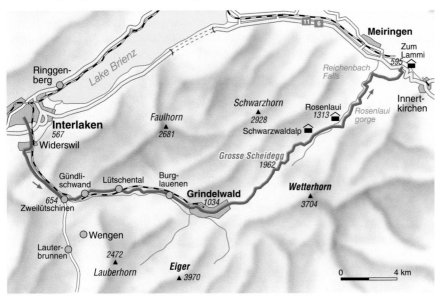

KIENTAL AND GRIESALP ROAD

Bern

TOUR PROFILE <<

Kiental and Griesalp Road: 1407m

Start: Reichenbach, 707m, about 5km south of Spiez on Lake Thun

Directions: Lucerne–Bern Authobahn A8, exit Spiez – Reichenbach

Level of Difficulty/Maximum gradient: Very difficult tour with a maximum gradient of 28 per cent over about 100m towards the top. Before that 24 per cent over about 1.5km, otherwise the gradient varies between 10 per cent and 12 per cent

Length: 14.0km

Total ascent: 740m

Time: 1¼–2 hrs

Suggested gearing: 39/29 or a triple chainset

Route: Reichenbach (0.0km) – Scharnachtal (1.0km) – Kiental (5.5km) – Gasthof Alpenruh (10.0km) – Tschingel alpine pasture (12.0km) – Griesalp mountain hotel (14.0km)

Road conditions: Tarmacked on the first 12km to Tschingel, then hard dirt road with hairpin bends, tarmacked in places

Pass open: This climb is usually free of snow from the end of May; officially the road is open from Easter until 31 October

Map: Euro Cart regional map 1:300,000, RV-Verlag, Switzerland sheet

The Kiental and Griesalp road climbs up to the top on an incline of up to 28 per cent, and is unsurfaced for short stretches.

Switzerland, too, can offer a mountain road whose gradient will push even well-trained cyclists to their limit. It's located in the canton of Bern and has Reichenbach as its point of departure, some 5km south of Spiez on Lake Thun. From there the route makes its way through Kiental and the Gornerengrund with gradients of up to a mammoth 28 per cent up to the Berghaus Griesalp, a well-run mountain hotel below the north-western slope of the Gspaltenhorn in the Bernese Alps. One important note: the steepest gradient on the upper part of the tour is on an unsurfaced dirt road. It should be rideable, even on narrow road bike tyres, but if you can't manage it you can always push your bike up. Even if you do ride, you can't expect high speeds, at least not on the way up.

There's no sign of the stiff climb ahead at the beginning of the tour in Reichenbach (0.0km), where you follow the signs for Kiental/Scharnachtal. The three hairpin bends over a grassy hillside up to Scharnachtal (1.0km) won't give anyone any problems and as you continue on to Kiental (5.5km) gradients of up to 8 per cent alternate with long flatter sections.

We follow the signposts for Gorneren/Griesalp, then the road goes downhill to the floor of a little valley (7.5km) and leads out of it again over a 1km long gradient of up to 12 per cent. Inclines of up to 10 per cent alternate with long flatter sections until we reach the tollbooth by the Gasthof Alpenruh (10.0km), then the extended high valley of the Gornerengrund, through which the road runs alongside the stream of the same name to the Tschingel alpine pasture (12.0km).

Then that's it: going around a boulder the tarmac suddenly changes to a dirt surface that climbs like a ramp. The road, which can still be managed with narrow clincher tyres, winds up a steep boulder-scattered slope at a gradient of 24 per cent, with narrow hairpin bends tarmacked in places. You struggle up this for about

1.5km and then on the last 100m just before a little crossroads (13.5km) you notch up an even more noticeable gradient of 28 per cent. Another 500m on a lesser gradient, then you can catch your breath again at the Hochschild chalet or the Griesalp mountain hotel (14.0km).

You won't see any electricity pylons and ski lift towers around here. That's because the area around the Griesalp isn't connected to the electricity grid, so you can enjoy pure, unadulterated nature. The countryside, with its centuries-old maple trees, is known as a peaceful retreat and so attracts many

visitors. Very few get here by bike as we did, but use the post bus, which also has to battle its way up the gradient. In doing so, it has set a European record: this is the steepest bus route in Europe.

Just after Reichenbach the Kiental and Griesalp road is still in good condition and only climbs slightly.

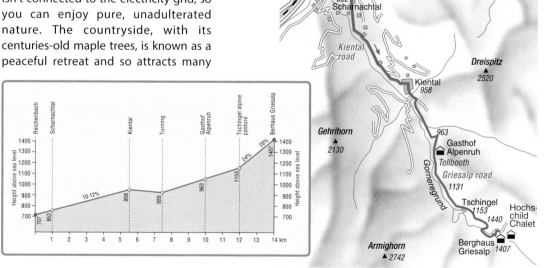

72 SAANENMÖSER PASS
Bern

TOUR PROFILE <<

Saanenmöser Pass: 1279m

WESTERN SIDE – Start: Bulle, 771m

Directions: A12 Bern–Vevey, exit Bulle

Level of Difficulty/Maximum gradient:
Easy, with a maximum gradient of
9 per cent

Length: 45.5km

Total ascent: 510m

Time: 2–3 hrs

Suggested gearing: 39/23

Route: Bulle (0.0km) – Villars sous Mont
(9.0km) – Montbovon (16.0km) – Les
Moulins (25.0km) – Château-d'Oex
(27.0km) – Flendruz (32.5km) – Saanen
(39.5km) – Schönried (43.5km) –
Saanenmöser (45.0km) – Top of the
pass (45.5km)

EASTERN SIDE – Start: Reidenbach,
845m

Directions: A8 Bern–Interlaken, exit
Wimmis – Erlenbach – Boltigen –
Reidenbach

Level of Difficulty/Maximum gradient:
Easy, with a maximum gradient of
6 per cent

Length: 16.5km

Total ascent: 435m

Time: 1–1½ hrs

Suggested gearing: 39/23

Route: Reidenbach (0.0km) –
Zweisimmen (9.5km) – Top of the pass
(16.5km)

Road conditions: Care is required
on the descent over the eastern side
because of blind bends, with traffic
mirrors in places

Pass open: All year

Map: Euro Cart regional map 1:300,000,
RV-Verlag, Switzerland sheet

*The maximum incline on the eastern side
of the Saanenmöser Pass is 6 per cent.*

The Frieburger or Waadtländer Alps are located between Lake
Geneva in the west and Lake Thun and Lake Brienz in the east
where the Bernese Alps fall away to the north into the Bernese
Oberland. This region is also called Haute Gruyère after the Lac de
la Gruyère, lying a little to the south of Freiburg, or rather Fribourg
since we're in the French-speaking part of Switzerland. The passes,
like the mountains, are not all that high but we find two worthwhile
climbs in the Saanmöser Pass and the Jaun Pass (Tour 73).

We leave Bulle (0.0km), situated 30km north of Montreux, in a
southerly direction via the suburb of La Tour-de-Trême. Between
the wooded hills, in which only isolated limestone cliffs suggest
anything like a mountain, there are long easy descents alternating
with short 6 per cent climbs as far as Villars-sous-Mont (9.0km). So
the road, which passes through several villages, makes little net
altitude gain.

Past Montbovon (16.0km) the valley narrows and after a short
gorge-like section you leave the main road on the little road
branching off to the right. This climbs at 8 per cent by the Hotel de
la Gare (19.5km) and descends again past a small lake; then gentle
climbs and downhill slopes alternate until you suddenly meet up
with the main road again (24.0km).

Past Les Moulins (25.0km) we cross the Saane, and the gradient
now increases to 9 per cent as far as Château-d'Oex (27.0km).
Through Flendruz (32.5km) and Rougemont this degree of gradient
occurs again and again on short uphill stretches, but interspersed
similarly with longer downhills.

In Saanen (39.5km) it's worth making a stop to look at the church
of St Mauritius. Although it's impressive from the outside with its
Romanesque tower that's visible for miles around, inside there are

important wall paintings from the 15th century. The actual road up to the pass starts just past the church with a gradient of 7 per cent on Saanenmöser Straße. This runs through the town then through the villages of Schönried (43.5km) and Saanenmöser (45.0km) and up to the top of the pass (45.5km) on a wide, grassy saddle.

From here it's just under 17km down a winding, but moderate, slope through the wooded Simme valley to Reidenbach.

The 2458m high Gummfluh rises above Château-d'Oex in the Pays-d'Enhaut.

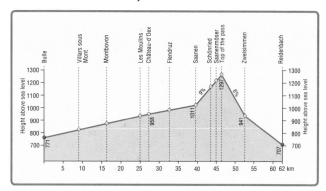

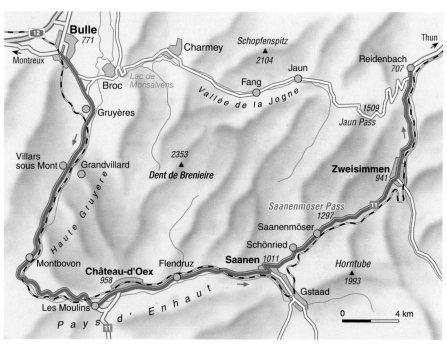

179

73 JAUN PASS
Bern/Freiburg/Fribourg

TOUR PROFILE <<

Jaun Pass: 1509m

EASTERN SIDE – Start: Reidenbach, 845m

Directions: A8 Bern–Interlaken, exit Wimmis – Erlenbach – Boltigen – Reidenbach

Level of Difficulty/Maximum gradient: Easy, with a maximum gradient of 11 per cent

Length: 8.5km

Total ascent: 435m

Time: 1–1½ hrs

Suggested gearing: 39/23

Route: Reidenbach (0.0km) – Eschihalten Restaurant (4.5km) – Top of the pass (8.5km)

WESTERN SIDE – Start: Broc, 717m

Directions: A12 Bern–Vevey, exit Bulle – Broc

Level of Difficulty/Maximum gradient: Easy to medium tour with a maximum gradient of 14 per cent

Length: 23.5km

Total ascent: 795m

Time: 1½–2¼ hrs

Suggested gearing: 39/26

Route: Broc (0.0km) – Charmey (9.5km) – Fang (13.5km) – Jaun (17.5km) – Top of the pass (23.5km)

Road conditions: Well-constructed roads

Pass open: All year

Map: Euro Cart regional map 1:300,000, RV-Verlag, Switzerland sheet

At 1509m high, the Jaun Pass is the highest pass in the Freiburger or Waadtländer Alps east of Lake Geneva. If you'd like to know more about the geography of this region read the section on the route to the Saanenmöser Saddle (Tour 72) or ride over to Reidenbach so that from there back over the Jaun Pass you've completed a good circular tour.

Reidenbach (0.0km) is surrounded by pleasant broad meadows on the border between the Obersimmen valley and the Untersimmen valley. However, we don't follow either of these two valleys but leave the village in a westerly direction over two hairpin bends with a slope of 11 per cent up a grassy hillside. A group of alpine huts marks a short decrease in the gradient but it increases again to 11 per cent after another hairpin bend. If you've already noticed signs of exhaustion you can stop at the Eschihalten restaurant (4.5km) for refreshments: there won't be another opportunity until the top of the pass.

The road now climbs over more hairpin bends on a gradient that stays resolutely at 11 per cent. It doesn't let up until just below the top of the pass at a hairpin bend with stone embankments, and a little later you reach the top of the pass (8.5km).

The gradient on the western side goes as high as 14 per cent, but we only have to tackle this on the way down. Even though the mountain summits of the Gastlosen in the west and the very rugged towering limestone peaks in the immediate vicinity do their best to impress, they seem more like foothills of the Alps. After the first steep descent the road goes more steadily downhill and in Fang, 10km later, we reach the end of the descent of the pass.

We still have further to go, as far as Charmey. The 6 per cent climb in the village lasts for a good 1.5km, then we cross the wide bridge over the Javro, which flows into the Montsalvens reservoir far below us. The road goes over several hairpin bends with a

A view of the Waadtländer Alps over the Zweisimmental.

The very rugged limestone peaks of the Gastlosen from the Jaun Pass.

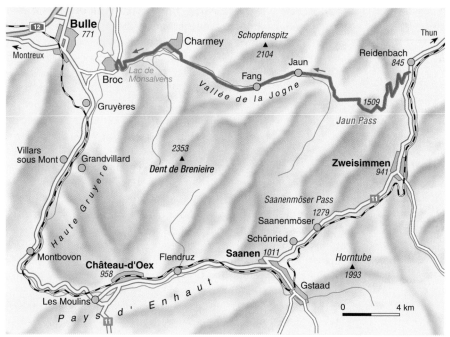

downhill slope of 10 per cent to Broc. Another short 4 per cent climb to a road junction and we go through La Tour-de-Trême to Bulle, 26.5km from the top of the pass.

Having got there you might need to know a bit of French to be able to find your way around, but the slogan the town uses to market itself – *Un site ouvert sur la poésie et l'amour, la sensualité et la sensibilité* – may not actually need any translation.

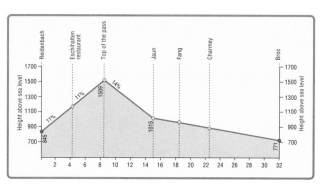

TOUR PROFILE <<

Simplon Pass: 2005m

NORTHERN SIDE – Start: Brig, 681m

Directions: Over the Furka Pass (Tour 65) or the Grimsel Pass (Tour 66) to Gletsch and through Oberwald and Ulrichen to Brig or over the Nufenen Pass (Tour 69) to Ulrichen then on to Brig

Level of Difficulty/Maximum gradient: Medium, with a maximum gradient of 9 per cent

Length: 22.5km

Total ascent: 1325m

Time: 1¾–2½ hrs

Suggested gearing: 39/23

Route: Brig (0.0km) – Ried (3.0km) – Schallberg (9.5km) – Ganter Bridge (12.0km) – Berisal (13.5km) – Rothwald (16.0km) – Schallbett (19.5km) – Hotel Bellevue (22.0km) – Top of the pass (22.5km)

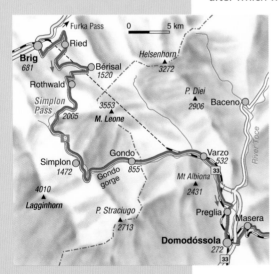

If you want to swap the mountains of the Valais for the mild, sun-drenched shores of Lake Maggiore or Lake Lugano in Ticino, fringed with agaves, acacia, cypresses, and orange and lemon trees, you have to go across the Simplon Pass. At the very least because it takes the shortest and easiest route, and has been a well-travelled trade road from time immemorial. The pass covers 64km from Brig in Valais to Domodossola in Piedmont, from where you have just under another 50km to go on to Locarno on Lake Maggiore. You have to tackle a total vertical climb of 1300m from Brig, but the road is in good condition and never exceeds a 9 per cent gradient, which, together with the continually changing scenery and places of interest en route, means that you don't tend to dwell on the difficulties.

Stockalper Castle in Brig, the main town in Upper Valais, is well worth seeing, with its three unmissable onion-domed towers. It commemorates the notable Valais merchant Kaspar Jodock von Stockalper, who laid the foundations for the town's prosperity in the 17th century through enterprising commercial activity with France and Italy. *Nihil solidum nisi solum* – there is nothing solid except the ground – is the motto over the main entrance to the palace, which was completed in 1678: we acknowledge the truth of this as we set off in the direction of the Simplon on our bikes.

We climb out of Brig (0.0km) over several hairpin bends with a gradient of 9 per cent over the Ried mountain to the south. From Ried (3.0km) the road goes up over another bend with a constant gradient and Brig and the Rhone Valley are soon far below us. Ahead are two short unlit tunnels and a 500m dimly lit tunnel, after which we turn into the Saltina gorge. Past Schallberg (9.5km) we cross the valley at a height of 160m on the gravity-defying spans of the Ganter Bridge, almost 700m long, where our admiration for the technical mastery of the bridge builders is distracted by the glacier mountains of the Valais Alps in the background.

After we cross this structure, which opened in 1980, shortening the old road by about 1.5km and one hairpin bend, the route narrows noticeably. Once through Berisal (13.5km) a sign informs us that the top of the pass is now only 9km away. The road climbs over many bends up the slopes of the Wasenhorn at a steady gradient of between 7 and 9 per cent through the Rothwald up to the village of the same name (16.0km). Now the top of the pass can just be seen through the opening of the valley, but the road up to it is not very pleasant.

The Simplon Pass road is in good condition, but not always as free of traffic as this picture might suggest.

The Simplon hostel at the top of the pass can accommodate up to 130 guests.

TOUR PROFILE <<

SOUTHERN SIDE – Start: Domodossola, 272m

Directions: A8 Milan–Domodossola, exit Domodossola

Level of Difficulty/Maximum gradient: Difficult, with a maximum gradient of 10 per cent

Length: 41.5km

Total ascent: 1735m

Time: 3¼–4½ hrs

Suggested gearing: 39/26

Route: Domodossola (0.0km) – Preglia (2.5km) – Varzo (12.5km) – Gondo (20.5km) – Top of the pass (41.5km)

Road conditions: Well-constructed roads

Pass open: All year

Things to see: Brig: Stockalper Castle, old town with Sebastian Chapel. Domodossola: history and folklore museum in the Palazzo Silva.

Map: Euro Cart regional map 1:300,000, RV-Verlag, Switzerland sheet

Notes: Lights are necessary because of the tunnels (up to 500m long) and the gallery tunnels (up to 750m long) on both sides of the pass

This is not because of the gradient, which at a maximum of 9 per cent is moderate, but because there are avalanche galleries soon after you leave the village. On the way up to the top of the pass there is only a short break in them, at Schallbett (19.5km), then they continue again up to the Hotel Bellevue (22.0km). Finally, after the semi-darkness of the galleries, our eyes have to become accustomed to the light again before we cover the last few metres up to the top of the pass (22.5km) on a level road. There a wonderful view opens up over the Rhone Valley across to the Bernese Alps with Monte Leone and the Fletschhorn. There has been a path here, leading from the Italian village of Varzo to the village of Simplon, for over three millennia. From the 13th century Milanese merchants used it to trade across the Alps. Napoleon had the road improved between 1800 and 1805 to take vehicles, mainly for military purposes. The pass was developed in its present form between 1960 and 1980 and is regarded as as one of the structural masterpieces in the southern Alps.

If you're hungry after the climb you should take a break in the village of Simplon just a little way away off-route. A snack of the excellent Alpenkäse cheese, Valais rye bread and air-dried beef will beat a protein bar hands down.

Thus fortified we can quickly ride through the next village of Gondo, which was a smugglers' haven as recently as the 1970s. Then we have to continue through five tunnels, one gallery tunnel, eight avalanche galleries and a descent of a 1700m down to Domodossola (64km), the eastern end point of the route over the Simplon Pass.

The daring Ganter Bridge over the Saltina gorge on the northern side of the Simplon Pass is 160m high and almost 700m long.

TOUR PROFILE <<

San Bernardino Pass: 2066m

NORTHERN SIDE – Start: Hinterrhein, 1620m, about 10km west of Splügen in the Hinterrhein valley

Directions: A13 Chur–Bellinzona (Rhine Valley Autobahn), exit Hinterrhein

Level of Difficulty/Maximum gradient: Easy, with a maximum gradient of 9 per cent

Length: 9.5km

Total ascent: 445m

Time: 1–1¾ hrs

Suggested gearing: 39/23

Route: Hinterrhein (0.0km) – Dürrenbüel alpine pasture (7.0km) – Top of the pass (9.5km)

SOUTHERN SIDE – Start: Mesocco, 791m

Directions: A13 Bellinzona–Chur (Rhine Valley Autobahn), exit Mesocco

Level of Difficulty/Maximum gradient: Medium, with a maximum gradient of 12 per cent

Length: 23.0km

Total ascent: 1275m

Time: 2¼–3¼ hrs

Suggested gearing: 39/26

Route: Mesocco (0.0km) – Pian San Giácomo (6.0km) – San Bernardino (16.0km) – Top of the pass (23.0km)

Road conditions: Well-constructed roads

Pass open: 1 May to 31 October

Map: Euro Cart regional map 1:300,000, RV-Verlag, Switzerland sheet

You can clearly see from the kit that this shot was taken some time ago in Hinterrhein at the beginning of the northern side of the San Bernardino Pass. But nothing has changed there since.

Deep down in the far end of the Rhine valley, in the so-called Rheinwald, a little west of the Splügen Pass (Tour 45), the San Bernardino Pass leads over the Ticino Alps to Lake Maggiore in Ticino. The dual carriageway, which also goes this way, soon disappears into a 6.6km tunnel and with it so does most of the traffic, so we can enjoy this rather easy crossing in peace.

The dual carriageway accompanies us from Hinterrhein (0.0km), the starting point of the northern route, for a short distance into the valley. As we go along we can see the Zapport glacier stretching down from the Rheinwald mountains, then we cross the Hinterrhein river (1.5km). While the traffic on the dual carriageway now has it rather easier as it heads off into the San Bernardino Tunnel, the hard part is just beginning for us. Harder still for the lorries and Swiss military vehicles that we sometimes see on the 9 per cent gradient, which have had to be abandoned on a hairpin bend because the road is so narrow.

The road is briefly a little more level on the way to the alpine huts at Dürrenbüel (7.0km), then it climbs at 9 per cent again over several hairpin bends. If you're wondering about the mysterious concrete construction at the side of the road (8.0km) whose security seems to have military overtones, it's actually a ventilation tower for the dual carriageway running through the tunnel beneath us.

The gradient decreases and you now ride up the road at a leisurely pace between bumpy glacier-worn rock formations. The gradient goes up again to 9 per cent for the last 500m over a hairpin bend to the top of the pass (9.5km). There you should enjoy the peace and solitude by Lagetto Moésola, a little mountain lake,

because it won't last long. After a 7km descent the traffic rejoins us as it emerges from the San Bernardino Tunnel in the resort of San Bernardino, and unfortunately it accompanies us down through the Val Mescolina, also known as Misox. Luckily for us most of the tourist traffic rushes through the valley on the dual carriageway but a lot of it still makes its way along the old main road with us. This is not really surprising, because the Misox is not just the most southerly, but also the most beautiful valley in Graubünden.

Unlike the Val Bregaglia, which you may know from the trip over the Maloja Pass (Tour 44) and the Val Poschiavo, to which the Bernina Pass (Tour 57) runs, the Misox is one of the valleys in Graubünden which lies to the south of the main alpine ridge where Italian is spoken rather than Swiss German or Rhaeto-Romanic. As you would expect, the atmosphere and architectural style we meet here in the area on the descent to Mesocco are obviously Italian.

Particularly well worth visiting here is the 12th-century church of St Maria al

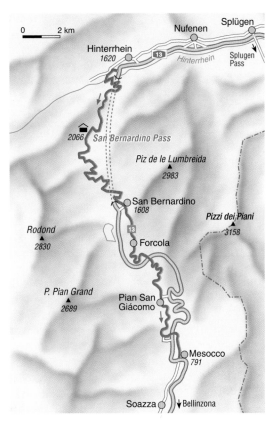

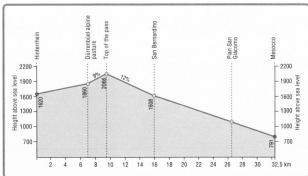

Castello at the foot of the castle hill with its coffered ceiling and paintings from the mid 15th century. If you'd rather visit a restaurant than go sightseeing you'll notice the Italian influence on the menu and be pleased to see the pasta dishes you'll need to replenish your lost energy.

187

TOUR PROFILE <<

Mattertal Road: 1616m

Start: Visp, 650m

Directions: A2 Lucerne–Bellinzona (Gotthard Autobahn), exit Göschenen – Andermatt – Realp – Furka Pass – Gletsch – Ulrichen – Münster – Brig – Visp

Level of Difficulty/Maximum gradient: Medium, with a maximum gradient of 10 per cent

Length: 35.0km

Total ascent: 970m

Time: 1½–2¾ hrs

Suggested gearing: 39/26

Route: Visp (0.0km) – Neubrück (4.5km) – Ackersand (5.5km) – Stalden (7.0km) – Stalden road junction (9.0km) – St Niklaus (15.5km) – Herbriggen (22.5km) – Randa (27.0km) – Täsch (30.0km) – Zermatt (35.0km)

Road conditions: Well-constructed roads from Visp to Täsch. From Täsch to Zermatt narrow in places with a slightly uneven surface

Pass open: All year

Things to see: View of the Matterhorn from Zermatt

Map: Euro Cart regional map 1:300,000, RV-Verlag, Switzerland sheet

Notes: There is a great deal of traffic on this route. An early start is therefore advisable. Between Täsch and Zermatt motor vehicles are only allowed with special authorisation from the canton police but you can still expect a considerable volume of traffic

The Breithorn with the dark rocky spur of the Klein Matterhorn seen from the climb over the Mattertal road.

The 4478m Matterhorn overlooking Zermatt in the Valais Alps is the best-known mountain in the Alps, if not the whole world. This is due partly to its distinctive twisted profile and partly to the history of its first ascent in 1865, which ended in tragedy. The Englishman Edward Whymper became the first man to set foot on the summit on 14 July 1865, after a tough struggle. Four of his companions, the Englishmen Lord Francis Douglas, Charles Hudson, Robert Douglas Hadow, and Michel Croz, a mountain guide from Chamonix, lost their lives when a rope broke on the descent. Only Whymper and two mountain guides from Zermatt, Peter Taugwalder and his son, survived the catastrophe. The story was revisited in the 1936 film produced by Louis Trenker, *The Mountain Calls*; its black and white cinematography has lost none of its drama even today.

Our journey will be a little easier. A good road leads from Visp in the Rhone Valley up to Zermatt, almost at the foot of the mountain. No particular drama should unfold in a total vertical climb of just under 1000m and gradients of up to 10 per cent. The worst dangers are likely to come from the high volume of traffic, since Zermatt is one of the biggest tourist destinations in the world, in summer as well as in winter. So we won't be the only ones following the signposts for Zermatt from Visp (0.0km) as we ride alongside the river of the same name on a level road into the Visp valley to Neubrück (4.5km). The gradient doesn't increase to 8 per cent until we've passed the next village, Ackersand (5.5km), then we cross the Mattervispa and ride over hairpin bends with a 10 per cent gradient

through the village of Stalden (7.0km). As we leave Stalden we again cross the river, which has carved out a deep gorge here, and turn into the Matter valley at the next junction (9.0km).

The road through the valley has an easy start. It climbs at 7 per cent for the next kilometre then descends gently to an avalanche gallery. There are only minor uphill gradients to overcome as far as St Niklaus (15.5), where a 9 per cent gradient descends again to Mattsand after a short gallery (19.5km). The valley widens out and before us rises the impressive Breithorn glacier and the dark rocky spur of the Klein Matterhorn that could be taken for a miniature version of its bigger namesake. Beyond Herbriggen (22.5km) is a 3km climb to Randa (27.0km), the starting point for mountaineers climbing the 4545m Dom, the highest peak located wholly in Switzerland. The Matterhorn, on the other hand, which the Swiss have to share with the Italians, doesn't show itself yet, and it still can't be seen in Täsch (30.0km).

In December 1972 it was decided in a referendum to end the road here and so the village functions as a giant car park, with the rest of the route only possible on a rack and pinion railway. But there's no problem riding a bike up the road from here up to Zermatt. It's rather narrow and bumpy, but is tarmacked throughout. If you think that you can cover the remaining 5km undisturbed by traffic, you are unfortunately mistaken. Road users are only allowed to drive further with the permission of the canton police, but the police seem to be very generous with their approval. Fortunately, passing cars aside, there aren't any great difficulties in store. Right from the beginning the road runs for a kilometre on a gradient of 10 per cent, then there follows a longer, almost

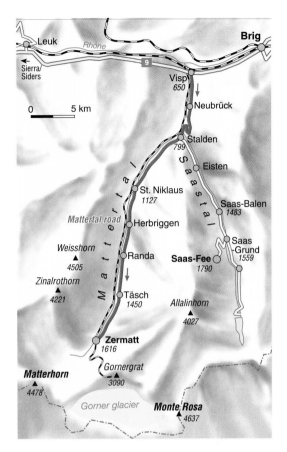

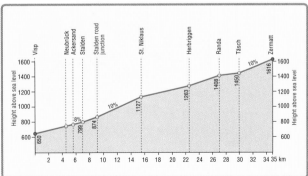

flat section before the incline increases to 10 per cent again for the final kilometre. The Matterhorn hides from us until the very last few metres. We don't actually see it until we reach the outskirts of Zermatt (35.0km).

77

SAASTAL AND MATTMARK ROAD

Valais

TOUR PROFILE <<

Saastal and Mattmark Road: 2197m

Start: Visp, 650m

Directions: A2 Lucerne–Bellinzona (Gotthard Autobahn), exit Göschenen – Andermatt – Realp – Furka Pass – Gletsch – Ulrichen – Münster – Brig – Visp

Level of Difficulty/Maximum gradient: Difficult, with a maximum gradient of 13 per cent on the last 3.5km

Length: 34.5km

Total ascent: 1550m

Time: 2½–3½ hrs

Suggested gearing: 39/28

Route: Visp (0.0km) – Neubrück (4.5km) – Ackersand (5.5km) – Stalden (7.0km) – Stalden road junction (9.0km) – Eisten (13.0km) – Niedergut (18.5km) – Saas-Balen (19.5km) – Saas-Tamatten (21.5km) – Saas-Grund (22.0km) – Saas-Almagell (26.5km) – Mattmark Restaurant (34.5km)

Road conditions: Well-constructed roads

Pass open: 1 June to 31 October

Map: Euro Cart regional map 1:300,000, RV-Verlag, Switzerland sheet

Notes: The road is very busy, particularly on the lower stretch to Saas-Grund; an early departure is therefore advisable

The only tunnel on the Mattmark Road is 100m long. There are also several avalanche galleries.

Visp in the Rhone Valley is not just the starting point for a climb through the Mattertal to Zermatt (Tour 76), but also for the Saastal, which runs into the Mischabel group. This massif can't offer such a well-known mountain as the Matterhorn, but it does have the highest peak lying completely within Switzerland, the 4545m Dom. Since the end point of the road at the Mattmark restaurant by the reservoir of the same name is a good 500m higher than Zermatt, the climb is rated a level higher and is thus graded as difficult.

From Visp (0.0km) we ride as described in Tour 76 to Stalden (7.0km), as far as the turning at the end of the village (9.0km) at the Saas-Fee/Mattmarksignpost. The valley doesn't provide us with a view and until you get to Eisten (13.0km) the gradient doesn't rise above 5 per cent. A series of avalanche galleries and one 100m tunnel have to be ridden through, with 8 per cent gradients alternating with flatter sections until you reach Niedergut (18.5km). Past Saas-Balen (19.5km) up to Saas-Tamatten (21.5km) the road climbs very gently, and then takes us to Saas-Grund (22.0km), a larger village.

If you want to you can take the turning here up a gradient of 8 per cent for 3.5km to Saas-Fee at a height of 1790m, but if you want to go higher up stay on the road going in the direction of Mattmark/Saas-Almagell. All the way to Saas-Almagell you can enjoy a wonderful view of the glacier in the Mischabel group as the road climbs moderately, but thereafter the gradient slowly increases to 9 per cent.

After crossing a stream (31.0km) it gets really hard: the gradient goes up to 13 per cent and stays there until you reach the end of the route at the Mattmark restaurant (34.5km), at the foot of the wall of the Mattmark reservoir. On a fine day you're almost dazzled up there by the gleaming white splendour of the Allalin glacier flowing down the 4027m Allalinhorn. There were once notorious smugglers' paths over the Monto Moro in front of us. You may well consider taking one or other of them on the return journey and riding up to Saas-Fee. The panorama over the proud 4000m mountains gathered in a semi-circle around the village counts as one of the most magnificent landscapes in Switzerland.

This region features in a book by the Valais author Adolf Fux, *Der Kilchherr von Saas* (*The Pastor of Saas*). It's dedicated to Johann Joseph Imseng, the well-known pastor who in the mid-19th century was one of the first to recognise that the only escape from poverty and destitution in

that area was through tourism. He directed all his energy towards this goal, overcoming a great deal of resistance. As you can see from the appearance of the place and the people, it was well worth the effort.

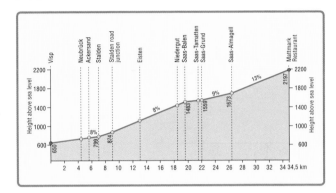

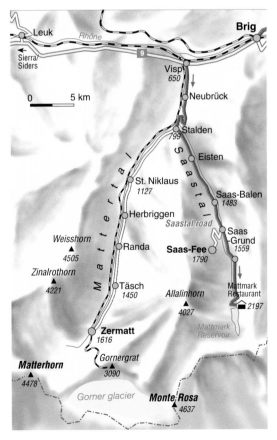

TOUR PROFILE <<

Anniviers and Zinal High Valley Road: 1700m

Start: Turning on the H9 Rhone Valley road, about 3km east of Sierre, 565m

Directions: A2 Lucerne–Bellinzona (Gotthard Autobahn), exit Göschenen – Andermatt – Realp – Furka Pass – Gletsch – Ulrichen – Münster – Brig – Visp – Sierre

Level of Difficulty/Maximum gradient: Medium, with a maximum gradient of 11 per cent on two short sections

Length: 25.5km

Total ascent: 1135m

Time: 1¾–2½ hrs

Suggested gearing: 39/26

Route: Turning (0.0km) – Niouc (4.5km) – Les Pontis Restaurant (7.0km) – Vissoie (13.0km) – Ayer (18.0km) – Navisence (20.0km) – Mottec (22.0km) – La Boulette (23.5km) – Zinal (24.0km) – Head of the valley (25.5km)

Road conditions: Some narrow stretches with passing places

Pass open: All year

Map: Euro Cart regional map 1:300,000, RV-Verlag, Switzerland sheet

Mattertal (Tour 76) and Saastal (Tour 77) are definitely the best-known valleys in Valais. But if you're talking about the most beautiful valley then you really have to mention another one, the Anniviers valley. This runs not very far west of the Mattertal in the Valais Alps and ends at the foot of the 4221m Zinalrothorn. Tourism hasn't gained as much of a foothold here as in other parts of Valais, which means that it has remained more unspoiled and less built-up. The mountain slopes of the valley are steep and the wooden houses with their shingle roofs crouch close together on the steep mountainside. A local saying goes that even the chickens have to wear crampons. We can leave our cleats undisturbed because the road runs at a rather more moderate gradient and at most just requires a little more stamina on the two short sections with an 11 per cent gradient.

The point of departure is a turning on the Rhone Valley road, the H9 main road, about 3km east of Sierre/Sitten where you find a signpost for Zinal/Grimetz. The road climbs up to Nious (4.5km), the first village in the valley, on a gradient of 9 per cent, where the initially straight road then switches into a group of tight hairpin bends.

The 11 per cent gradient leading out of Nious soon decreases and you make progress quickly on an almost level section before hitting 11 per cent again just before the Les Pontis restaurant (7.0km). Two short avalanche galleries (11.5km) are followed by a

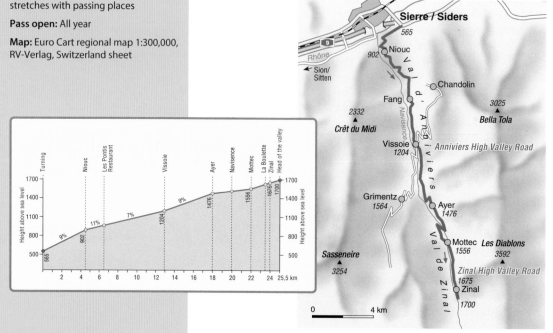

Ayer is a well-known mountain and winters sports region.

Wooden houses with shingle roofs in the Anniviers valley are often crowded onto the steep mountain slopes.

100m unlit tunnel, and we reach the village of Vissoie (13.0km) over gradients of up to 7 per cent, though most are well below this.

The sharply pointed glaciated pyramid of the Zinalrothorn now appears over the head of the valley and the 9 per cent gradient drops temporarily before an increase to 8 per cent after Mission (16.0km) up two hairpin bends to Ayer (18.0km). Beautiful old wooden houses at the edge of the road draw your attention. Carrying on gently downhill you approach the head of the valley, riding over the little Navisence river (20.0km) on a tight bend before going up over another hairpin bend with a 9 per cent gradient. This stretch of the climb ends by a little chapel just before Mottec (22.0km) and there's an enjoyable flat stretch to the Gasthof Pralong before the gradient increases once more to 9 per cent on the way up to the wooden huts of La Boulette (23.5km).

Another bend and the signboard for Zinal (24.0km) is there in front of us, and soon after the tour ends at the head of the valley (25.5km), modest in comparison to the impressive high-mountain landscape on all sides.

193

79 GREAT ST BERNARD PASS
Valais/Aosta

TOUR PROFILE <<

Great St Bernard Pass: 2473m

NORTHERN SIDE – Start: Martigny, 471m

Directions: A12 then A9 Bern–Martigny, exit Martigny or over the Furka Pass (Tour 65), the Grimsel Pass (Tour 66) or the Nufenen Pass (Tour 69) through the Rhone Valley (Valais) to Martigny

Level of Difficulty/Maximum gradient: Difficult, with a maximum gradient of 11 per cent on long sections

Length: 43.5km

Total ascent: 2005m

Time: 3¼–5 hrs

Suggested gearing: 39/26

Route: Martigny (0.0km) – Les Valettes (6.0km) – Sembrancher (11.5km) – La Duay (15.5km) – Orsières (17.0km) – Fontaine-Dessous (22.5km) – Rive-Haute (23.5km) – Liddes (25.5km) – Bourg-St-Pierre (30.5km) – Old pass road (36.5km) – Top of the pass (43.5km)

SOUTHERN SIDE – Start: Aosta, 583m

Directions: A5 Turin–Aosta, exit Aosta

Level of Difficulty/Maximum gradient: Difficult, with a maximum gradient of 10 per cent

Length: 31.0km

Total ascent: 1850m

Time: 3¼–5 hrs

Suggested gearing: 39/26

Route: Aosta (0.0km) – Signayes (2.5km) – Gignod (7.0km) – Etroubles (15.5km) – Saint Oyen (17.5km) – Saint Rhémy (19.0km) – Top of the pass (31.0km)

Road conditions: Surface damage on the old pass road at the entrances to the tunnels. Otherwise well-constructed roads

Pass open: The old pass road is open from 1 June to 15 October

Things to see: Hostel at the top of the pass with museum on the St Bernard dog breed. Aosta: Augustinian arch, Roman theatre, museum

Map: Euro Cart regional map 1:300,000, RV-Verlag, Switzerland sheet

On the section of the road called the Combe des Mortes on the upper part of the northern side of the Great St Bernard Pass.

A whole catalogue of well-known people have crossed the Great St Bernard Pass, which links the Swiss Valais with the Italian Aosta valley, before us. The most famous was probably Napoleon, who made the traverse with 45,000 soldiers, 5000 horses and 60 heavy guns and defeated the Austrians at the Battle of Marengo. Before him Charlemagne had used this route on his way to be crowned as emperor in Rome, and even earlier than that Julius Caesar's legions were here in the course of the conquest of Gaul. The most famous of all was the Carthaginian general Hannibal, on account of the elephants he supposedly planned to use to defeat Rome, though their presence is hotly disputed by historians. Anyway, it seems, according to the history books, that the elephants, real or invented, weren't very successful anyway. It's reckoned that he made the attempt in winter and suffered heavy losses due to avalanches and snowstorms.

These days the way over the Great St Bernard Pass is through the almost 6km long tunnel at the summit and is safe even in winter, but since we prefer to use the old pass road we have to wait until the beginning of June. To prevent our own undertaking from coming to grief we need to have trained hard for this, because a vertical climb of 2000m with a bike over maximum gradients of 11 per cent demands a high level of fitness.

A visit to the Pierre Gianadda Foundation museum is recommended if you arrive in Martigny the day before. It was built on the remains of a Roman temple, which was discovered in 1976 during construction work, and showcases Roman finds along with art exhibitions and a motor museum with rarities from around the world dating from 1897 to 1939. You'll see many more cars on the road out of Martigny (0.0km) into the Val d'Entremont, which starts out as a dual-carriageway, though all of a much later date.

After La Valette (6.0km) the road hardly climbs at all, with the first 10 per cent slopes not in evidence until after Sembrancher

(11.5km). Flatter sections through La Duay (15.5km) allow us to progress quickly while saving our strength, and we soon reach Orsières (17.0km). This is where the surroundings start to look appropriately pass-like, and past the village we start to climb over two hairpin bends with a gradient of 10 per cent.

The road is also narrower now and ascends at the same rate over many bends to Fontaine-Dessous (22.5km). After more hairpin bends we reach Rive-Haute (23.5km) and then, going downhill, Liddes (25.5km). Hannibal would likely have welcomed the long tunnel (29.0km) up to Bourg-St-Pierre (30.5km) if it had existed when he was here, but we can't take much pleasure in either the tunnel or the galleries which follow. The road goes on up past the Lac de Toules on a gradient that's down to 6 per cent. Watch for the exit to the old pass road (36.5km) or you'll end up in the 5828m tunnel at the summit, where you'll be sent straight back from the Swiss border. Having put the galleries behind you, you pass the 'Super-St-Bernard' cable car valley station along a narrow road into a high valley that becomes more and more desolate. On this stretch the gradient hardly ever falls below 11 per cent and you'll have to work really hard to get up the very winding road. There's a section called the Combe de Mortes over four hairpin bends whose stony embankments can hardly be distinguished from the surroundings, then suddenly the top of the pass (43.5km) is in front of us. The souvenir stalls up there are piled high with soft toys of the famous Saint Bernard dogs in various sizes. A good dozen pure-bred dogs were kept in the hostel nearby until they stopped breeding them in 2004. The most famous of them, Barry I, who between 1800 and 1812 saved the lives

of about 40 people stranded due to a sudden drop in temperature or buried by avalanches, was stuffed and is displayed in the Historical Museum in Bern.

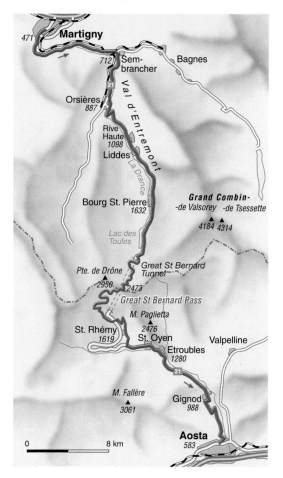

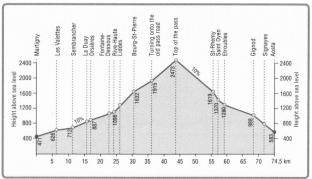

ALPINE PASSES
IN FRANCE

80 COL DE L'ISERAN
Savoy

TOUR PROFILE <<

Col de l'Iseran: 2770m

NORTHERN SIDE – Start: Séez, 904m

Directions: over the Little St Bernard Pass to Séez (Tour 48) or A43 Chambery–Moûtiers – Séez

Level of Difficulty/Maximum gradient: Difficult, with a maximum gradient of 12 per cent for a short distance on the lower part of the tour

Length: 45.0km

Total ascent: 1870m

Time: 3½–5 hrs

Suggested gearing: 39/26

Route: Séez (0.0km) – Ste-Foy (8.5km) – Lac du Chevril (21.5km) – Val d'Isère (27.0km) – St Charles bridge (33.5km) – Viewpoint (41.5km) – Top of the pass (45.0km)

On the northern side of the Col de l'Iseran just after the Val d'Isère.

At 2770m the Col de l'Iseran is the second highest pass road in the Alps, after the Col de Restefond/Col de la Bonette (Tour 94). It's completely tarmacked and even accessible by public transport. The northern approach along the Val d'Isère is both longer than the Col de Restefond/Col de la Bonette and also climbs further, which makes it a little more difficult. So a hearty dinner is in order the day before, perhaps a *Gratin savoyard*, a traditional vegetable dish of sliced potatoes baked in the oven with stock and grated cheese, and a chunk of Beaufort for afters, one of Savoy's best cheeses, similar to Emmenthal but without the holes.

Thus fortified we leave Séez (0.0km), at the intersection of two pass roads, the Little St Bernard (Tour 48) and the Col de l'Iseran, whose name derives from the sixth milestone of an earlier road running between Milan and Lyon, on a road that slopes gently downhill at first. After a 3.5km descent alongside the Isère the road climbs gently for about the same distance, then the gradient increases to 10 per cent over two hairpin bends up to Ste-Foy (8.5km). Through the village, whose grey stone houses with slate roofs huddle around a little church, the road narrows and the gradient goes up to 12 per cent. There are two short natural tunnels (12.0km), then the gradient decreases a little and the road leads into a gorge-like section and to the foot of the fearsome hanging glacier of Mont Pourri.

After a 300m unlit tunnel the valley broadens out again and we reach the gleaming deep-green Lac du Chevril (21.5km) up a climb of between 10 per cent and 12 per cent. We ride along the eastern bank of the lake, an impressive 11 square kilometres, to Val d'Isère (27.0km) on a level road through a series of unlit tunnels and galleries with considerable damage to the road surface in places. Even though at first sight the town looks like one of those purpose-built French ski resorts that sprang up in the 1960s and 1970s with the sole purpose of cramming as many tourists as possible into as little space as possible, the centre at least still retains its original Savoyard mountain village character. It's famous because the 1992 Winter Olympics were held in nearby Albertville and some of the ski runs came in here, and also as one of the most beautiful skiing regions in the world, with pistes going up to a height of 3700m. We won't be going quite that far up today, but the top of the pass is nonetheless still a good way off.

Once we've crossed little St Charles Bridge (33.5km) over the equally little Isère here, we reach the prettiest part of the route. The gradient increases to 10 per cent and the road, bumpy in places, goes on up over many bends and hairpins. It blends well into the landscape, which becomes more and more attractive the higher you go. After 41.5km, it's well worth getting off to walk the short distance to the Belvédère de la Tarentaise viewpoint. Not long after that the gradient decreases, the top of the pass comes into sight and you finally get there (45.0km) over the last two hairpin bends with a gradient that reaches 10 per cent again.

When you're up there you can take a photo to commemorate your climb in front of the stone-built sign giving the altitude. Other than that you won't find

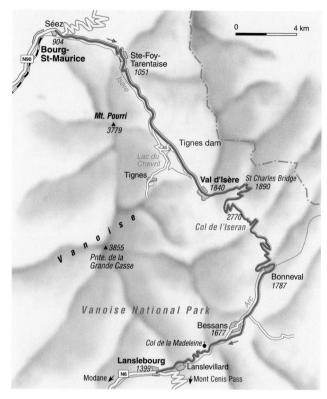

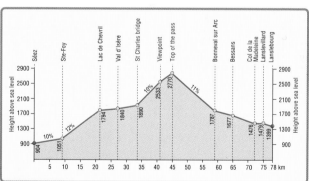

much – no shelters, no restaurant, just a stone chapel and sometimes a sweet-seller with a portable wooden stall. A last look at the surroundings with the 3000m peaks of the Vanoise National Park and the precipitous rock formations of the Gran Paradiso National Park, then you need to concentrate on the descent.

TOUR PROFILE <<

SOUTHERN SIDE – Start: Lanslebourg, 1399m

Directions: A32 Turin–Fréjus, exit Venaus – Mont Cenis Pass – Lanslebourg

Level of Difficulty/Maximum gradient: Medium to difficult tour with a maximum gradient of 11 per cent

Length: 33.0km

Total ascent: 1375m

Time: 2½–3½ hrs

Suggested gearing: 39/26

Route: Lanslebourg (0.0km) – Lanslevillard (3.0km) – Col de la Madeleine (6.0km) – Bessans (13.0km) – Bonneval sur Arc (19.0km) – Top of the pass (33.0km)

Road conditions: Well-constructed roads on the lower section of the northern side. Unlit tunnels with large potholes in places before Val d'Isère. The road then becomes narrower, with numerous bends with surface damage

Pass open: 1 July to 30 September

Things to see: Belvédère de la Tarentaise viewpoint on the northern side and Belvédère de la Maurienne viewpoint on the southern side, both just below the top of the pass. Bessans: St Antoine chapel with frescoes and wall paintings. Lanslevillard: St Sebastian chapel

Map: Euro Cart regional map 1:300,000, RV-Verlag, Sheet 8 Provence/Rhône-Alpes/Côte d'Azur

View of the glacier fields around Albaron on the descent over the southern side of the Col de l'Iseran.

Concentrate above all on the poor state of the road as well the hairpin bends, which are tight in places.

After 13km of winding descent, the first inhabited settlement you reach is Bonneval-sur-Arc. Up here the beauty of the valley is still unspoiled, barren mountain slopes contrasting with the green meadows of the valley bottom. The next settlements are typical mountain villages with old, grey stone houses the same colour as the rocks all around them. Time hasn't stood still here, but it does seem to run noticeably more slowly. You should give yourself plenty of it here, because the modern industrial age catches up with us in Lanslebourg, after a 20km descent containing a 1.5km upward climb with a gradient of 6 per cent to the Col de la Madeleine (not to be confused with the Col de la Madeleine described in Tour 86).

Col de l'Iseran

Apart from these road signs and the stone chapel there is little to be seen at the top of the Col de l'Iseran.

81 MONT CENIS PASS
Savoy/Piedmont

TOUR PROFILE <<

Mont Cenis Pass: 2100m

NORTHERN SIDE – Start: Lanslebourg, 1399m

Directions: Over the Col de l'Iseran to Lanslebourg (Tour 80) or A43 then A32 link Chambéry–Turin–Mondane – Lanslebourg

Level of Difficulty/Maximum gradient: Easy to medium tour with a maximum gradient of 11 per cent

Length: 10.0km

Total ascent: 705m

Time: 1¼–2 hrs

Suggested gearing: 39/26

Route: Lanslebourg (0.0km) – Top of the pass (10.0km)

SOUTHERN SIDE – Start: Susa, 505m

Directions: A32 Turin – Fréjus, exit Susa

Level of Difficulty/Maximum gradient: Difficult, with a maximum gradient of 11 per cent

Length: 31.0km

Total ascent: 1595m

Time: 2¾–4 hrs

Suggested gearing: 39/26

Route: Susa (0.0km) – Costa (10.5km) – Bar Cenisio (15.5km) – Top of the pass (31.0km)

Road conditions: Well-constructed roads

Pass open: 15 May to 15 October

Things to see: Old fort on the southern shore of the Mont Cenis Reservoir

Map: Euro Cart regional map 1:300,000, RV-Verlag, Sheet 8 Provence/Rhône-Alpes/Côte d'Azur

Notes: There is a particularly high volume of heavy goods traffic on this road as it's the main link between Turin and Lyons. The smooth tarmac surface (very slippery because of skid marks and traces of oil, particularly when wet) is dangerous on the descent

The Mont Cenis Pass is known today as the most important traffic link between Geneva, Lyons and Grenoble on one side and the industrial region around Turin on the other. Even though the Fréjus Tunnel takes away most of the traffic, a large number of lorries from the valley of the River Arc, called the Maurienne, still battle their way over the pass into the Italian Susa valley to avoid paying the tunnel fees. Many centuries ago the Holy Roman Emperor, Henry IV, is believed to have followed the same route in 1077 on his famous journey to Canossa to beg Pope Gregory VII for forgiveness. It's also said that, long before, in 218BC, Hannibal chose this easier crossing over Mont Cenis instead of the difficult route over the St Gotthard Pass (Tour 64) with his Punic army, with 20,000 infantry and 6000 cavalry.

Certainly conditions were different in those days. We start our climb on a wide, well-made road at Lanslebourg (0.0km), perhaps after coming down from the Col de l'Iseran (Tour 80). We wind up over wide hairpin bends with a gradient of 8 per cent at first, which then increases to, but doesn't exceed, 10 per cent. Looking back, the light larch woods give a wonderful view of the Dent Parachée and Dôme de Chasseforêt glaciers in the Vanoise massif, a view that widens out as we cross the tree line (7.5km). The top of the

It's always worth keeping an eye out for hazards ahead.

Henry IV, the Holy Roman Emperor, once crossed the Mont Cenis Pass on his way to Canossa.

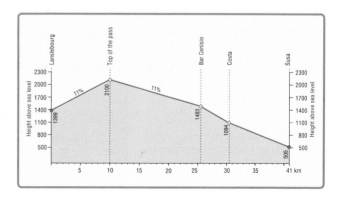

pass (10.0km), which is also the border between the Graian Alps and the Cottian Alps, named after the Roman prefect Cottius who ruled this country under the Emperor Augustus, is then quickly reached over a gradient of 8 per cent. The wide plateau at the foot of Mont Malamot is almost completely filled by the Lac du Mont Cenis, one of the largest reservoirs in the Alps. An old hostel from the ninth century disappeared beneath the waters of the lake, and was replaced by a very modern-looking new building. On the south-western shore of this long lake we can make out the ruins of an old fort, then we reach the the reservoir wall, 130m high and almost 2.5km long. A 31km descent follows with a downhill slope of up to 11 per cent and 14 hairpin bends. It's particularly dangerous where skid marks and traces of oil make the smooth tarmac surface greasy.

TOUR PROFILE <<

Col du Télégraphe: 1600m

NORTHERN SIDE – Start: St-Michel-de-Maurienne, 712m

Directions: Either over the Col de l'Iseran (Tour 80) or the Mont Cenis Pass (Tour 81) and via Modane to St-Michel-de-Maurienne or A32 then A43 link Turin–Chambéry to St-Michel-de-Maurienne

Level of Difficulty/Maximum gradient: Medium, with a maximum gradient of 10 per cent

Length: 12.5km

Total ascent: 890m

Time: 1¼–2 hrs

Suggested gearing: 39/26

Route: St-Michel-de-Maurienne (0.0km) – Les Seignères (2.5km) – Top of the pass (12.5km)

SOUTHERN SIDE: On the southern side the pass road drops 170m on a 5km downhill slope of 9 per cent to Valloire (1430m), the northern starting point for the Col du Galibier (Tour 83)

Road conditions: Well-constructed roads

Pass open: All year

Map: Euro Cart regional map 1:300,000, RV-Verlag, Sheet 8 Provence/Rhône-Alpes/Côte d'Azur

The Col du Télégraphe is really only the lower part of the climb to the Col du Galibier (Tour 83), upstream of it, as it were. But because it has its own summit, with a 5km, 170m descent on the other side, it's seen as a separate pass road. It can be ridden on its own for training purposes, but in most cases it's done on the way to the significantly higher and better-known Col du Galibier.

If you don't see any signs for the Col du Télégraphe in St-Michel-de-Maurienne (0.0km), a rather plain industrial town in the Arc valley, just follow directions for the Col du Galibier. Leave the town on the Rue de Télégraphe through a narrow railway underpass and then across a wooden bridge over the Arc. A little later you arrive in St-Martin-d'Arc.

The surprisingly wide, well-constructed road winds its way up over many bends and hairpins with a moderate gradient of between 8 and 10 per cent on its way to Les Seignères (2.5km). The wooded mountain slopes don't offer any particularly interesting views or detours, although if you keep a close eye ahead you can see on a rocky ledge a little above the head of the pass the old Télégraphe fort from which the pass takes its name. Fourteen hairpins later and you're at the top. It's really just a clearing in thick forest with a sign saying Col du Télégraphe: there are no views worth mentioning. You may as well continue straight on to the descent, which is almost 5km long with a gradient of up to 9 per cent, although it's mostly less than that and as a result you're obliged to pedal. In Valloire, a little holiday resort in the Valloirette valley, the pass over the Col du Télégraphe ends and you reach the start of the climb to the Col du Galibier.

An opportunity for reflection at the top of the Col du Télégraphe.

The Col du Télégraphe and the Col du Galibier (Tour 83) that follows it first featured in the Tour de France in 1911 on the fifth stage, from Chamonix to Grenoble. The winner of that stage was the Frenchman Emile Georget, but Paul Duboc and Gustave Garrigou also hit the headlines as the only two riders to make it to the top without having to get off and push. It is hard to believe today, but if you look at photos of cyclists and the state of the roads in those days you'll be surprised that anyone ever managed the climb on a bike at all. The only advantage that riders had in those days was that they could take the tunnel at the top of the pass, saving a vertical climb of almost 100m.

Once the board says 'Ouvert' (open) there's nothing to stop you climbing the pass any more.

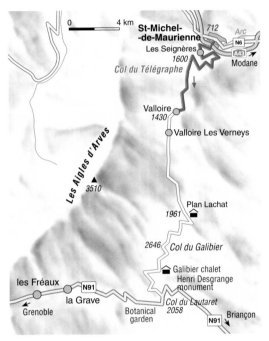

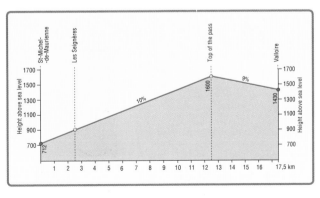

83 COL DU GALIBIER
Savoy/Dauphiné

TOUR PROFILE <<

Col du Galibier: 2646m

NORTHERN SIDE – Start: Valloire, 1430m

Directions: From the north Valloire can only be reached over the Col du Télégraphe (Tour 82)

Level of Difficulty/Maximum gradient: Medium to difficult tour with a maximum gradient of 12 per cent

Length: 18.5km

Total ascent: 588m

Time: 1¾–2½ hrs

Suggested gearing: 39/26

Route: Valloire (0.0km) – Valloire Les Verneys (2.0km) – Plan Lachat Restaurant (9.5km) – North tunnel entrance (15.5km) – Top of the pass (18.5km)

SOUTHERN SIDE – Start: Top of the Col du Lautaret, 2058m

Directions: Either from Briançon or Le Clapier on the Col du Lautaret (Tour 87)

Level of Difficulty/Maximum gradient: Easy to medium tour with a maximum gradient of 12 per cent over the last kilometre of the climb

Length: 9.0km

Total ascent: 590m

Time: 1¼–2 hrs

Suggested gearing: 39/26

Route: Top of the Col du Lautaret (0.0km) – South Galibier chalet/South tunnel entrance (8.0km) – Top of the pass (9.0km)

Road conditions: Considerable surface damage in places, especially at the top

Pass open: 15 June to 15 October

Things to see: Monument to Henri Desgrange (founder of the Tour de France) in the car park in front of the South Galibier chalet on the southern side. Botanical garden at the top of the Col du Lautaret

Map: Euro Cart regional map 1:300,000, RV-Verlag, Sheet 8 Provence/Rhône-Alpes/Côte d'Azur

The Col du Galibier is known in cycling circles as the 'Roof of the Tour', an allusion to the fact that it is the highest point in the Tour de France, the best-known cycling race in the world. It is, however, only the fifth highest pass in the Alps. The Col de Restefond/Col de la Bonette (Tour 94) in Provence, the Col de l'Iseran (Tour 80) in Savoy, the Stelvio Pass in Italy (Tour 40) and the Col Agnel in Italian Piedmont are higher. That isn't to say that it's a pushover: far from it, especially when you start the climb on the northern side and already have the Col du Télégraphe (Tour 82) under your belt. That means a total vertical climb of 2100m, which none of the higher passes can match.

From Valloire (0.0km), the starting point for the Col du Galibier on the northern side, there's a further vertical climb of around 1200m, which kicks in immediately at 12 per cent. The town takes its name from the Latin *vallis aurea*, which means 'golden, rich valley', but the exact nature of these historic riches is unclear, in the days before the arrival of the alpine tourism and outdoor pursuits that fuel today's economy. In Les Verneys (2.0km) the gradient finally decreases and you can get up some speed on a wide valley floor before the gradient increases again to 8 per cent after two hairpin bends (5.0km). There are no particular obstacles to overcome among the barren high meadows alongside the Valloirette until you reach Plan Lachat restaurant (9.5km), where things start to get serious. Once you've crossed the river the road climbs upwards over many bends and hairpins at a gradient of 12 per cent through a desolate landscape of scree and boulders. The gradient doesn't go down appreciably until the 13.5km mark, when the road also becomes

The Massif des Écrins with the Meije glacier and the 4102m high Barre des Écrins on the descent over the southern side of the Col du Galibier.

straighter. You can already see the hairpin bends climbing to the summit ahead, which begin at the entrance of the tunnel that cuts through to the other side of the pass. This is closed to cyclists, so instead you have to ascend to the top via four hairpins winding up the last 100m of the climb at a moderate gradient of between 10 and 12 per cent. The top of the pass (16.5km) is barely the size of a large tennis court, but the view is breathtaking. The Pelvoux group in front of us, also called the Massif des Écrins, is almost close enough to touch, with its highest peak, the 4102m Barre des Écrins, rising at the back. It's a massive bulwark of granite and ice with mighty rock walls, sharp ridges and pointed needles carved by huge hanging glaciers. The Meije glacier in particular, which covers the north side of the mountain of the same name with savage seracs and crevasse fields, presents a sight unique in the alpine region. Edward Whymper, none other than the first person to climb the Matterhorn, called this mountain group the wildest part of the Alps and wrote in his notes: 'Its rocks, mountain streams and gorges are unforgettable, their wild, deep valleys present bold, sublime spectacles and as far as the boldness of the mountain shapes is concerned, they are a match for any other landscape'. It was also Whymper who was the first to climb the Barre des Écrins in 1864, well before the first edition of the Tour de France in 1903. Their achievments are all the more worthy of our respect given their primitive equipment, especially when compared to the technical kit and gadgetry of today.

If on the way up we appreciated our lightweight bikes and multiple gears, on the way down we should be particularly grateful for good brakes, because the road drops quickly over three tight hairpin bends at a gradient of 12 per cent. Just a

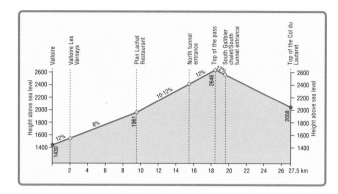

kilometre lower down, stop by the restaurant at the mouth of the tunnel. A stone column commemorates Henri Desgrange, the 'Father of the Tour de France', who rode over this pass for the first time in 1911 in the early days of the race.

After another 8km with a 10 per cent downhill our pass route ends, rather unusually, at another pass. This is the Col du Lautaret (Tour 87), 2058m high, which links Grenoble with Briançon and, further on, Turin.

TOUR PROFILE <<

Col de la Croix de Fer: 2067m

NORTHERN SIDE – Start: St-Jean-de-Maurienne, 546m

Directions: A43 then A32 Chambéry–Turin link to St-Jean-de-Maurienne in the Arc valley

Level of Difficulty/Maximum gradient: Difficult, with a maximum gradient of 14 per cent on a short section in St-Sorlin-d'Arves. Otherwise long stretches at 12 per cent

Length: 30.0km

Total ascent: 1645m

Time: 2¾–4 hrs

Suggested gearing: 39/26

Route: St-Jean-de-Maurienne (0.0km) – La Brevière (8.5km) – St-Jean-d'Arves (19.5km) – St-Sorlin-d'Arves (23.0km) – Top of the pass

SOUTHERN SIDE – Start: Rochetaillée, 711m

Directions: Grenoble – Le-Pont-de-Claix – Vizille – Rochetaillée

Level of Difficulty/Maximum gradient: Medium to difficult tour with a maximum gradient of 12 per cent

Length: 28.0km

Total ascent: 1240m

Time: 2¼–3½ hrs

Suggested gearing: 39/26

Route: Rochetaillée (0.0km) – Allemont (5.0km) – Rivier d'Allemont (14.0km) – Top of the pass (28.0km)

Road conditions: Narrow in places on the Combe Genin on the northern side and on the Combe d'Olle and the Défilé de Maupas on the southern side as well as slight surface damage on the upper part of the route

Pass open: 15 May to 31 October

Map: Euro Cart regional map 1:300,000, RV-Verlag, Sheet 8 Provence/Rhône-Alpes/Côte d'Azur

Croix de Fer means 'iron cross', and you should train to be iron-hard if you're going to ride up it on a bike, because with gradients of up to 14 per cent and a vertical climb of 1500m over a route 30km long this pass on the northern edge of Haute-Dauphiné counts as one of our hardest tours. Cycle sport fans may know the name from the Tour de France, which has occasionally included it. But if you're not familiar with it, it lies west of the Col du Galibier (Tour 83) and so forms a link from the valley of the river Arc, the Maurienne, over into the Romanche valley in the area round Grenoble. A tip: in the tourist season you should consider doing the Col de la Croix de Fer rather than the Col du Galibier because there's far less traffic on it. You'll also save yourself almost 500m of vertical climb, the only reservation being that you don't want to go on to Briançon because that would add on the Col du Lautaret and a vertical climb of 1200m.

In St-Jean-de-Maurienne (0.0km) take the turning to the Col de la Croix de Fer. The road starts to climb at once with a gradient of 10 per cent through the town and then goes on up over a mountain slope overgrown with sun-scorched scrub. Make sure not to miss the left-hand turning past a little quarry after almost exactly 4km of the route. The road goes gently downhill for some time (6.5km) then you zoom along quite a level valley before the gradient increases again after a bridge to between 10 per cent and 12 per cent until you reach La Brevière (8.5km). You ride over a hairpin bend into a wood and then need a great deal of effort to make it to the top over more hairpin bends, because the gradient rarely drops below 10 per cent, and more often than not reaches 12 per cent.

When you reach Combe Genin (11.5km) the slope decreases as you go through a narrow, gorge-like part of the valley and you make rapid progress, although you have to ride through five tunnels between 30m and 450m long. A short descent to a little dam (15.5km) does your legs some good, but you soon have to struggle to regain the height you lost. Apart from one short 10 per cent climb the road runs quite gently up to St-Jean-d'Arves (19.5km) and there are no particular difficulties as far as St-Sorlin-d'Arves (23.0km). Here it's a good idea to switch to quite a large sprocket because the gradient increases substantially through the village to 14 per cent. You fight your way past old, almost ruined stone houses, to which the modern hotel offers a not particularly pleasing constrast.

Once you leave Combe Genin you've done the hardest part of the climb, but now the road is noticeably narrower and in worse condition. You ride into a treeless high valley whose alpine pastures are littered with moss-covered boulders and try your utmost to avoid the deepest potholes. If you're worrying about negotiating this kind of road damage on the descent ahead, don't worry: the road is considerably better there. First you have to reach the top of the pass and that's not so easy because the gradients hit 12 per cent. There are 10 hairpin bends to tackle before you suddenly arrive at the top of the pass (30.0km) at the Col de la Croix de Fer chalet. A little rocky hillock just above the

top of the pass then affords you the most wonderful view over the Aiguilles d'Arves, the Rocher Blanc, the Aiguilles de la Saussaz and the mighty Meije.

The description of the descent over the western side can be confusing. Strictly speaking it ends after a 2.5km, 7 per cent descent where the road joins the Col du Glandon road (Tour 75). From here there are just a few hundred more metres and a vertical climb of just 40m or so to the top of the Col du Glandon, or just 27.5km and a drop in height of almost 1200m over the southern side down to Rochetaillée. A glance at the map should make the options clear.

Opposite: Participants in the 'Marmotte' cycle tour which takes place over the Col de la Croix de Fer (pictured), the Col du Galibier and up the Alpe d'Huez.

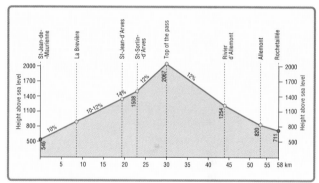

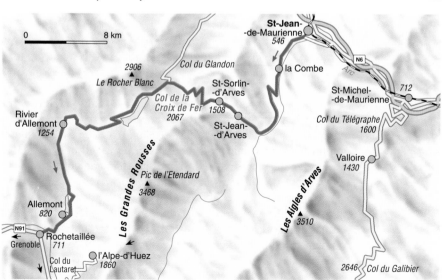

TOUR PROFILE <<

Col du Glandon: 1951m

NORTHERN SIDE – Start: St-Avre, 450m

Directions: Over the A43 then A32 Chambéry–Turin link to St-Arve in the Arc valley

Level of Difficulty/Maximum gradient: Difficult, with a maximum gradient of 15 per cent on the last 3km up to the top of the pass

Length: 21.5km

Total ascent: 1505m

Time: 2¼–3½ hrs

Suggested gearing: 39/28

Route: St-Avre (0.0km) – Le Villard-Martinan (10.0km) – St-Colomban-des-Villards (10.5km) – Top of the pass (21.5km)

SOUTHERN SIDE: On the southern side the road descends by 16m over a 0.5km stretch down to the junction with the southern side of the Col de la Croix de Fer (Tour 84), then descends by 160m over a 2.5km stretch with gradients of up to 7 per cent below the top of the Col de la Croix de Fer

Road conditions: Well-constructed roads

Pass open: 15 May to 31 October

Map: Euro Cart regional map 1:300,000, RV-Verlag, Sheet 8 Provence/Rhône-Alpes/Côte d'Azur

The Col du Glandon is a bit of a tricky one too. You may already have heard the name from editions of the Tour de France, but you can't quite place it. It's not quite as difficult if you've already got to grips with the route of the Col de la Croix de Fer (Tour 84). The beginning of the Col du Glandon is also in the valley of the river Arc, known as the Maurienne, which it links with the Romanche valley over the mountains of the Belledonne chain. St-Avre, the starting point to the north-east of the Col du Glandon, is situated only 10km down the valley from St-Jean-de-Maurienne, the starting point for the Col de la Croix de Fer, and the two passes almost bump into each other at the top. If you have to choose between them, both are hard on a bike, but the Col du Glandon is perhaps one level more difficult because its maximum gradient is 15 per cent, maintained over a 3km stretch.

We leave St-Avre and the rather uninteresting Arc valley on a road with a moderate gradient. After leaving the village the gradient increases to 10 per cent and the road snakes its way up through thick deciduous woods with no view. We reach Le Villard-Martinan (10.0km) on a road that winds tortuously even though there are only two real hairpin bends along its 5.5km length, at a gradient that hardly ever drops below 8 per cent. It then descends slightly through St-Colomban-des-Villards (10.5km) and maintains this slope for a kilometre. There's little say about the scenery; only the little vegetable plots growing in the mountain pastures spring to mind. As, of course, does the 12 per cent gradient, which now starts to make itself felt. But flatter sections regularly allow you to rest and slowly the surroundings become more interesting. Be sure to take a look back by a bridge at 14.5km. Far away to the north-east, if you look very carefully, you'll see a snow-covered peak emerging above the cleft of the Col de la Madeleine (Tour 86). This disappears again as the road makes its way up over a 12 per cent gradient with many bends. Once you cross the tree line after 16.5km the gradient decreases to between 8 and 10 per cent and the peak will reappear when you look back.

From now on the more immediate vicinity requires our attention, and all our strength too, because the gradient increases to a challenging 15 per cent. And it doesn't decrease again any time soon, so you won't be spending too much time thinking about the mountain peak to the north-east. You'll find out just how much 3km can wear you down when you're cycling here, but you do finally reach the top of the pass (21.5km).

There's no great hustle and bustle here at the top, probably because apart from a few tourists in cars you're the only one there, and there's not a lot to detain you here, neither a restaurant nor much of a view. But peace and tranquillity can have their advantages, and if you finally want to know what that mountain peak to the

On the northern side of the Col du Glandon with a view over the mountains of the Belledonne chain.

north-east is called, it's actually Mont Blanc, at 4807m the highest mountain in Europe. From where we're standing it's hard to grasp that mountaineers on its slopes, who may at this moment be watching us take a breather, are exactly 2856m higher than we are.

Now you can set about the descent and decide whether to notch up another pass. To do that you have only to cycle 500m on a 7 per cent downhill slope to the N91 and then, if you can face 2.5km with a total vertical climb of 160m up to the Col de la Croix de la Fer, you're almost home and dry. At the top of the Croix de la Fer is a restaurant as well as a wonderful view.

From the long, scenically attractive and varied descent over the south-western side of the Col du Glandon to Rochetaillée (49.5km) in the Romanche valley, there is an opportunity for another climb of about 1.5km with a 6 per cent gradient past a reservoir on the upper part of the climb.

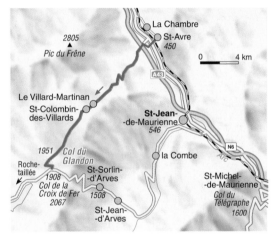

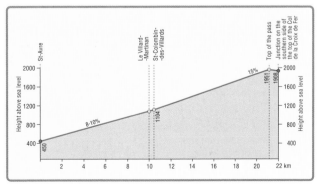

86 COL DE LA MADELEINE
Savoy

The Maurienne, as the upper part of the Arc valley from the Col de l'iseran (Tour 80) down in the direction of Chambéry is also known, has a whole range of pass roads, from the Col du Télégraphe and the Col du Galibier (Tours 82 and 83) to the Col de la Croix de Fer (Tour 84) and the Col du Glandon (Tour 85). However, while these tours lead out of the valley towards the south, the Col de la Madeleine chooses the opposite direction, to the north and into the Val d'Isère, also called the Tarentaise valley, at the edge of the Vanoise massif.

Following the signposts for Col de la Madeleine in the little town of La Chambre (0.0km), not far from Saint-Avre, you soon reach the village of Saint-Martin-sur-la-Chambre (1.5km) on a straight road that climbs at 8 per cent. The gradient then increases to 10 per cent over a series of hairpin bends and stays up here for a long time. Sparse mixed woodland lines the road, which makes its way uphill without offering much in the way of views. Faded words scribbled on the tarmac indicate that the Tour de France has been over this pass. In the annals of the greatest cycling spectacle in the world you can read that this first happened in 1969, when Eddy Merckx won the event.

View from the Col de la Madeleine of the Belledonne mountain chain.

Past Le Planet (9.5km) the woods recede, the gradient remains constant and you reach the winter sports resort of Saint-François-Longchamp (14.0km) via L'Épalaud (10.5km). On the barren slopes above, completely empty of both trees and bushes, we can already clearly see the hairpin bends zigzagging to the top of the pass. First the road climbs hairpin bends, then wide, looping curves with a constant gradient of between 8 and 10 per cent, which add considerably to the distance. The top of the pass (19.5km) with its mountain refuge offers us a panoramic view of the Belledonne mountains, familiar from the climb to the Col de la Croix de Fer (Tour 84) and the Col du Glandon (Tour 85). Next to them is the Grandes Rousses glacier and the Massif des Écrins to the south-east, while to the north-east, as well as the Massif de Beaufort, you can admire Mont Blanc.

Though there were 27 hairpin bends to tackle on the way up, there are only 14 on the 27km descent to Notre Dame de Briançon, with downhill gradients of up to 12 per cent. If you want to do the climb here from the north out of the Val d'Isère you'd do well not to confuse this town with the Briançon situated further to the west in the Durance valley. That Briançon has three passes to offer, the Col du Lautaret (Tour 87), the Col de Montgenèvre (Tour 49) and the Col d'Izoard (Tour 89).

The Tour de France has another story about the Col de la Madeleine. It came this way on the sixth stage of the Tour in 1996 from Chambéry to Les Arcs. The Spaniard Miguel Indurain, who had appeared until then to be invincible, suffered considerable difficulties. He lost over seven minutes to the eventual stage winner Luc Leblanc and was given a 20-second penalty because he broke the rules by accepting a drinks bottle from a

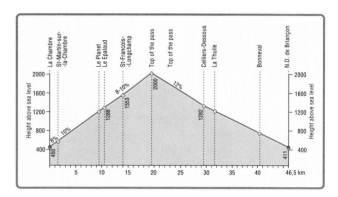

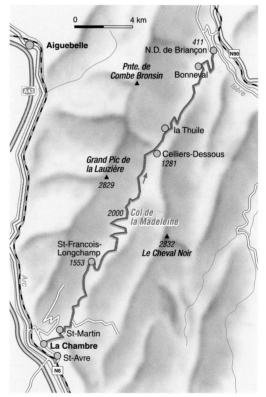

support vehicle in the last kilometre before the finishing line in Les Arcs. Indurain's dream of a sixth Tour win was over, and he retired from cycling soon after. The Col de la Madeleine was partly responsible for ending one of the greatest careers in the history of the sport of cycling.

87 COL DU LAUTARET
Dauphiné

TOUR PROFILE <<

Col du Lautaret: 2058m

WESTERN SIDE – Start: Le Clapier, 742m, about 5km east of Le Bourg-d'Oisans

Directions: either over the Col du Glandon (Tour 85) or the Col de la Croix de Fer (Tour 84) to Le Clapier or Grenoble – Le Pont-de-Claix – Vizille – Rochetaillée – Le Bourg-d'Oisans

Level of Difficulty/Maximum gradient: Medium, with a maximum gradient of 10 per cent

Length: 34.5km

Total ascent: 1320m

Time: 2½–3½ hrs

Suggested gearing: 39/26

Route: Le Clapier (0.0km) – Le Freney (6.0km) – Lac de Chambon (8.5km) – Les Fréaux (21.5km) – La Grave (23.0km) – Top of the pass (34.5km)

EASTERN SIDE – Start: Briançon, 1321m

Directions: Over the Col de Montgenèvre (Tour 49) or the Col d'Izoard (Tour 89) to Briançon or Grenoble – Gap – Embrun – Guillestre – Briançon

Level of Difficulty/Maximum gradient: Easy to medium tour with a maximum gradient of 7 per cent

Length: 27.5km

Total ascent: 740m

Time: 1½–2½ hrs

Suggested gearing: 39/23

Route: Briançon (0.0km) – Chantemerle (5.5km) – Villeneuve-la-Salle (7.5km) – Les Monétiers-les-Bains (13.0km) – Top of the pass (27.5km)

Road conditions: Well-constructed roads

Pass open: All year

Map: Euro Cart regional map 1:300,000, RV-Verlag, Sheet 8 Provence/Rhône-Alpes/Côte d'Azur

Notes: Lights are compulsory because of the 10 tunnels and gallery tunnels, unlit in places, on the western side and the tunnel on the eastern side

The performance of these older riders on the Col du Lautaret deserves recognition.

With a total route length of almost 70km between Le Bourg-d'Oisans in the west and Briançon in the east, the Col du Lautaret is a very long pass road. But it's not all that high, reaching only 2058m, and the vertical climb of 737m on the eastern side isn't too dramatic, although the western side's net gain of 1334m is rather more impressive. If this isn't enough you can bolt on a trip up to the top of the Col du Galibier (Tour 83), which would add another 588m of height.

Western side

Leaving Le Bourg-d'Oisans on the N91 in a south-easterly direction we go past the turning for the Alpe d'Huez (Tour 88) and on to Le Clapier (0.0km). Our road, following the signposts for Briançon, turns into the Gorges de l'Infernet, the Gorges of Hell, and climbs at 10 per cent. This gradient is maintained for almost 4km along the right-hand side of the gorge before the road suddenly descends after a bend. You reach Le Freney (6.0km), where the incline increases again to 10 per cent up to the Lac du Chambon reservoir (8.5km). Tunnels along the left-hand shore of this lake, which are unlit in places, need care, then we ride into the Combe de Malaval. There are no problems on this gently climbing road between vertical rock walls along the Romanche as far as Les Fréaux (21.5km), where the gradient increases to between 8 per cent and 10 per cent up to La Grave (23.0km). Massive glaciers from the Massif des Écrins stretch down to the old mountaineering village, which is increasingly becoming a mecca for skiers. The surroundings change again after a 600m dimly lit tunnel. Through alpine meadows and grey rain-eroded terrain the road climbs up over many bends with a gradient of between 8 per cent and 10 per cent to the top of the pass (34.5km), which lies imposingly at the foot of the 3982m Meije glacier. The long descent down to Briançon is so gentle that for most of the way you have to pedal.

Eastern side

Briançon, which stretches out over a south-facing valley at the confluence of the Guisane and the Durance rivers, is, according to the tourist information brochures, the highest town in the Alps. But, at a height of 1560m, the Swiss town of Davos is disputing this ranking. We don't want to get involved in that, but we can say that Briançon's altitude means that the vertical climb on the Col du Lautaret isn't all that much. It also gives a leg up to riders starting the climbs up to the Col de Mongenèvre (Tour 49) and the Col de l'Izoard (Tour 89).

The most difficult part of the ascent is in the centre of the town, where the road climbs at a continuous 10 per cent. Then the wide Guisane valley takes us in and we ride up its exposed slopes at a gradient of 7 per cent. This soon turns into a gentle descent, and there are no difficulties awaiting further on. The road is wide and

only narrows as we go through little villages such as Chantemerle (5.5km) and Villeneuve-la-Salle (7.5km). The south-western side of the valley obscures the view of the Barre des Écrins, whose magnificent peaks can only be glimpsed now and again through the valley mouths. The gradient increases to 7 per cent for longer stretches as we go further up and a more or less straight road takes us into a rather barren region. A 350m dimly lit tunnel (23.5km) is rather unpleasant, but, emerging, we finally have a wonderful view of the cliffs and glaciers of the Meije. A shorter, unlit tunnel follows, then all that separates us from the top of the pass (27.5km) is another longer gallery.

On the eastern side of the Col du Lautaret.

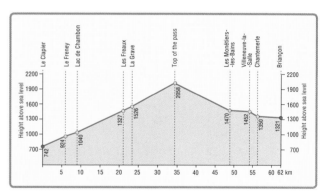

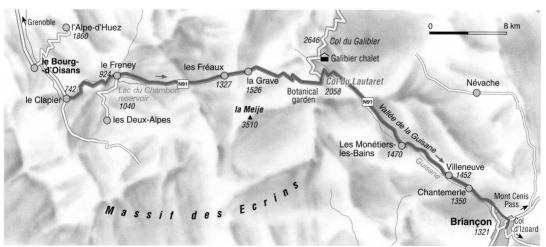

TOUR PROFILE <<

L'Alpe d'Huez Mountain Road: 1860m

Start: Le Bourg-d'Oisans, 724m, about 45km east of Grenoble

Directions: Grenoble – Le Pont-de-Claix – Vizille – Rochetaillée – Le Bourg-d'Oisans

Level of Difficulty/Maximum gradient: Medium, with a maximum gradient of 10 per cent nearly all the way

Length: 13.5km

Total ascent: 1140m

Time: 1½–2½ hrs

Suggested gearing: 39/26

Route: Le Bourg-d'Oisans (0.0km) – La Garde (3.5km) – Le Ribaut-d'Huez (5.5km) – Huez Village (9.0km) – Huez en Oisans (10.5km) – L'Alpe d'Huez (13.5km)

Road conditions: Well-constructed roads

Pass open: All year

Map: Euro Cart regional map 1:300,000, RV-Verlag, Sheet 8 Provence/Rhône-Alpes/Côte d'Azur

Little Alpe d'Huez, situated high over the Romanche valley, is a well-known winter sports resort in the Dauphiné Alps in France. It's a little less busy in summer unless the Tour de France chooses it as the end point for an alpine stage, in which case it is likely to be the longest and most difficult. The total of 19 hairpin bends up to the top are crowded with tens of thousands of spectators and sometimes there's hardly any room for the cycling professionals to get through.

By contrast, at any other time riders will be almost all alone on the road once they follow the signposts for La Garde/L'Alpe d'Huez at the end of the town of Le Bourg-d'Oisans (0.0km). You cross the Romanche and the gradient of the road increases to 10 per cent. The first hairpin bend after 2.5km, is indicated by a sign with the number 19, which means that there are another 18 to come. You

This is what the climb to the Alpe d'Huez near Le Ribaut d'Huez looks like when the Tour de France isn't taking place.

can see exposed slate, painted here and there by cycling fans with the names of their idols, as the gradient only decreases briefly in the curve of the hairpin bends.

In the small village of La Garde (3.5km) Tour riders will have the briefest of glimpses of the beautiful Gothic stone church, and it's more likely they'll be thankful for the brief levelling out of the route. But this doesn't last long, and as you leave the village the gradient increases again to 10 per cent and several hairpin bends take you further up to Le Ribaut-d'Huez (5.5km).

Instead of crowds of spectators we're accompanied up to Huez Village (9.0km) by well-manicured flowerbeds at the edge of the road and dark wood-clad chalets, with Huez en Oisans (10.5km) following on almost immediately. At the end of the village we reach hairpin bend number 4 and at the next junction (11.5km) we follow the road straight on, just like the professionals do, as you can see from the inscriptions on the road. We reach hairpin bend number 2 over the predictable 10 per cent gradient just as we enter the ski resort of L'Alpe d'Huez (12.5km), whose centre (13.5km) is the goal of the Tour de France stage.

If at the top you want to compare your time with that of the Tour de France pros, in 1997 the Italian Marco Pantani took 37 minutes and 35 seconds. But he already had more than 200km over several passes behind him. In the individual time trials staged for the first time in 2004 the American Lance Armstrong took 39 minutes and 41 seconds.

Unfortunately you can't make an exact comparison between these times because while Marco Pantani's was measured from the beginning of the climb, the 2km from the starting line to the middle of Le Bourg-d'Oisans were added to Lance Armstrong's time. The

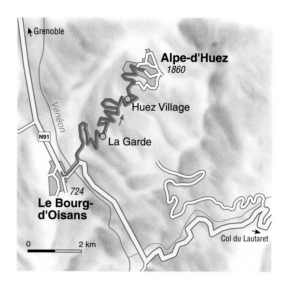

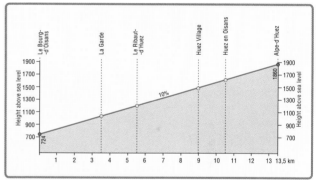

timekeepers established that Armstrong's time from the beginning of the climb was 37 minutes and 36 seconds and so he remained just one second over Pantani's time.

Signpost in Le Bourg-d'Oisans

217

89 COL D'IZOARD
Dauphiné

The Col de l'Izoard is one of three pass roads that start/end at Briançon, the others being the Col de Montgenèvre (Tour 49) and the Col du Lautaret (Tour 87). All three pass through beautiful scenery, but the Col de l'Izoard can offer a geological feature unique in the alpine region: the Casses Désertes, which translates as a broken, shattered desert. But more of that later.

For the time being we'll stay with the urban landscape and take a look at Briançon. Louis XIV, better known by many as the Sun King, had the town developed as a fortified garrison in the 17th century by the brilliant engineer and military architect Vauban. The fact that the Austrians failed to capture Briançon in 1850 in spite of having forces 20 times stronger shows that he must have been a master of his craft. The successful defence was due in particular to the fortifications, of which there is nothing left now apart from their double walls and a few bulwarks and ditches overgrown with grass. We ride up through the old town on a very steep road with a gradient of 12 per cent. From the square with its allegorical Statue de France, you have a wonderful view not only over the town, but also over the sides of the valley where other fortifications are visible.

The last few metres on the northern side of the Col d'Izoard.

The way to the Col d'Izoard is well signposted.

The enemies, against whom these offered protection, came mostly from the north over the Col de Montgenèvre, which these days forms the border with Italy. Our route, though, takes us out of town (0.0km) in a south-westerly direction over a wide-angled hairpin bend with a gradient of 12 per cent. Soon after the gradient decreases first to 10 per cent and then even lower beyond the little village of Fontchristianne (3.5km). We have a 1.5km gentle descent before us on the left-hand side of an immense gorge which the Cerveyette has carved through the soft limestone and dolomite rock; then gradients of up to 10 per cent alternate with flatter sections until we reach Cervières (10.0km). This is a little hamlet with two churches and a hotel at the foot of the Cime de la Charvie.

We cross the Cerveyette, the road climbs at 10 per cent over hairpin bends, then turns sharply towards the south. Along the Cime de la Charvie we come to several old stone buildings in Le Laus (12.5km). The road now winds its way up over wide hairpin bends with gradients of up to 12 per cent through sparse pinewoods on the right-hand side of the valley. Soon the trees start to peter out, and the Refuge Napoléon appears above us; we reach it after 19.5km. It consists of six shelters, built by the famous Corsican. In all probability we won't need to avail ourselves of its facilities, because we can already see the top of the pass above us. There are just a few more wide bends on a gradient of 10 per cent before we're at the top and can park our bikes by the stone obelisk (20.5km) erected to commemorate the French troops who built the road.

There is no view but if you think that you can manage it in your cycling shoes

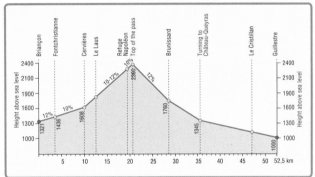

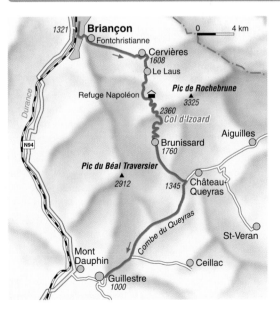

219

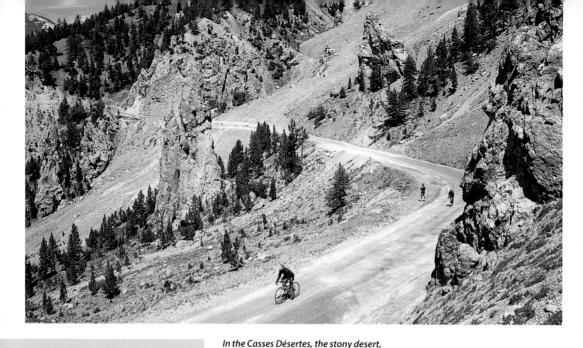

In the Casses Désertes, the stony desert, on the southern side of the Col d'Izoard.

TOUR PROFILE <<

SOUTHERN SIDE – Start: Guillestre, 1000m

Directions: Over the Col de Vars (Tour 92) to Guillestre or Grenoble – Gap – Embrun – Guillestre

Level of Difficulty/Maximum gradient: Medium to difficult tour with a maximum gradient of 12 per cent

Length: 32.0km

Total ascent: 1360m

Time: 2¼–3½ hrs

Suggested gearing: 39/26

Route: Guillestre (0.0km) – Le Cristillan (5.5km) – turning to Château-Queyras (17.0km) – Brunissard (24.0km) – Top of the pass (32.0km)

Road conditions: Considerable surface damage in places at the top

Pass open: 15 June to 15 October

Things to see: Briançon: Porte Pignerol (northern city gate), Maison Jean Prat at 37 Grande Rue with a Renaissance facade, castle; Casses Désertes, scree desert on the southern side just below the top of the pass.

Map: Euro Cart regional map 1:300,000, RV-Verlag, Sheet 8 Provence/Rhône-Alpes/Côte d'Azur

Notes: Lights are necessary because of the five 30- to 300m tunnels on the southern side

you can climb up the 30m or so to the top of a little hill above the top of the pass. Here you'll be rewarded by a wonderful view of the mountains of the Briançonnais area to the north, the top of the Durance valley from where we set off and the Queyras in the south, which may be our next destination. At the time of writing there was a little Tour de France museum housed in a hut at the side of the road, with impressive photos from the early days of the sport. The achievements of two of the greatest cyclists of all time, Fausto Coppi and Louison Bobet, are commemorated by a plaque on a huge rock on the right of the road just after the summit.

Fausto Coppi (1919-1960) was the greatest Italian cyclist of all time. He won the Tour de France in 1949 and 1952 and the Giro d'Italia five times in all. He was the World Champion in cycling pursuit in 1947 and 1949 and the World Road Racing Champion in 1953. The list of his victories would have been longer if the Second World War hadn't cost him the best years of his career.

The Frenchman Louison Bobet (1925-1983) won the Tour de France three years in succession, from 1953 to 1955, and was World Road Racing Champion in 1954. His career came to an end in 1961 when he broke his femur in a car crash.

The only sight worth seeing is the Casses Désertes landscape, a huge expanse of scree that stretches out over the slopes to the left of the road punctuated by huge, bizarrely shaped rocks exposed by erosion. In a landscape that is otherwise completely free of vegetation a few hardy larch trees soften the impression of a moonscape a little. We leave this unique natural spectacle up a short 6 per cent gradient followed by a 32km run to Guillestre descending at up to 12 per cent.

The surroundings of the Col d'Izoard are barren and devoid of vegetation but still grand and impressive.

TOUR PROFILE <<

Sommet Bucher Mountain Road: 2257m

Start: Château-Queyras, 1384m

Directions: Either over the southern side of the Col de l'Izoard (Tour 89) down to the turning for Guillestre/ Château-Queyras to Château-Queyras or over the northern side of the Col de Vars (Tour 92) to Guillestre and then on to Château Queyras

Level of Difficulty/Maximum gradient: Medium, with a maximum gradient of 14 per cent on short sections

Length: 11.0km

Total ascent: 875m

Time: 1¾–2¾ hrs

Suggested gearing: 39/28

Route: Château-Queyras (0.0km) – Top of the pass (11.0km)

Road conditions: Considerable surface damage throughout the route

Pass open: All year

Things to see: Château Queyras, a 13th/14th century castle

Map: Euro Cart regional map 1:300,000, RV-Verlag, Sheet 8 Provence/Rhône-Alpes/Côte d'Azur

Notes: Extreme caution is needed because of the poor state of the road, particularly on the descent, and in places it's advisable to ride at a walking pace

Coming down the southern side of the Col d'Izoard (Tour 89) you reach the junction of the Guillestre/Aiguilles roads after almost exactly 14km. If you're in a hurry and want to go further on to the Col de Vars (Tour 92) you'll follow the D902 to the right through the Queyras gorge to Guillestre. But if you do you'll miss two of the most beautiful scenic tours that the Guil valley has to offer. One of them is the Belvédère-du-Cirque-du-Mont-Viso road (Tour 91) to Mont Viso (Monviso in Italian), the other goes up to Sommet Bucher, a wonderful viewpoint for this region. But if you do decide to take the turning to the left to Château-Queyras or Aiguilles

In this picture of the turning on the southern side of the Col d'Izoard you can see in the background the little village of Château-Queyras, the starting point for the Sommet-Bucher.

Château Queyras was built in the 13th and 14th centuries.

you should be aware that both roads, although tarmacked throughout, are in very poor condition in places. If you're not careful enough, particularly on the descent, you can quickly find yourself with a bent rim or a broken spoke.

The starting point is the village of Château-Queyras (0.0km), only 2km after the turning for Aiguilles. Just before the village, whose 13th- to 14th-century castle has already caught the eye, a signpost marked 'Sommet Bucher' points the way. We cross the Guil and although we can't go any further on the only road going east here, we still find another signpost to our goal.

The road climbs at 10 per cent, then the gradient decreases briefly after 3km, only to increase again, not just to 10 per cent but to as much as 14 per cent on short stretches. The climb doesn't offer much in the way of features, but you have to give the road your undivided attention anyway because it's riddled with large potholes. Football goalposts in a little meadow after 7.5km mark a decrease in gradient to 12 per cent. Then after 11km the climb ends by a car park.

The view is elusive. You have to push your bike up an unmade road for 500m before it finally reveals itself. A board gives information about the many peaks, including the 3841m Mont Viso, the highest mountain in the Cottian Alps. Unfortunately, this distant peak is often hidden by a veil of mist.

The range is named after Cottius, the Ligurian king, who was appointed governor of this region in 8BC by the Roman emperor Augustus. The slopes around Mont Viso are also the source of the River Po, the longest river in Italy, which has a journey from here to the Adriatic of 652km. Whereas now we just have to go back down to Château-Queyras.

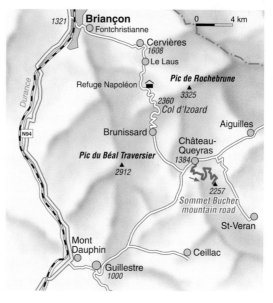

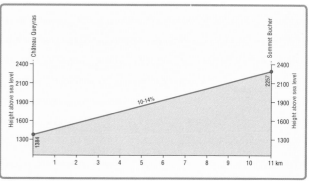

TOUR PROFILE <<

Belvédère-du-Cirque-du-Mont-Viso Road: 2127m

Start: Abriès, 1522m, about 25km east of Guillestre

Directions: Either over the southern side of the Col d'Izoard (Tour 89) down to the turning for Guillestre/Château-Queyras and through Château-Queyras and Aiguilles to Abriès or over the northern side of the Col de Vars (Tour 92) to Guillestre and through Château-Queyras and Aiguilles to Abriès

Level of Difficulty/Maximum gradient: Easy to medium tour with a maximum gradient of 14 per cent over two sections about 1km long in the middle of the climb. But mostly under 8 per cent

Length: 15.0km

Total ascent: 605m

Time: 1¼–2 hrs

Suggested gearing: 39/28

Route: Abriès (0.0km) – Ristolas (3.5km) – L'Echalp (6.5km) – end point in turning area (15.0km)

Road conditions: Well-constructed roads for the first 9km, then considerable surface damage in places

Pass open: 15 May to 31 October

Things to see: Vantage point at the end of the road on the western side of Mont Viso

Map: Euro Cart regional map 1:300,000, RV-Verlag, Sheet 8 Provence/Rhône-Alpes/Côte d'Azur

Notes: The road, which is closed to the public from the 9.0km point, is very badly damaged. You must exercise extreme caution, particularly on the descent

Opposite: The view over the western side of Mont Viso is compensation for the badly damaged state of the Belvédère-du-Cirque-du-Mont-Viso road.

The Belvédère-du-Cirque-du-Mont-Viso road is unfortunately not always in the best of condition.

The Belvédère-du-Cirque-du-Mont-Viso road is the second most worthwhile tour in Queyras, the hinterland of the Guil, after the Sommet Bucher road (Tour 90). It's a level easier than the Sommet Bucher and although it doesn't offer 360° panoramas it does give you impressive views of the western side of the 3841m Mont Viso. This is the highest mountain in the Cottian Alps, whose craggy triangular peak can be clearly seen from just about every high point in the region and at whose foot the River Po, the longest river in Italy, has its source. There is one slight reservation: this road is in a badly damaged state for at least the last 2km. It's not as bad as the road to the Sommet Bucher, however, and can be ridden on narrow tyres if you take care.

If you start your tour in Abriès (0.0km), quite deep in the Guil valley, on a Wednesday morning you can visit the market, where traders from the surrounding areas offer their products for sale. Hard to believe amid all this activity, but this remote little place was badly bombed during the Second World War and what was left was washed away in 1957 when the Guil flooded. A lovely village has grown up here now, but as we ride to Ristolas (3.5km) we look at the river alongside us with rather different eyes. The road presents no problems, offering views of the plate-like slabs of the rock walls of Monte Granero in front of us, upstream of Mont Viso. Until we reach L'Echalp (6.5km) it remains almost level before starting to climb gently up to a large car park (9.0km).

A massive barrier blocks the way to motor traffic from here, but we can pass, and now cross the Guil (9.5km), where the gradient hikes up to 14 per cent. It stays like this for a kilometre, climbing steeply over hairpin bends, where patches of dirt road threaten to overwhelm the tarmac, before decreasing again, first to 8 per cent (11.0km) and then even less. A pleasant, almost flat road takes us between meadows along a long high valley and then steps up into a another valley (14.0km). Here you have to pedal harder again, as the gradient increases once more to 14 per cent over a 1km stretch.

A little turning circle (15.0km) constitutes the end point. You won't be disappointed by the magnificent view it offers over the beautifully shaped Mont Viso, streaked with bands of snow and crevices. Lovely to look at, but tough to conquer: the ascent takes two days and and includes some demanding climbs.

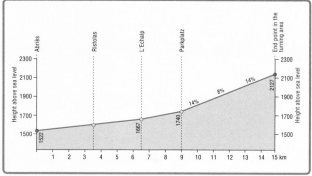

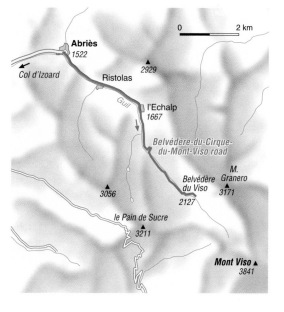

TOUR PROFILE <<

Col de Vars: 2109m

NORTHERN SIDE – Start: Guillestre, 1000m

Directions: either over the Col d'Izoard (Tour 89) to Guillestre or Grenoble – Gap – Embrun – Guillestre

Level of Difficulty/Maximum gradient: Medium, with a maximum gradient of 12 per cent

Length: 20.0km

Total ascent: 1110m

Time: 2–3 hrs

Suggested gearing: 39/26

Route: Guillestre (0.0km) – Saint-Marcellin (10.5km) – Sainte-Marie (12.0km) – Les Claux (14.0km) – Top of the pass (20.0km)

SOUTHERN SIDE – Start: Les Gleizolles, 1307m in the Ubaye valley about 1.5km north-east of Barcelonnette

Directions: Grenoble – Gap – Tallard – Le Lanzet – Barcelonnette – Jausiers – Les Gleizolles or Cuneo – Borgo S. Dalmazzo – Maddalena Pass – Les Gleizolles

Level of Difficulty/Maximum gradient: Easy to medium tour with a maximum gradient of 10 per cent

Length: 15.0km

Total ascent: 805m

Time: 1¼–2 hrs

Suggested gearing: 39/26

Route: Les Gleizolles (0.0km) – St-Paul-sur-Ubaye (5.5km) – Top of the pass (15.0km)

Road conditions: Well-constructed roads apart from slight surface damage at the top

Pass open: All year

Things to see: Small mountain zoo at the top of the pass, Demoiselles Coiffées, earth pyramids halfway up the southern side of the pass

Map: Euro Cart regional map 1:300,000, RV-Verlag, Sheet 8 Provence/Rhône-Alpes/Côte d'Azur

The Col de Vars follows the Col d'Izoard (Tour 89) passing from the Durance valley over the Montagne de Parpaillon into the Ubaye valley. As well as the Maddalena Pass (Tour 93), there's another very special pass there, the Col de Restefond/Col de la Bonette (Tour 94), the highest pass in the Alps open to traffic. The Col de Vars doesn't come anywhere near in terms of height, but still demands a vertical climb of 1100m with gradients of up to 12 per cent, and, like the Col d'Izoard, takes us into a unique landscape.

If you come straight from the Col d'Izoard to start the climb to the Col de Vars you should skirt round the little town of Guillestre in the Durance valley. This is no hardship: the Durance valley, known here as the Embrunoisis, is one of the most densely populated alpine valleys and often choked with traffic. The route along the side of the mountain is usually quieter, except during tourist season and France's annual August holiday shut-down.

The road is wide and in good condition as it winds its way up from the valley floor over numerous bends and hairpins with a gradient of between 8 per cent and 10 per cent. Each bend gives wonderful views back towards the Massif des Écrins over the wide valley floor, until the road disappears into another valley. The gradient goes down a little as you pass grassy meadows and arable farming once you're through the first hairpin bends (6.5km). The road remains in good condition and, with not-too-demanding gradients topping out at 8 per cent alternating with long flat stretches, the ride to Vars-Saint-Marcellin (10.5km) and through to Sainte-Marie-de-Vars (12.0km), another notably unspoiled holiday village, is a pleasant one. On the other side of the village there's even a short descent, before the climb increases to 10 per cent and we reach the significantly more modern ski resort of Les Claux (14.0km) on a road that is getting increasingly narrow.

This last stop before the top of the pass offers an opportunity to top up on food and water supplies, and if it weren't for the 12 per cent gradient through the village you'd have pleasant memories of it. On leaving the village the gradient decreases and as we continue two short 10 per cent climbs alternate with more moderate uphills, flatter sections and even a brief descent. This way we make good progress, even if we're not gaining much height. But there's no reason to rush in this peaceful landscape. You could even take a rest here, as the Refuge Napoléon invites you to do. Set peacefully between wide mountain crests by a little lake, this is one of six mountain shelters in the French Alps that were set up at the Corsican's expense. The road goes on a little further to the top of the pass (20.0km), but at only a moderate gradient. A slight saddle marks the summit which, as well as being the border between the *départments* of Dauphiné and Haute-Provence, is home to a little alpine zoo.

The 15km descent down to Les Gleizolles is more interesting than the climb up, though not for its 10 per cent gradients and six hairpin bends. About halfway down, pyramids rise up at the side of the road, grotesque structures of moraine scree, which are known here as the Demoiselles Coiffées, that is, fairies turned into stone. In Saint-Paul-sur-Ubaye we arrive in the valley of the Ubaye, a crystal-clear torrent, and we follow the course of its light gravel banks. Finally we tackle the Pas de la Reysolle, a narrow valley in which dark slate curves above us, before reaching the end of the pass at Les Gleizolles (35.0km).

Opposite: This part of the route in the Ubaye valley, known as the Pas de la Reysolle, doesn't really inspire confidence.

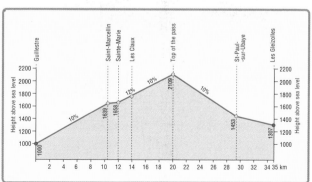

TOUR PROFILE <<

Maddalena Pass: 1996m

WESTERN SIDE – Start: Junction of the D902 and D900 just outside Les Gleizolles, 1307m

Directions: Grenoble – Gap – Tallard – Le Lauzet – Barcelonnette – Jausiers – Les Gleizolles

Level of Difficulty/Maximum gradient: Easy, with a maximum gradient of 12 per cent on a short section in Meyronnes

Length: 16.5km

Total ascent: 690m

Time: 1¼–2 hrs

Suggested gearing: 39/26

Route: Junction just outside Les Gleizolles (0.0km) – Meyronnes (6.0km) – Larche (11.0km) – Top of the pass (16.5km)

EASTERN SIDE – Start: Vinádio, 904m

Directions: A6 Turin–Savona, exit Fossano – Cuneo – Borgo San Dalmazzo – Vinádio

Level of Difficulty/Maximum gradient: Medium, with a maximum gradient of 8 per cent

Length: 33.0km

Total ascent: 1095m

Time: 1¾–2½ hrs

Suggested gearing: 39/23

Route: Vinádio (0.0km) – Pietropórzio (15.0km) – Argentera (27.0km) – Top of the pass (33.0km)

Road conditions: Well-constructed roads

Pass open: All year

Map: Euro Cart regional map 1:300,000, RV-Verlag, Sheet 8 Provence/Rhône-Alpes/Côte d'Azur

Notes: Lights are advisable on the eastern side because of the three tunnels, 100-400m long and unlit in places, and the three gallery tunnels, 100-150m long

To reach the Italian region of Piedmont from the Ubaye valley, which, from the north usually means riding over the Col de Vars (Tour 92), take the Maddalena Pass, a connecting road without too much traffic which is in good condition and passable throughout the year. A navigation tip: it's called the Colle della Maddalena in Italian and the Col de la Madeleine or Col de l'Argentière in French.

Just to confuse things, if we start the climb on the French side at the junction of the D902 and D900 just outside Les Gleizolles (0.0km) we have to follow signposts for Col de Larche. The road goes up at a constant 8 per cent gradient to Meyronnes (6.0km), where it increases briefly to 12 per cent. The hardest part of the climb is now behind us and on the rest of the route through Certamussat and Larche (11.0km), the main village in the valley, the gradient never exceeds 8 per cent and is often less than that. We

soon reach the top of the pass (16.5km), which not only forms the border between France and Italy but also between the Maritime Alps and the Cottian Alps, named after Cottius, the Roman prefect of Liguria.

The eastern side now slopes slowly down to the Stura valley on a fairly straight road with a downhill gradient that's also fairly level, topping out at 8 per cent but generally lower than that, requiring you to employ the big chainring. The most scenic part of the route lies between the Ponte delle Barricate and the small village of Pontebernardo, where the river and the road are squeezed between vertical rock walls over 300m high with characteristic wave-form banding. These narrows are known quite logically as 'barricate', 'barricades'. These are the last obstacles before the end point of the eastern pass in Vinádio, 33km away from the top. From here it's another 40km to Cuneo. If you want to take on another pass, the climb from Vinádio to the Lombard Pass (Tour 50) is a beautiful, but demanding, option.

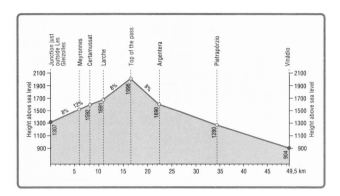

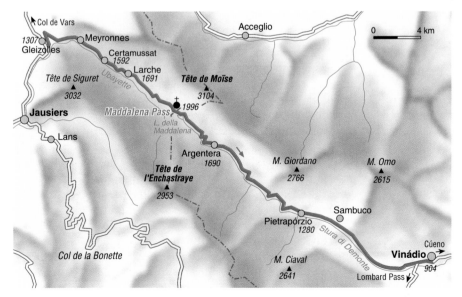

The western ascent of the Maddalena Pass is laid out in long loops.

Opposite: Characteristic wave-like banding of the rocks in the Ponte delle Barricate on the eastern side of the Maddalena Pass.

TOUR PROFILE <<

Col de Restefond/Col de la Bonette:
2802m

Level of Difficulty/Maximum gradient:
Difficult, with a maximum gradient of
14 per cent over 1km from the top of
the Col de Restefond to the top of the
Col de la Bonette. Long stretches of up
to 12 per cent

NORTHERN SIDE – Start: Jausiers, 1220m

Directions: Over the Col de Vars (Tour
92) or the Maddalena Pass (Tour 93) to
Jausiers or Grenoble – Gap – Tallard –
Le Lauzet – Barcelonnette – Jausiers

Length: 23.5km

Total ascent: 1585m

Time: 2¾–4 hrs

Suggested gearing: 39/28

Route: Jausiers (0.0km) – Lans (3.5km) –
Chalet Halte 2000 (10.5km) – Restefond
barracks (19.0km) – Col de Restefond
(22.5km) – Col de la Bonette (23.5km)

SOUTHERN SIDE – Start: St-Etienne-
de-Tinée, 1144m

Directions: Nice – Plan-du-Var
– St-Sauveur-sur-Tinée – Isola –
St-Etienne-de-Tinée

Length: 26.5km

Total ascent: 1660m

Time: 3–4 hrs

Suggested gearing: 39/28

Route: St-Etienne-de-Tinée (0.0km)
– St-Dalmaas-de-Tende (5.0km) –
Bousiéyas (13.0km) – Col de Restefond
(25.5km) – Col de la Bonette (26.5km)

Road conditions: Well-constructed
roads on the first 7km on the northern
side, then numerous bends with surface
damage

Pass open: 15 June to 30 September

Things to see: Ruins of the Restefond
barracks on the northern side. Short
detour (15 minutes) from the top of
the Col de la Bonette to the Cime de la
Bonette and its panorama board

Map: Euro Cart regional map 1:300,000,
RV-Verlag, Sheet 8 Provence/Rhône-
Alpes/Côte d'Azur

*Just a few more metres, and you've conquered the
highest Alpine pass from its northern side.*

The highest pass road in the Alps, the 2802m Col de Restefond/Col
de la Bonette lies almost at the end of the Alps, barely 100km from
Nice and the Côte d'Azur. Both sides of the climb, starting from
Jausiers in the north-west in the Ubaye valley and from St-Etienne-
de-Tinée in the south-east in the eponymous Tinée valley, are
about the same length, with almost the same vertical climb, and
both classed as difficult.

If you follow the sign for the 'Col de la Bonette – Plus Haut Col
d'Europe' in Jausiers (0.0km), you'll note that it gives the height as
2804m, but it's officially 2802m, as marked on a board by a boulder
at the top of the pass. Either way, it's a long way up and two metres
more or less isn't going to make much difference.

A wide road in good condition leads out of the town at a
moderate gradient. It crosses the Ubaye (1.0km), after which the
gradient increases to 10 per cent over hairpin bends. Past chalets
with little gardens dotted among the meadows we reach Lans
(3.5km), the last village before the top of the pass.

Numerous bends now climb at between 8 per cent and 10 per
cent until after about 6.5km the road narrows and, unfortunately,
the surface deteriorates. A rock wall, over which a waterfall tumbles,
looms in front of us. We wind our way around it over hairpin bends
with gradients of up to 12 per cent along the eastern side of the

valley. The valley becomes a little wider again and we reach the Chalet Halte 2000, a solitary stone building almost hidden by an embankment next to the road and the highest property to be inhabited at least some of the time.

Here you can refresh yourself with produce from the alpine meadows before going further up over hairpin bends with a gradient of 10 per cent. After about a kilometre there's a surprise in the form of a short descent: take advantage of the momentum for the next 12 per cent stretch of hairpin bends. This takes us into a barren landscape of heaps of brown rubble and boulders through which trickles of water run here and there, with no indication that we're approaching the highest alpine pass.

The course of the road, constantly alternating between shallow depressions and deeper valleys, passing a small lake (15.5km), going over steep scarps and across slopes with gradients of between 8 per cent and 12 per cent, never gets boring. Suddenly a group of stone buildings appears in front of us, the long-since ruined remains of former military quarters from the 19th century, when Napoleon III built this road for tactical reasons and named it 'Route Impériale'.

Imperial indeed, the road loops upwards at a gradient of 8 per cent along the slopes of the Restefond to the 2678m summit of the Col de Restefond (22.5km). But our climb doesn't end here. A sign indicates a road to the right that loops the Cime de la Bonette summit. Naturally we aren't going to miss out on this one, and so, after another kilometre of hard going with a gradient of 14 per cent all the way, we stand at the highest pass crossing in the Alps that's open to traffic. As well as a rock needle that looks like a menhir and a board noting the altitude, 2802m, you'll sometimes find a small

kiosk selling sausages, sweets and sugary drinks, and you'll have a panoramic, but not too intoxicating view over the mountains of the Mercantour National Park. You can get a better view if you walk 60m further up to the viewpoint at the top of the Cime de la Bonette.

If your shoes aren't suitable you should move straight on to the descent. This takes you down to the Col de Restefond on a 14 per cent gradient and from there down 27km and 14 hairpin bends to St-Etienne-de-Tinée.

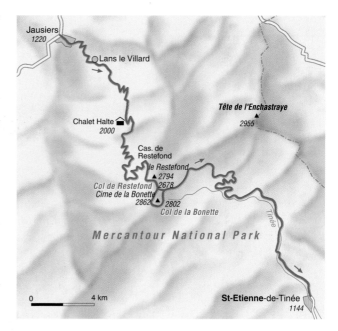

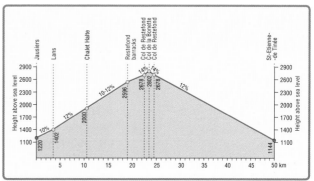

95 COL D'ALLOS
Provence

The route on the northern side of the Col d'Allos is very narrow in some places.

If you've worked your way south through the French Alps and arrived in the Ubaye valley you can take the Col de Restefond/Col de la Bonette (Tour 94) down towards the sea. Just as you'd expect from the Alps' highest pass, it's a very difficult route. If you'd prefer something a little less strenuous, the road over the Col d'Allos is an attractive alternative.

Our starting point is the little town of Barcelonnette in the Ubaye valley, situated just 8km or so from Jausiers down the valley, at the start of the Restefond. It's the most northerly town in Provence and was originally called Barcelone in honour of Count Raymond Bérenguer V who was descended from the Counts of Barcelona, and founded the town in 1231. The old town centre was built by emigrants returning home after making their fortunes in Mexico from the cloth trade. An exhibition in a little museum tells us about the living conditions of the emigrants during their time in Mexico.

We leave Barcelonnette (0.0km) on the D902, cross the Ubaye and then follow signposts to Col de la Cayolle and Col d'Allos. After 2.5km on the flat we reach the fork in the road to the two passes, and while the D902 branches off over the bridge over the Bachelard,

we follow the D908 over the rather more scenic route in the direction of the Col d'Allos.

Past the turning to Pra Loup, a little winter sports resort at an altitude of 1630m, our road now climbs at a gradient of 10 per cent. The gradient decreases after 5km and you should make good progress through the conifer forests along the western side of the valley. After 6.5km you cross the Pont de Fau and soon after that come to the first signs for 'Garage'. This is the French word for a car or lorry workshop, but there's no such thing to be seen. 'Garage' here means a passing place cut out of the rock on narrow roads. They're not something we should need to use: the road is easily wide enough for both cyclists and cars, though drivers don't necessarily realise this and sometimes overtake without leaving a safe margin. This isn't too much of a cause for concern because fortunately, except during the busy August holiday period, the pass isn't particularly busy.

After 9km the road turns sharply to the west and we ride around the Gorges de la Malune, down the slopes of the Tête de la Sestrière, in a wide loop with an 8 per cent gradient and reach Les Agneliers (12.5km). In a barren mountain landscape, where high meadows are dotted with isolated groups of pines or larches, the gradient increases again to 10 per cent. If you look to the east, you can make out the peak of the Cime de la Bonette. Congratulating ourselves on avoiding that climb, we tackle gradients of between 8 per cent and 10 per cent to the refuge (20.5km) much more easily. We have just one more hairpin bend in front of us to take us up to the top of the pass (21.0km) via a gap between the Cheval de Bois and the Tête de Vascal.

Now the road, very narrow at first then widening out lower down, descends over

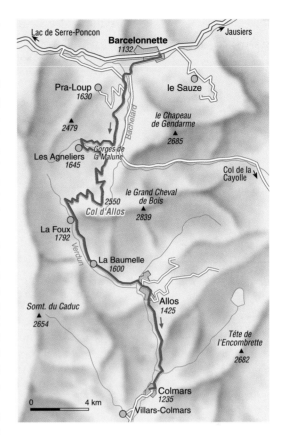

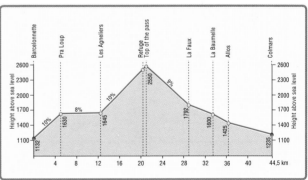

14 hairpin bends with a gradient of 9 per cent into the Verdon valley to Colmars (44.5km), a little town that's worth seeing, with a notable fort. If you follow the River Verdon you can do a circuit of the Verdon gorge (Tour 99), one of the most beautiful tours in the Alps.

96 COL DE TENDE
Provence/Piedmont

TOUR PROFILE <<

Col de Tende: 1908m

SOUTHERN SIDE – Start: Car park on the highest hairpin bend about 200m from the southern tunnel entrance and the former French customs post on the new Col de Tende pass road, 1275m

Directions: A10 then A8 Genoa–Nice, exit Ventimiglia – Breil-sur-Roya – Tende – Car park in front of the southern tunnel entrance

Level of Difficulty/Maximum gradient: Easy to medium tour with a maximum gradient of 12 per cent on a short section. Otherwise a 9-10 per cent gradient almost the whole way

Length: 8.0km

Total ascent: 635m

Time: 1¼–2 hrs

Suggested gearing: 39/26

Route: Car park (0.0km) – First house (2.5km) – Ruined house (4.5km) – Top of the pass (8.0km)

NORTHERN SIDE – Start: Al Connone d'Oro di Bragard, 1250m near Limone Piemonte, about 19km south of Borgo San Dalmazzo

Directions: A6 Turin–Savona, exit Fossano – Cuneo – Borgo San Dalmazzo – Limone Piemonte – Al Connone d'Oro di Bragard

Level of Difficulty/Maximum gradient: Easy to medium tour with a maximum gradient of 10 per cent

Length: 9.0km

Total ascent: 660m

Time: 1¼–2 hrs

Suggested gearing: 39/26

Route: Al Connone d'Oro di Bragard (0.0km) – Top of the pass (9.0km)

Road conditions: The southern side is a hard dirt road that's easy to ride if you're careful. The northern side is tarmacked, but with surface damage

Pass open: 15 May to 31 October

Map: Euro Cart regional map 1:300,000, RV-Verlag, Sheet 8 Provence/Rhône-Alpes/Côte d'Azur

First the bad news: the Col de Tende road is unfortunately unmade, at least on its southern side, which is the one we're concerned with here. Now the good news: you can easily ride it on narrow tyres, with no need to worry about bent rims or broken spokes. You'll have to adapt your riding style of course, both on the ascent and the descent. Why is this good news? There are two reasons. The first is that the fastest route from the Côte d'Azur, from San Remo, Menton, Monaco or even Nice, to the Turin area is the Col de Tende. It does have a tunnel 3.2km long at the top, which while not prohibited for cyclists is fortunately complemented by the old pass road, which bypasses the tunnel. The second reason: this pass offers a special experience, unique in the Alps.

The old pass road is only 8km long on the southern, that is the French, side and with a vertical climb of only 650m to deal with is classed as easy. However, it boasts one feature that sets it apart from other passes: it has a total of 48 linked hairpin bends that represent a masterly achievement of road building, the like of which is not to be found anywhere else. The closest you get to it is perhaps the old road through the Tremola valley to the St Gotthard Pass (Tour 64), though this is tarmacked.

The old Col de Tende pass road is open to traffic, though there is a ban on vehicles over 3.5 tonnes and a speed restriction of 20km an hour. Unlikely to be a problem for us: bikes don't officially count as vehicles for the purposes of road traffic regulations; even if they did, they'd be unlikely to exceed even the 10 kilogram mark; and the chances of reaching 20km an hour going uphill are slim.

If you want to put the theory to the test, start off at the car park (0.0km) on the upper hairpin bends about 200m from the southern tunnel entrance and the former French customs post on the new Col de Tende pass. There we take a road that climbs at a gradient of 9 per cent, leading us up over a series of hairpin bends following seamlessly one after another. The foundation of the road is solid, only washed away a little in the hairpins, and the maximum

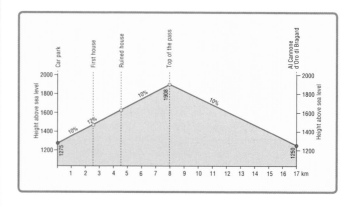

gradient is 10 per cent. After about 2.5km of hairpin bends following each other in swift succession we reach a large house and here you may have to switch to the large sprocket because the gradient increases to 12 per cent. On these few steeper metres of the climb the road is tarmacked, but the gradient quickly goes back down to 10 per cent and the surface is once more dirt.

The immediate surroundings are not very exciting. The road climbs up over predominantly scree-strewn slopes with sparse clumps of grass and the odd tree here and there on slightly more widely spaced hairpin bends. Then there's another house at the side of the road (4.5km), which appears uninhabited and quite dilapidated.

Although we can already make out the old fort high above us at the top of the pass, the view behind us over the hairpin bends stretched out one after the other is much more interesting. You should definitely stop and take a photo of this unique serpentine route.

Now there are just a few bends set wider apart taking us up to the top of the pass (8.0km) on a constant gradient of 10 per cent. The view is unfortunately quite restricted, but we're on tarmac again here. This brings us to the old Fort Central situated a little further up and then a little more comfortably, apart from a few minor potholes, down the 9km to Al Connone d'Oro di Bragard (17.0km), where we meet up again with the traffic coming through the tunnel.

Even though the Col de Tende road is unmade on the southern side you shouldn't miss out on this hairpin bend dream.

Just where the foothills of the French Maritime Alps appear to plummet into the Mediterranean there is another interesting pass: the Col de Turini. Interesting not just for motorsport fans who know it as part of the Monte Carlo Rally, even if only from television broadcasts, but interesting too for sports cyclists. And you really need to be a sports cyclist, even though the pass is only 1607m high. The route starts in Menton barely metres above sea level and en route you drop 350m on the descent from the Col de Castillon to Sospel, so the total vertical climb is 1950m and thus equals the Stelvio Pass (Tour 40) or the Großglockner High Mountain Road (Tour 9).

Southern side

In Menton (0.0km) we follow the signposts for Sospeland and ride under the autoroute into a valley overgrown with lush vegetation. Inclines of up to 10 per cent bring us to Monti (3.5km), then the gradient decreases to 8 per cent and we cross beneath the Caramel Viaduct (9.0km), a relic from Roman times. Slopes of between 6 per cent and 8 per cent take us past the village of Castillon (11.0km) to a 40m unlit tunnel through the rock that forms the top of the Col de Castillon (13.5km). Now we cruise down a wide, well-built road to the picturesque little town of Sospel (20.5km), where signposts for Moulinet/Col de Turini direct us to the floor of the Bévera valley. The road climbs on a moderate gradient for the first kilometre then after a short descent the rock walls crowd in as the road takes us up over countless bends at 8 per cent to Moulinet (26.0km). You go through a short tunnel through the rock (29.0km), at a gradient of mainly between 6 per cent and 8 per cent, only rising now and then to 10 per cent. The sign '8 Lacet' indicates the last group of hairpin bends that leads up to the top of the pass (38.5km) at 10 per cent. The junction of the descent on the northwestern side acts as the end point just outside Roquebillière in the Vésubie valley, which you can ride through for 50km to Nice if you'd rather not go back over the western side of the pass.

Northern side

Our starting point, the junction of the D70 and the D2565, lies out of the way in the Vésubie valley, just outside the small town of Roquebillière (0.0km). We can't miss the signposts for La Bollène/Turini and so find ourselves on the D2565, which climbs over several hairpin bends with a gradient of 10 per cent for the first kilometre. The more numerals a D-road has in France, the less important it is for traffic, which suits us down to the ground. We get to La Bollène-Vésubie (2.5km), the first and only village on this side of the pass, on a gradient decreasing to 6 per cent. Past the village the climb increases again to 10 per cent and maintains this more or less throughout the route to the top of the pass. A short tunnel through the rock (5.0km) means that we're exactly a third of the way through. The road isn't all that wide, but it's in good condition. To the left rocks jut out, and massive stone escarpments can be seen on the valley slopes. It's easy to imagine the fast cars on the Monte Carlo Rally precision-drifting around the corners past the stone walls and revving their engines through the group of hairpin bends which begins after 6.5km. We take things rather more slowly as a little bridge (8.5km) gives us a view of the slope and the bends we've taken lying below us. Hairpin after hairpin, bend after bend, the road climbs at a constant rate of 10 per cent. The valley narrows, the rocks retreat, the woods swallow us up and the gradient comes to a sudden halt in front of the hotel at the top of the pass (15.0km). Allow yourself a quiet coffee, remembering that a total vertical climb of almost 360m up to the Col de Castillon awaits on the next stage down to Menton.

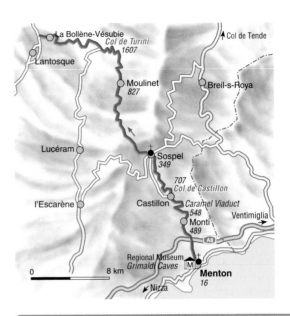

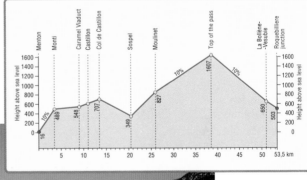

The port of Menton on the Mediterranean Sea is the starting point for the difficult climb to the Col de Turini.

237

TOUR PROFILE <<

Nice, Braus and Brouis Passes: 1002m

Start: La Trinité suburb of Nice, 19m, end point La Giandola, 308m

Directions: A10 Genoa–Nice, exit Nice-East

Level of Difficulty/Maximum gradient: Difficult, with a maximum gradient of 15 per cent on one 700m section and a shorter section on the Braus Pass

Length: 55.0km

Total ascent: 1570m

Time: 3¼–4½ hrs

Suggested gearing: 39/28

Route: La Trinité suburb of Nice (0.0km) – Drap (6.5km) – La Pointe (10.0km) – Nice Pass (17.0) – L'Escarène (17.5km) – Touët-de-l'Escarène (20.0km) – Braus Pass (28.5km) – Sospel (39.5km) – Brouis Pass (52.5km) – La Giandola (55.0km)

Road conditions: Well-constructed roads. Caution is necessary on the descent from the Braus Pass to Sospel because of the hairpin bends

Pass open: All year

Things to see: Nice: old town, local history museum in the Lascaris Palace, fish market in the Place St François, Promenade des Anglais

Map: Euro Cart regional map 1:300,000, RV-Verlag, Sheet 8 Provence/Rhône-Alpes/Côte d'Azur

Notes: It's a total of around 60km from the end point in La Giandola down the Roya valley to Ventimiglia and through Menton, Monte Carlo and Eze along the coast road back to Nice

As well as the climb to the Col de Turini (Tour 97) the area inland of the Côte d'Azur offers further possibilities to collect kilometres and vertical climbs. One of them is the Nice, Braus and Brouis pass road, which takes you from Nice over the three passes mentioned into the Roya valley, which stretches from the coast at Ventimiglia up to the Col de Tende (Tour 96). Even though the highest pass, the Braus Pass, exceeds the 1000m mark by just 2m, there's a vertical climb of a good 1550m in total on the tour, and a maximum gradient of 15 per cent. You can shorten the tour at L'Escarène at the start of the Braus Pass and in Sospel at the foot of the Brouis Pass, and return to the Côte d'Azur, so the tour will be of interest if you're riding here in spring and don't yet have enough training kilometres under your belt. If you don't have a support vehicle, remember to take into account that it's a good 60km from the end point through the Roya valley to the coast road back to Nice.

To reach the starting point in Nice-East, follow signposts for the autoroute to Genoa, passing the road to Drap and Sospel. Set off on the bike from the suburb of La Trinité (0.0km), through which you'll be constantly accompanied by industrial estates until you reach Drap (6.5km). Here follow the signposts for L'Escarène/Sospel. The road becomes quieter and you ride into a wooded valley as the gradient increases to 5 per cent. Pass through the little town of La Pointe (10.0km) and keep going to the next junction (12.5km) on the road signposted to Col de Nice or alternatively to L'Escarène. At the edge of a little gorge a well-made road takes us up a gradient of 9 per cent, we have to tackle four hairpin bends and then we've done the Nice Pass (17.0km), the first pass of the day. At a height of 402m the pass doesn't present too much of a challenge and the descent that follows it to L'Escarène (17.5km), 50m lower down, is

The stretch of hairpin bends on the Brouis Pass is very impressive.

very short. With the Braus Pass, which comes next, things get a little more serious. The initial 7 per cent may be negligible, but it soon increases to 10 per cent up to Touët-de-l'Escarène(20.0km). Then things get really tough: the 15 per cent gradient you hit here is a real challenge on a bike, particularly since it's maintained for 700m. Finally you ride up the second group of hairpin bends, 15 in all, with a gradient of between 8 per cent and 10 per cent, with a significantly increased pulse rate. Once again a gradient of 15 per cent gets you out of the saddle with your heart racing, but then you reach the top of the pass (28.5km), marked by another ruined house.

Now you bowl along down several tight hairpin bends to Sospel (39.5km) in the Bévera valley. If you're considering shortening the tour here bear in mind that the alternative in the deep valley to the south takes you over the Col de Castillon (Tour 97), where you'll face a vertical climb of almost 360m over a 7km stretch. The route further on to the Brouis Pass isn't much more difficult. Follow the signposts to Breil-sur-Roya on a road that climbs gently at first. Leave the floor of

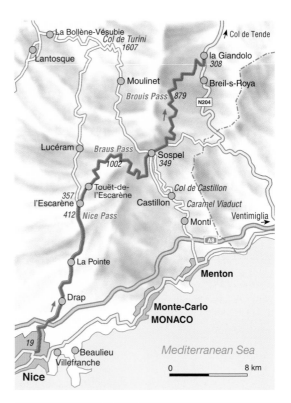

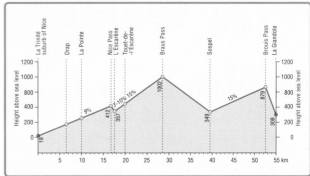

the valley over 11 hairpin bends with a gradient of 6 per cent, increasing a kilometre further on to 8 per cent. Take four more hairpins at 6 per cent, and then you're at the top of the pass (52.5km). Then go to the end of the pass road in La Giandola (55.0km) at the entrance to the Roya valley down a gradient of up to 12 per cent.

239

TOUR PROFILE <<

Verdon Gorge Circuit: 1406m

Start/finish: Comps-sur-Artuby, 895m

Directions: From Nice on the Route Napoléon through Grasse to Le Logis-du-Pin and turning to Comps-sur-Artuby

Level of Difficulty/Maximum gradient: Difficult, with a maximum gradient of 14 per cent on short sections of the circular crest road on the climb to Collet Barris

Length: 122.0km

Total ascent: 1500m

Time: 6½–9 hrs

Suggested gearing: 39/28

Route: Comps-sur-Artuby (0.0km) – Balcons de la Mescla (13.5km) – Pont de l'Artuby (16.0km) – Fayette tunnel (20.0km) – Auberge des Cavaliers (23.0km) – Falaise de Baucher (26.5km) – Cirque de Vaumale (32.5km) – Col de l'Iloire (35.5km) – Aiguines (38.0km) – Galetas Bridge (46.5km) – 'Gorges du Verdon' junction (51.0km) – Col d'Ayen (66.0km) – La Palud-sur-Verdon (68.5km) – turning for the circular crest road (70.0km) – Collet Barris (78.5km) – La Palud-sur-Verdon (92.5km) – Point-Sublime restaurant (100.0km) – Pont-de-Soleis (106.0km) – Jabron (117.0km) - Comps-sur-Artuby (122.0km)

Road conditions: Roads narrow in places with rough tarmac

Pass open: All year, with the exception of the circular crest road, which is open from 1 April to 15 November

Things to see: Vantage points on the route, in particular at the Balcons de la Mescla Restaurant, Pont de l'Artuby, Fayette tunnels, Col d'Ayen and on the circular crest ring-road) Lac de Ste-Croix (pedalo ride in the Verdon Gorge); Moustiers-Ste-Marie (little Provençal town, chapel of Notre-Dame-de-Beauvoir)

Map: Euro Cart regional map 1:300,000, RV-Verlag, Sheet 8 Provence/Rhône-Alpes/Côte d'Azur

Some readers might be wondering what a gorge is doing in a guide to mountain passes, even if it is the biggest and most impressive gorge not just in France, but in the whole of Europe. Once they've ridden the route and have 122km and a total vertical climb of close to 1500m under their belt, they'll know. The circuit includes several passes, including the Col d'Ayen and the Collet Barris, with climbs from about 500m above sea level to a good 1400m, and gradients of up to 14 per cent, which makes it the equal of any mountain pass proper.

If you're coming from Grasse on the Route Napoléon turn off after about 60km at Castellane onto the D952 for Pont-de-Soleis and then carry on along the D955 to Comps-sur-Artuby (0.0km), the starting point. Follow the signposts for 'Rive gauche' and ride on coarse tarmac on a well-maintained road between thick undergrowth. After about 2.5km the moderate incline becomes a gentle descent with long flatter sections, and after 10km you can get up speed on a downhill slope of up to 8 per cent into Balcons de la Mescla (13.5km). The valley suddenly opens up in front of us. Limestone walls plunge 250m straight down into the depths of the Verdon river as it rounds a bend, foaming as it joins the waters of the rivers flowing in from the south.

A short climb, then you ride down again to the 110m Pont de l'Artuby (16.0km). Over the reinforced concrete bridge the road climbs at 10 per cent and maintains this gradient, apart from a 500m descent, until it reaches the two short Fayette tunnels (20.0km). A good 300m below us the Verdon winds sluggishly through the narrowest part of the gorge that it's worn away over 50 million years. This is probably the most beautiful view down into the depths on the southern side of the circuit. However, there are fascinating views of it again and again further down its course, such as the one by the Auberge des Cavaliers (23.0km), whose restaurant terrace ends precipitously almost 300m above the river. From here, gentle uphills alternate with equally gentle descents as far as

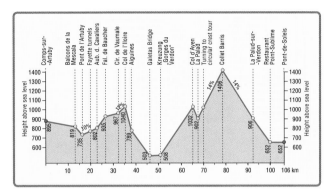

Falaise de Baucher (26.5km). After this the road climbs gradients of up to 12 per cent close to the edge of the gorge up to the highest point on the southern side just outside Cirque de Vaumale (32.5km), at 800m. There are numerous bends on the descent. We leave the gorge at Col de l'Iloire and cruise past the red-tiled roofs of Aiguines (38.0km) and its 17th-century castle to a crossroads (44.5km).

Follow the signposts for Moustiers-Ste-Marie and cross the Galetas Bridge (46.5km). Here you could hire a pedalo and take a trip a few hundred metres into the gorge, until it narrows and the water starts to run much more wildly. Back on

Opposite: Limestone cliffs dominate the surroundings of the Verdon Gorge, the biggest gorge in Europe.

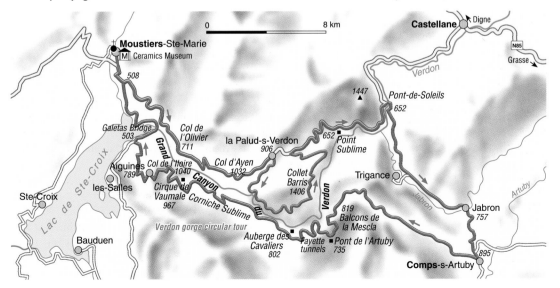

The road along the Verdon Gorge has had to be blasted through the rock in some places.

Opposite: View from high above the gleaming green waters of the Verdon, which gives this gorge its name.

the road, long gentle climbs and descents bring you to a junction (51.0km). Where you can either follow the signposts for Gorges du Verdon to begin the return over the other side of the gorge or make a short detour to the little Provençal town of Moustiers-Ste-Marie, which is well worth seeing.

Then you quickly gain height on a gradient of 8 per cent, which decreases again after 3km (54.0km) only to go back up to 8 per cent after about 60km. You go down again past viewpoints, hidden 200m into the lavender bushes next to the road, at Mayreste (62km) and Col d'Ayen (66.0km), to La-Palud-sur-Verdon (68.5km). If you don't set off immediately on the return journey following the signposts to Castellane, but instead take the turning to the right not long after La-Palud-sur-Verdon and follow the one-way Route des Crêtes, you have a 23km long circular tour ahead. This has been blasted through the rock to some dizzyingly high locations and lots of

viewpoints. The most spectacular is probably the Belvédère des Trescaires where climbers can abseil down and work their way back up again on mirror-smooth rock walls. On the circular tour we have to cope with gradients of up to 14 per cent as far as Collet Barris (78.5km), with the highest at 1406m; it's pretty strenuous.

Back in La Palud (92.5km) the difficulties lie behind us. The road descends for 5km, then climbs again at 6 per cent to the Point-Sublime restaurant (100.0km). You roll along through a short tunnel in the Carjuan gorge (104.0km) down to the level of the Verdon and past the Roman Tusset Bridge, which is more than 2000 years old, to the crossroads at Pont-de-Soleis (106.0km). You should already be familiar from the drive from Castellane with the gently rolling slopes in the meadow valley of the Jabron to the village of the same name (117.0km), and the 3km climb at a gradient of 8-10 per cent before the final descent back into Comps-sur-Artuby (122.0km).

100 MONT VENTOUX
Provence

The poles at the side of the road mark the course of the road after snow has fallen.

It isn't the difficulty of the Ventoux route that lures cyclists deep into Provence to experience this isolated mountain. A vertical climb of 1640m and gradients of up to 12 per cent only barely add up to a rating of difficult and nothing marks the scenery out as particularly impressive. But if you want to conquer a legend rather than a pass, then a trip here is essential. Ventoux embodies the legend of cycling like no other climb. On 13 July 1967 the British professional cyclist Tom Simpson lost his life during the 13th stage of the Tour de France, slipping from his bike less than 2km from the summit. Exhausted, dehydrated and exposed to temperatures of up to 54°C, he had suffered heart failure. His post-mortem also revealed traces of alcohol and amphetamine in his blood. The tragedy sent shockwaves of grief and controversy through the world. The Tour looked for a different route, but with the ever-increasing interest in cycle sport, organisers were loth to dispense with a mountain that epitomised like no other the suffering to which professionals on the Tour de France were exposed.

How much suffering amateur riders will experience depends on their fitness and speed, but the weather will also play its part. The name of the mountain derives from 'vent', the French for wind, and when the Mistral in particular begins to blow things quickly start to get uncomfortable. I've always been lucky with the weather but the pictures from the television broadcast of the Tour de France show that this isn't always the case. In July 2000, for example, patchy fog drifted over the mountain and completely enveloped the spectators standing at the side of the road. At the summit the temperature was only just above freezing, and at that time it was definitely not a good place to be, even though weather conditions like those have to be considered as part and parcel of cycling in the Alps.

Of course it'll be much nicer if the sun's shining when we leave Malaucène (0.0km) on a road climbing at 6 per cent. As you leave

This cyclist is training on a mountain road near Bard at the foot of Mont Ventoux.

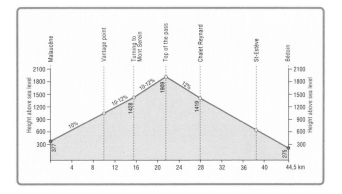

the town the gradient decreases briefly, but then increases to between 8 per cent and 11 per cent after the source of the Grozau. The road is wide and well made and maintains that steep gradient as it goes up into densely wooded terrain. These woods don't give much shade, but the gradient does decrease after 5km, first to 6 per cent and then to even lower. After a short flat stretch the climb gets steeper again, but at least the 10 per cent uphills alternate with long flat sections at first.

After 10km a little viewing platform just below the road offers a good opportunity for a rest; then things become more difficult. The signs here may indicate a maximum gradient of only 10 per cent, but if you're riding a bike it's classed as 12 per cent and lasts for 4km. Past the turning for the little holiday resort of Mont Serein (15.5km, the gradient finally decreases and a sign indicates that the top of the pass is only 6km away. The road becomes noticeably narrower, and the woods denser, as the gradient increases to 12 per cent for 1km.

The summit slope lies in front of us; we approach over tight hairpin bends with a gradient of between 8 per cent and 10 per cent. A little ski tow hints at winter sports, above us the transmitting mast and the buildings of the observatory at the summit can be seen, then the wood peters out. Greyish-white limestone blocks, the work of constant climate change and heavy rainfall, accompany us now, while at the edge of the road on the valley side yellow and black marker poles show the course of the road in snowdrifts. There are now just two more hairpins left, with a gradient of 8 per cent to 10 per cent, before the top of the pass (21.5km), which we reach soon after. We can admire the panoramic view, which on clear days is said to stretch as far as the Pyrenees 300km away, and dream of passes such as the Aubisque, the Tourmalet and the Peyresourde, which may be our destination some other day.

If you relish a challenge, you could ride down over the eastern side to Bédoin and from there take on Ventoux again from the other direction. As you push up, take a moment to contemplate the Spaniard Iban Mayo's achievement of completing the 21.6km climb to the summit in the record time of 55.51 minutes during a mountain time trial in the Dauphiné Libéré stage race in 2004.

Opposite: Amateur cyclists can also measure their strength in various cycling events on Mont Ventoux.

It's not difficult to guess that this is Mont Ventoux during the Tour de France.

CIRCULAR TOURS IN THE ALPS

If the 100 alpine passes described have whetted your appetite you might like to spend some time doing a longer, more challenging circular tour. The following four routes in Austria, Italy, Switzerland and France should serve as a taster.

THROUGH THE LECHTAL ALPS

North Tyrol, Austria

TOUR PROFILE <<

Start: Reutte, 854m

Directions: A96 Munich–Memmingen, exit Buchloe West – Markt Oberdorf – Füssen – Reutte or Munich–Starnberg – Weilheim – Peißenberg – Peiting – Steingaden – Trauchgau – Füssen – Reutte

Level of Difficulty/Maximum gradient: Because the gradients on the west side of the Hahntennjoch reach 18 per cent and 15 per cent on longer sections, this route is classified as medium to difficult.

Length: 104.5km

Total ascent: 1430m

Time: Day tour. Riding time (no stops included) is between about 4½ and 6 hours.

Suggested gearing: 39/28

Route/Directions: Reutte (0.0km) – Weißenbach (8.0km) – Johannisbrücke (12.0km) – Stanzach (18.5km) – Elmen (24.0km) – Bschlabs (31.5km) – Pfafflar (37.5km) – Hahntennjoch (41.0km) – Imst (51.0km) – Nassereith (65.0km) – Fernstein Castle (70.5km) – Fern Pass (75.5km) – Turning for the Weißensee (80.0km) – Lermoos (84.5km) – Heiterwang (93.5km) – Reutte (104.5km)

Road conditions: Road narrow and single lane in places on the climb to the Hahntennjoch (with occasional passing places). Many blind bends and cattle grids (take great care on the descent and in wet weather)

Pass open: Hahntennjoch open 1 June to 30 October

Things to see: Reutte: ruins of Ehrenberg castle, local history museum, merchants' houses in town centre; Pfafflar: 13th-century alpine cottages; Imst: Old noblemen's houses dating from the 18th century, parish church of St Lawrence

Map: Euro Cart regional map 1:300,000, RV-Verlag, Austria sheet

Over the Hahntennjoch and the Fern Pass

Austria has some of the Alps' most breathtaking and challenging mountain passes. But for our first circular tour, rather than linking big-hitting climbs such as the Großglockner High Alpine Road, we'll start with something a bit smaller. Instead of the High Taurus we've chosen the Lechtal Alps in the Tyrol. If you're not familiar with the name, they stretch some 60km from the Flexen Pass and the Lech valley in the west to the Fern Pass in the east and and include such peaks as Freispitze (2887m), Muttekopf (2777m) and Namloser Wetterspitze (2551m). As for passes, there aren't many of them, but the Hahntennjoch, which sits roughly across the middle of the range, more than meets our needs. The 28km long road, which takes us up to 1894m and features gradients of up to 18 per cent, demands a lot but doesn't quite push us to our limits.

In combination with the easier Fern Pass this northern part of the Lechtal Alps offers a great opportunity to test your stamina and mountain fitness. The down side is that the Fern Pass is busy, especially during rush hour and when heavy traffic is returning from holiday areas to the south.

Our starting point is the marketplace in Reutte, which we leave heading south-west following the signpost to Ehenbichl into the valley to the left of the Lech. At Weißenbach we cross the Lech and join the B198, which briefly runs straight along beside the river. Some 4km further on we cross the Johannis bridge onto the other bank of the Inn. We get up some speed along the still-flat road to Stanzach below the steep cliffs of the Liegfeist range and the mountains around the Schwarzwasser valley with the Lailach and Hochvogel ranges opposite. We ride on past the turn-off to the Namlos valley, sometimes only a hairsbreadth from the gravel banks of the Lech, continuing upstream and reaching the start of the western side of the Hahntennjoch Pass at Elmen.

It's immediately clear what we're up against. The road climbs at 18 per cent and anyone who's ever been up this kind of gradient on a bike knows what that means. The only thing to do is to team the smallest chainring with the largest sprocket and get up out of the saddle, pushing on the pedals with all your strength. That way, even if the 2km climb might seem to drag on, you will be able to get through it. The gradient only decreases to an almost pleasant 10 per cent as you enter the Bschlabs valley, lessening a little more as you go through a short tunnel in the rock.

You reach Bschlabs on ever-narrower roads and if you want you can take a break at the Gasthof Zur Gemütlichkeit. Right up till the 1960s this was run by the local priest as a parish property in order to provide an income for the clergy. Reinvigorated, we set off again and

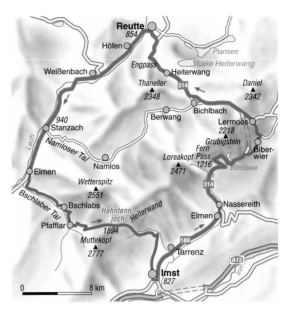

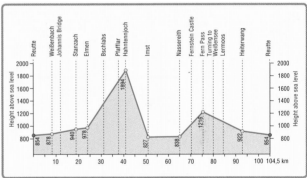

Opposite: The Ehrwald valley with a view of the 2417m-high Ehrwalder Sonnenspitze in the Mieming mountains.

The Chapel of the Auxiliary Saints.

calmly see off two hairpin bends with a gradient of 12 per cent at the entrance to the Plötzig valley; even the 15 per cent gradient from the entrance to the Pfafflar valley up to the alpine houses in Pfafflar shouldn't give us much of a problem.

This village is an interesting cluster of old wooden houses right on the edge of the road built from dark weatherbeaten timber dating in parts from the 13th century, making them among the oldest houses in the Tyrol. One of them has been converted into a kiosk and a little refreshment surely can't hurt, for the climb up to the top of the pass almost 4km away continues at a fairly steady 10 per cent.

Unfortunately there's no view to be had up here and no restaurant either, so it's not long before we make the long descent down the eastern slope to Imst. The road has more bends than it seems at first glance and the surface is also more uneven than it looks. Downhills of up to 15 per cent and a few cattle grids add to the problems, so you need to be careful here and concentrate on the job in hand in order to arrive safely in Imst.

This is a beautiful little town that has grown up at the foot of the mighty Tschirgant in the Inn valley, with strikingly beautiful old noblemen's houses and many attractive fountains that in earlier times served as watering places for teams of horses passing through. We can fill our water bottles here in the shadow of the soaring Gothic spire of St Lawrence's Church before we begin the journey to the Fern Pass.

Some 2000 years ago the Romans built a supply route running north from here in order to secure the area they had conquered on the northern side of the Alps. Today this has become a well-built road that hugs the left-hand side of the broad valley floor all the way to Nassereith

and climbs at only a moderate 6 per cent. Past the 13th-century Fernstein castle that lies on the edge of the deep-green lake of the same name there's only one hairpin bend left before the top of the pass with its inns and souvenir stalls. As we leave we first get a view of the Ehrwald Sonnenspitze and then the mighty Wetterstein mountain range.

Once past the Weißensee we leave the new road with the tunnel under the Grubigstein, which takes the main traffic. Turn off to the left and follow the gently descending road to Biberwier, named after the beavers that once lived here, before we follow gentle ups and downs to Lermoos on the left side of the Ehrwald valley. A gentle climb brings us once more to the B14 main road which alternates gentle climbs and descents to Heiterwang before we descend into our starting point of Reutte.

The climb to the Fern Pass starts in Nassereith.

Opposite: You could shorten your journey considerably by going via the Namlos Saddle here near Stanach.

AROUND THE ROCK KINGDOM OF THE BRENTA

Trentino, Italy

TOUR PROFILE <<

Start: Mezzolombardo in the Adige valley, 227m

Directions: Brenner Autobahn exit S. Michele All'Adige/Mezzocorona – Mezzolombardo

Level of Difficulty/Maximum gradient: Medium, with a maximum gradient of 12 per cent on the climb to the Molveno saddle

Length: 142.5km

Total ascent: 2260m

Time: Well-trained riders can do the tour in a day. Riding time (no stops included) is an estimated 8 hours

Suggested gearing: 39/26-28

Route/Directions: Mezzolombardo (0.0km) – Fai della Paganella (9.5km) – Andalo (16.0km) – Molveno (21.0km) – San Lorenze in Banale (32.0km) – Dorsino (33.5km) – Outskirts of Tavodo (35.5km) – Sclemo (38.0km) – Ponte Arche (41.5km) – Preore (50.0km) – Tione di Trento (53.5km) – Pinzolo (70.5km) – Sant'António di Mavignola (77.0km) – Madonna di Campiglio (82.5km) – Campo Carlomagno Pass (87.0km) – Dimaro (102.0km) – Malé (107.5km) – Cles (124.0km) – Mezzolombardo (142.5km)

Road conditions: Narrow in places on the descent from the Molveno Saddle with several short tunnels

Pass open: All year

Things to see: Pinzolo: Church of St Vigilius; view of the Brenta Mountains from Lake Molveno and Madonna di Campiglio

Map: Euro Cart regional map 1:300,000, RV-Verlag, South Tyrol/Veneto sheet

Over the Molveno Saddle and the Campo Carlomagno Pass

There's no doubt that the Dolomites provide one of the most beautiful mountain landscapes in the world. At the same time there are certainly higher summits with more spectacular glacial scenery and better-known peaks, but there's hardly another mountain range where mountains, people, culture and scenery have come together in such a unique symbiosis. It is worth seeing and experiencing this unique cultural pocket between the Puster valley in the north, the Isarco valley in the west and far down to the heights of Trento in the south. When people talk about the Dolomites, they generally mean the south Tyrol area, which rises east of the Isarco and Adige valleys and boasts such well-known passes as the Sella Joch, the Grödner Joch, the Campolongo Pass, the Fedáia Pass and the Falzarégo Pass, which snake around massifs such as the Sella group, the Langkofel and the Marmolada.

There's another Dolomite range stretching west of the Adige valley from round about Bozen down to Trento – in the area called Trentino – the Brenta Dolomites. Not quite as big, not quite as high, not quite as spectacular and perhaps not as well known as their South Tyrol neighbours but still a mountain range that can match the landscape of any other region of the Alps. But the fact that this area isn't quite so crowded, and we can freely explore the mountain range by bike, definitely makes it more appealing to us cyclists.

The ruins of Belfort castle at Andalo date from the 14th century.

254

Our starting point is the town of Mezzolombardo in the Adige valley, which we reach from the exit for S. Michele/Mezzocorona. We ride a short way, a few hundred metres, from the town out into the Nons valley, following the signs for Molveno/Andalo, before turning off onto the very busy main road. We engage a low gear because the road immediately winds up the slopes of Monte Corno on a gradient of 10 per cent. Soon we get a view to the east over the neighbouring peaks of the Dolomites, and after the village of Fai della Paganella, situated on a plateau at the foot of Monte Fausior, we have to pedal even harder on sudden gradients of up to 12 per cent before the route takes us down past the valley station of the Paganella cable-car and into the green hollow of Andalo.

Not having to make a huge amount of effort on what is – for the most part – a gently descending road down to Molveno, we can enjoy the view of the eastern side of the Brenta range, whose smooth high walls, jagged peaks and sharp towers rise sheer over the calm waters of Lake Molveno. We ride along the shore of the lake to its southern end, where past the small, mostly dried-up Lake Nembia we wind down a narrowing road that in places has been cut into the cliff, gently descending through five short tunnels to San Lorenzo in Banale. Here the valley widens out again and the southern slopes of the Brenta become visible,

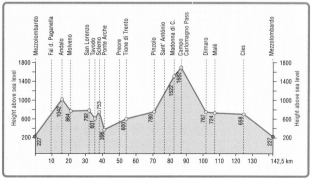

The descent from the Molveno saddle to San Lorenzo in Banale.

joined a little further west by the peaks of the Adamello group. But we mustn't let this view make us miss the turning for Tione/Stenico just before Tavodo, or we won't get over into the Sarca valley to Tione di Trento, the southernmost point of the Campo Carlomagno Pass road. The climb begins in a leisurely way, with a short 8 per cent gradient in the town, then the road keeps mostly to the valley floor as far as Pinzolo, apart from a few short gentle climbs. Before we leave the valley's main town it's worth having a look at the towering Church of St Vigilius of Trent where there's a fresco of the Dance of Death by the 16th-century artist Simone Baschenis on the outer wall, something rarely found here in the southern Alps. In Carisolo, which immediately becomes Pinzolo, we cross the wide stony bed of the Sarca stream and start the actual climb to the pass.

The road goes up round several bends through thick mixed woods to Sant'Antonio di Mavignola where the woods start to give way to alpine meadows and slowly the west side of the Brenta range comes into view, its peaks, the Cima Tosa and the Cima Brenta, both over 3000m high. We should then take in the view in the popular tourist resort of Madonna di Campiglio, which we approach on a slope that is hardly ever less than 10 per cent. It's named after a small church built here in 1182 dedicated to the Virgin Mary. Since the area had been called Campiglio since time immemorial, the town which grew up round the church was given the name Madonna di Campiglio. The old church was unfortunately destroyed by fire in 1877. Although luckily, the carved Gothic altar was saved and then reinstalled in the church when it was rebuilt in 1894. We're rewarded with a view over the surrounding area, for which there can be only one word: spectacular. You'd have to go a long way to find such a fantastic mountain panorama as at the rock bastion of the Brenta, soaring high to the east of the town.

Nevertheless at some point we have to tear our eyes away from the view and continue our journey up to the top of the pass, which is barely 5km away now. Having negotiated the 11 per cent slope into the town, the gradient as we leave the town only gradually decreases but then settles at a comfortable 7 per cent all the way to the highest point of our tour, the Campo Carlomagno. It gets its name from no less a person than the Frankish emperor Charlemagne, who once halted here with his army on the way to northern Italy. Other than the name, which translates literally as 'Charlemagne's Field', there is nothing at all to prove that the emperor was ever here, and the view over to the mountains is hidden by tall forests. This is neither here nor there, our attention drawn instead to the bends and hairpins on the long descent that follows, with gradients of up to 9 per cent. The road down from the pass finishes in Dimaro, and we arrive in the broad Val di Sole. If you haven't had enough of cycling over passes you could turn off at this point and follow the road that goes to the west to the Tonale Pass – though the top of the pass is still almost 28km and a vertical climb of a good 1110m away. All of which might convince us it's a better idea to turn back around now, especially because the 40km or so back to our starting point has longer, flatter sections as well as shorter slopes of up to 8 per cent to ride. Back at the start the feeling that we have completed one of the more breathtaking cycle routes in the world is reward enough for the efforts we have expended.

The Presanella group south of the Tonale Pass also has its charms.

THE HÖLLENSCHLUCHT AND THE ZITTERN VALLEY

Graubünden/Ticino/Uri, Switzerland

Over the Lukmanier, St Gotthard and Oberal Passes

Switzerland must surely be the number one choice for ambitious pass cyclists. This should in no way be taken as a slur on the other alpine countries since these countries definitely offer pass routes comparable to the route profile and the challenges seen here. But the ice-clad peaks and razor-sharp crests of the Swiss mountains, heaving in glaciers, give rise to magnificent scenery the like of which is rarely found elsewhere.

Our tour takes us into the high alpine area of Switzerland where passes such as the Lukmanier, St Gotthard and Oberalp have illustrious-sounding names, even though one or two may only be known from radio or television coverage of closures during the winter. This also shows the alpine character of this tour, which is clearly underlined further by names like Höllenschlucht and Tal des

In the Blenio Valley south of the Lukmanier Pass – the little church of San Pietro e Paolo in Motto near Ludiano in Ticino.

Zitterns (respectively 'hell's gorge' and 'shaking valley'). Don't let these names put you off: these descriptions of sections of the routes to the Lukmanier and St Gotthard Passes date from earlier times when travel here was really dangerous and an adventure. Today these passes are generally well constructed and no problem to cycle over, provided conditions are good.

So we set off from Disentis/Munstér, which is dominated by the massive wall and two towers of the 13th-century Benedictine Abbey, and take the turn-off for the Lukmanier Pass, which for the first 2km takes us down to the Vorderrhein river at the valley floor. There the rock faces cluster closely together leaving hardly any room for the road, which now has a gradient of 10 per cent and pushes through three tunnels. Two of these are almost 100m long and one is a 600m dimly lit gallery tunnel. In Curaglia the valley then widens a bit and we leave the Höllenschlucht behind us. The road climbs slowly through several smaller villages, then once past Acla and after 10km the gradient increases to 10 per cent again. The rocky surroundings and sparse vegetation give no hint that the name of the pass was originally Lucus Magnus, which basically means 'large wood', referring to the thick forest once prevalent here. In front of us lies the more than 100m-high concrete wall of the Sontga Maria Lake, which we get to after climbs of up to 8 per cent and several short tunnels and gallery tunnels. Then we ride along the left-hand bank of the lake into a long avalanche gallery that gently descends halfway through to the top of the pass and its hotel, the Hospezi San Maria.

There are two 100m long tunnels, one short gallery and five hairpin bends on a gradient of up to 8 per cent on the 43km

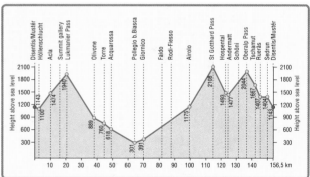

descent to Pollegio, not far from the main town of Biasca, which we bypass. We've arrived in the northern part of Ticino, known as Sopraceneri, with its glorious colours and flowers, but there's not much time to enjoy them. A good 35km now lie before us through the Levantina valley and on to Airolo, a journey we cover in several stages, the gradient never exceeding 10 per cent and mostly far less than that.

TOUR PROFILE <<

Road conditions: The route to the
St Gotthard Pass on the old road
through the Tremola valley with its 24
cobblestone hairpin bends should only
be attempted in good, safe weather
conditions. Otherwise use the bypass.
The descent from the Oberalp Pass is
narrow in places with surface damage.
Lights are necessary because of tunnels
and galleries at the Lukmanier and
Oberalp Passes

Pass open: Lukmanier Pass 15 May
to 30 November; St Gotthard Pass 15
May to 15 November; old road through
Tremola valley subject to weather
conditions with closures possible.
Oberalp Pass 15 May to 15 November

Map: Euro Cart regional map 1:300,000,
RV-Verlag, Switzerland sheet

In Airolo we come face to face with what was long considered to
be the most dangerous and most dreaded pass road in the Alps,
the southern ramp of the St Gotthard Pass through the Val Tremola
or 'shaking valley'. The danger used to come mainly from the
avalanches against which the area is almost defenceless. But we
shouldn't have any problems in high summer, and the cobblestones
on the 24 narrow hairpin bends shouldn't cause any difficulties.
Nevertheless, I'd like to point out that this route should only be
attempted in good, safe weather conditions because after heavy
rain, rockfalls can occur here, and I myself once saw how a huge
rockfall blocked a stretch of the route. In that case you should
switch to the safe, well-constructed new route used by almost all
traffic to the top of the pass.

In good weather conditions the climb over the old south ramp,
where the skilfully engineered system of 24 hairpin bends one after
the other never exceed 10 per cent, is a really unique experience. If
you're lucky you'll see the old stage coach built in 1830, for which
the route was surfaced and which still travels the route today as a
tourist attraction.

Once at the top of the pass, it is worth visiting the former
mountain hostel that now houses a museum, whose exhibits
creatively illustrate the dangers of earlier times. The top of the pass
itself is a rather barren plateau littered with smooth polished stones
and dotted with very small lakes. We start the descent with gradients
of up to 10 per cent down to Hospental, riding on from there on a

level road to Andermatt, the starting point for our last climb to a pass, the Oberalp. Even though there's very little strength left in our legs, we should be able to manage the near-600m ascent. At first the road climbs at 10 per cent around wide hairpin bends up a grassy slope, then the gradient decreases to 6 per cent through the hamlet of Schöni, just over halfway on this section of the climb, and the lush grasses give way to sparse alpine meadows. Towards the top the gradient decreases a little again and through a very long, lit gallery tunnel we reach the top of the pass, which is almost completely covered by the 2.5km-long Oberalp Lake

– to be frank one of the less impressive alpine lakes.

However, we can feel pleased because the difficulties are behind us and we're riding down a winding route with gradients of up to 10 per cent back into the Vorderrhein valley, which is called the Tavetsch here. After Tschamut the valley broadens out, the gradient decreases and we have to pedal again on flat sections. After Sedrun what had been up till now a narrow route is replaced by a broad, well-maintained road. It descends gently, interrupted only by a few short level sections and we reach our starting point again.

Opposite: There are 24 hairpin bends on the old road through the Tremola valley on the southern side of the St Gotthard pass.

Taking a break on the descent from the Lukmanier pass.

DIFFICULT PASSES AT THE END OF THE ALPS
Provence/Piedmont, France

TOUR PROFILE <<

Start: Menton, 16m

Directions: A8 Genoa–Nice, Ventimiglia – Menton exit

Level of Difficulty/Maximum gradient: Difficult, with a maximum gradient of 11 per cent on short stretches on the Col de la Lombarde

Length: 285.0km

Total ascent: 5850m

Time: Only cyclists who have trained hard can manage the route in two days. Therefore three days should be allowed

Suggested gearing: 39/28

Route/Directions: Menton (0.0) – Monti (3.5km) – Caramel Viaduct (9.0km) – Castillon (11.0km) – Col de Castillon (13.5km) – Sospel (20.5km) – Moulinet (26.0km) – Col de Turini Pass (38.5km) – La Bollène-Vésubie (51.5km) – D2565/ D70 junction (53.5km) – Rouquebillière (57.5km) – Saint Martin-Vésubie (66.5km) – Col Saint Martin (74.5km) – Saint Dalmas (77.5km) – La Bolline (81.5km) – D2565/D2205 junction (91.5km) – Saint Sauveur-sur-Tinée (95.5km) – Isola (108.5km) – Isola 2000 (125.0km) – Col de la Lombarde (129.5km) – Vinádio (151.0km) – Demonte (161.5km) – Borgo San Dalmazzo (179.0km) – Robilante (182.5km) – Vernante (190.5km) – Limone-Piemonte (197.0km) – Al Cannone d'Oro Bragard (201.5km) – Col de Tende (210.5km) – tunnel southern exit (219.5km) – Tende (229.5km) – Breil-sur-Roya (247.5km) – Ventimiglia (274.0km) – Menton (285.0km)

Road conditions: The Col de la Lombarde pass road is well constructed as far as Isola 2000; further on up to the top of the pass and on the descent it is narrow with considerable damage to the road surface. The descent from the Col de Tende is on an unpaved dirt road that is rather worn away on the bends and has minor potholes

A rather barren, inhospitable Alpine world awaits us on the northern side of the Col de la Lombarde.

Over the Col de Turini, the Col Saint Martin, the Col de la Lombarde and Col de Tende

If we assume that you've worked your way through this guide to passes and have got as far as France, in the saddle of course, then you must have the one thing that you're definitely going to need on this tour, namely, stamina. Although the Alps seem almost at an end here in the immediate vicinity of the Côte d'Azur, there are still pass roads which by their height, challenging conditions and landscape features are on a par with other better-known alpine passes. The Col de Turini, the first of four pass roads we'll be climbing on our tour, is probably the best known at 1607m high. The final stage of the Monte Carlo Rally runs over it and perhaps has made it familiar to one or two from television pictures of high-performance cars bombing over the summit, the crest an inferno of flashing lights and headlamps, during what is known as the Night of the Long Knives.

However, we needn't worry about too much traffic here: the Col de Turini, just like the other pass roads, is rather isolated, and traffic is light. Problems come more from its total vertical climb, which, with an interim descent from the Col de Castillon on the way, adds up to a good 2000m. Already an impressive figure on its own but add to that the 1000m to the Col Saint Martin, followed by the

262

1500m of the Col de la Lombarde, a high alpine crossing from the French Tinée valley over to the Italian Stura valley near Cuneo. This takes us through the Mercantour National Park, an unspoiled landscape where the winding and occasionally narrow road seems to discourage too much traffic. Then from Borgo San Dalmazzo up to the Col de Tende it's a good 1300m, but the fourth pass of the group we're crossing has something special that lifts it above other pass roads. The old pass road on the southern, French side that we ride down actually has a total of 48 hairpin bends, sited very tidily one after the other and unlike any other pass road in the Alps – an unequalled masterpiece of road-building. The nearest comparison here in terms of construction is perhaps the old road through the Tremola valley to the St Gotthard Pass (see also the tour of

Switzerland), but while this is surfaced the Col de Tende pass road is a dirt road. However, its unmade surface is so well maintained that it can also be ridden on our narrow clincher tyres. As well as the obligatory puncture repair kit we should

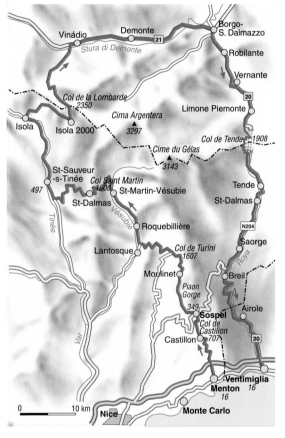

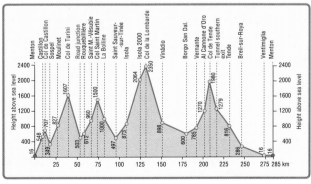

TOUR PROFILE <<

Pass open: Col de la Lombarde 15 June to 31 October. Border station at the top of the pass closed from 10pm to 7am. Col de Tende open 15 May to 31 October.

Things to see: Col de Castillon: the Caramel Viaduct on the climb; Sospel: St Michael's Church; the top of the Col de Turini: detour from the top of the pass on the D68 to L'Anthion and Pointe des Tres Communes vantage points, 2082m with a view over the Mercantour National Park; Tende: old town, Church of the Assumption of Our Lady; Menton: Palais Cornolès, Biovès Garden, Regional Museum, St Michael's Church, Grimaldi caves.

Map: Euro Cart regional map 1:300,000, RV-Verlag, France, sheet 8 Provence/Rhône-Alpes/Côte d'Azur

perhaps carry a spare inner tube, although we probably won't need it, providing we ride carefully of course.

You can see there's a lot waiting for us as we set off from Menton, and if you don't spot any signposts here for the Col de Turini then just keep following the signposts to Sospel, riding under the road's high-soaring pillars and continuing upwards with gradients of up to 10 per cent throughout. After barely 10km you catch sight of the Caramel Viaduct, bypass the town of Castillon, and then suddenly a 40m-long, unlit tunnel announces the top of the Col de Castillon. A good two-lane road with gradients of up to 10 per cent goes down to Sospel sprawling in a wide hollow along the river Bévera. There's nothing much to look at here, but the next part of the route is well signposted to Moulinet/Col de Turini. We ride along a road with no more than an 8 per cent gradient to start with into an unspoiled landscape. The rock walls of the Piaon Gorge crowd in on the road, then it's up again through the woods to Moulinet, the last town before the top of the pass, round countless bends, the odd one even with a gradient of 10 per cent. A short rock tunnel, a sign saying '8 Lacet', then we can rest at the top of the pass where we realise that on the other side the route finally goes back down again. It does this on a narrow, winding road with gradients of up to 10 per cent down to La Bollène-Vésubie and on to the junction

of the D2565 and the D70, where we turn off for Roquebillière. We climb up the Vésubie valley and if you think you can take it easy here you're wrong because the road climbs 1500m up to the Col Saint Martin before it finally goes down into the Tinée valley. We ride up this gently rising valley to the little village of Isola and reach the turning for the Col de la Lombarde, a very well-constructed road, but in return there's a total vertical climb of almost exactly 1480m with a gradient of no less than 8 per cent and no more than 11 per cent.

The top of the pass, just above the architect-designed ski resort of Isola 2000, is a barren, rock-strewn landscape without even a restaurant to visit. So we set off on the long, winding descent to Italian territory over the eastern side, its steepest gradient reaching 13 per cent down in the lowest part near Vinádio at

the mouth of the Stura valley, which we now follow to Borgo San Dalmazzo.

The climb to the Col de Tende is nothing out of the ordinary. We follow the traffic heading for France on a good, wide road with a gradient of no more than 9 per cent until we get to the little village of Al Cannone d'Oro di Bragard, where we mustn't miss the turning to the old route up to the pass. At first this road too is unexceptional, though it gets distinctly narrower and the condition of the road surface worsens. The road climbs for 9km at no more than 10 per cent and then we're up at the top of the pass in unspoiled, isolated surroundings. The tarmac ends here and becomes an unsurfaced road which now goes down hairpin bend after hairpin bend, only once briefly reaching a gradient of 12 per cent. Nowhere on the route is difficult, exposed or dangerous but given the desolate surroundings and the unmade road there's a feeling of being back in the previous century when the Alps were first opened up on tracks like these.

The route then takes us back onto the new pass road, where we join the traffic going through the tunnel and reach the Côte d'Azur at Ventimiglia, still 11km or so from our starting point in Menton.

The town of Saorge on the southern side of the Col de Tende nestles on the mountain ridges.

The 48 hairpin bends on unsurfaced roads on the southern side of the Col de Tende are fine to ride on your narrow clincher tyres if you take care.

265

The 'Casses Désertes' (Fossil Desert) on the southern side of the Col d'Izoard offers a landscape that is unique in the whole of the Alps.

Summary of pass and mountain roads <<

Pass and mountain roads	Height	Length	Maximum Incline	Open	Country	Tour
Albula Pass	2315 m	west 31.5 km/east 9.5 km	west 12%/east 12%	01/06–31/10	Switzerland	54
Alpe-d'Huez Mountain Road	1860 m	13.5 km	10%	01/01–31/12	France	88
Anniviers and Zinal High Valley Road	1700 m	25.5 km	11%	01/01–31/12	Switzerland	78
Belvédère-du-Cirque-du-Mont-Viso Road	2127 m	15.0 km	14%	15/05–31/10	France	91
Bernina Pass	2330 m	north 15.0 km/south 34.5 km	north 10%/south 10%	01/01–31/12	Switzerland/Italy	57
Campo Carlomagno Pass	1682 m	north 15.0 km/south 32.5 km	north 9%/south 11%	01/01–31/12	Italy	43
Campolongo Pass	1875 m	north 6.5 km/south 4.0 km	north 10%/south 10%	01/01–31/12	Italy	26
Col d'Allos	2250 m	north 21.0 km/south 23.5 km	north 11%/south 9%	15/06–15.11	France	95
Col d'Izoard	2360 m	north 20.5 km/south 32.0 km	north 12%/south 12%	15/06–15/10	France	89
Col de l'Iseran	2770 m	north 45.0 km/south 33.0 km	north 12%/south 11%	01/06–30/09	France	80
Col de la Croix de Fer	2067 m	north 30.0 km/south 28.0 km	north 14%/south 12%	15/05–31/10	France	84
Col de la Lombarde	2351 m	north 21.5 km/south 21.0 km	north 13%/south 11%	15/06–31/10	Italy/France	50
Col de la Madeleine	2000 m	north 19.5 km/south 27.0 km	north 12%/south 12%	15/06–31/10	France	86
Col de Mongenèvre Pass	1850 m	east 7.5 km/west 14.0 km	east 10%/west 10%	01/01–31/12	Italy/France	49
Col de Restefond/Col de la Bonette	2802 m	north 23.5 km/south 26.5 km	north 14%/south 14%	15/06–30/09	France	94
Col de Tende	1908 m	south 8.0 km/north 9.0 km	south 12%/north 10%	15/05–31/10	France/Italy	96
Col de Turini and Col de Castillon	1607 m	south 38.5 km/north 15.0 km	south 10%/north 10%	01/01–31/12	France	97
Col de Vars	2109 m	north 20 km/south 15.0 km	north 12%/south 10%	01/01–31/12	France	92
Col du Galibier	2646 m	north 18.5 km/south 9.0 km	north 12%/south 12%	15/06–15/10	France	83
Col du Glandon	1951 m	north 21.5 km/south 0.5 km	north 15%/south 7%	15/05–31/10	France	85
Col du Lautaret	2058 m	west 34.5 km/east 27.5 km	west 10%/east 7%	01/01–31/12	France	87
Col du Télégraphe	1600 m	north 12.5 km/south 5.0 km	north 10%/south 9%	01/01–31/12	France	82
Costalunga Pass	1752 m	west 24.5 km/east 10.0 km	west 18%/east 10%	01/01–31/12	Italy	31
Engstlenalp Mountain Road	1837 m	14.5 km	12%	01/05–31/10	Switzerland	68
Falzárego Pass	2117 m	east 16.5 km/west 11.0 km	east 11%/west 8%	01/01–31/12	Italy	22
Fedáia Pass	2056 m	west 14.5 km/ east 14.5 km	west 10%/east 15%	15/04–15/10	Italy	32
Flüela Pass	2383 m	west 13.0 km/east 13.5 km	west 10%/east 11%	01/01–31/12	Switzerland	53
Fuorn Pass	2149 m	west 22.0 km/east 16.0 km	west 10%/east 10%	01/01–31/12	Switzerland	52
Furka Pass	2436 m	east 17.5 km/west 7.5 km	east 11%/west 11%	01/06–31/10	Switzerland	65
Gardena Pass	2137 m	west 9.5 km/east 9.5 km	west 10%/east 12%	01/01–31/12	Italy	25
Gavia Pass	2652 m	north 26.5 km/south 17.0 km	north 16%/south 16%	01/06–15/10	Italy	41
Giau Pass	2236 m	north 16.0 km/south 10.0 km	north 12%/south 14%	01/05–31/10	Italy	23
Gressoney High Valley Road	1825 m	38.0 km	12%	01/01–31/12	Italy	46
Grimsel Pass	2165 m	south 6.0 km/north 27.5 km	south 9%/north 11%	15/06–15/10	Switzerland	66
Great St Bernard Pass	2473 m	north 43.5 km/south 31.0 km	north 11%/south 10%	01/06–15/10	Switzerland/France	79
Große Scheidegg Pass	1962 m	west 31.0 km/east 16.5 km	west 12%/east 14%	May–October	Switzerland	70
Grossglockner High Alpine Road	2505 m	north 33.5 km/south 15.0 km	north 12%/south 10%	01/05–01/11	Austria	9
Hahntennjoch	1894 m	west 17.0 km/east 14.0 km	west 18%/east 15%	01/05–31/10	Austria	15
Jaufen Pass	2094 m	east 18.5 km/west 19.5 km	west 10%/east 12%	01/05–30/11	Italy	35
Jaun Pass	1509 m	east 8.5 km/west 23.5 km	east 11%/west 14%	01/01–31/12	Switzerland	73
Julier Pass	2284 m	north 37.0 km/south 7.5 km	north 10%/south 11%	01/01–31/12	Switzerland	55
Kiental and Griesalp Road	1407 m	14.0 km	28%	Easter–31/10	Switzerland	71
Kitzbüheler Horn	1966 m	8.5 km or 11.0 km	16% or 18%	01/01–31/12	Austria	10
Klausen Pass	1952 m	east 39.0 km/west 25.0 km	east 10%/west 9%	15/05–31/10	Switzerland	60
Kühtai Saddle	2020 m	west 18.5 km/east 23.5 km	west 16%/east 16%	01/01–31/12	Austria	12
Little St Bernard Pass	2188 m	north 23.5 km/south 27.5 km	north 9%/south 12%	15/06–31/10	Italy/France	48
Livigno, Foscagno and Eira Passes	2315 m	50.0 km	12%	15/06–06/11 or 10/05–15/12	Switzerland	56
Lukmanier Pass	1940 m	north 20.5 km/south 43.0 km	north 10%/south 8%	15/05–31/10	Switzerland	63
Maddalena Pass	1996 m	west 16.5 km/east 33.0 km	west 12%/east 8%	01/01–31/12	France/Italy	93

Pass and mountain roads	Height	Length	Maximum Incline	Open	Country	Tour
Maloja Pass	1815 m	west 32.5 km/east 10.0 km	west 12%/east 6%	01/01–31/12	Italy/Switzerland	44
Malta Alpine Road	1920 m	28.5 km	13%	01/06–31/10	Austria	8
Mattertal Road	1616 m	35.0 km	10%	01/01–31/12	Switzerland	76
Mendel Pass	1363 m	east 16.0 km/west 9.5 km	east 10%/west 12%	01/01–31/12	Italy	39
Mont Cenis Pass	2100 m	north 10.0 km/south 31.0 km	north 11%/south 11%	15/05–15/10	France/Italy	81
Mont Ventoux	1909 m	west 21.5 km/east 23.0 km	west 12%/east 12%	15/05–31/10	France	100
Nice, Braus and Brouis Passes	1002 m	55.0 km	15%	01/01–31/12	France	98
Nigerpass	1774 m	25.0 km	24%	01/01–31/12	Italy	30
Nockalm Mountain Road	2040 m	south 32.5/north 18.0 km	south 12%/north 12%	Whitsun–31/10	Austria	7
Nufenen Pass	2478 m	east 24.0 km/west 14.5 km	east 10%/west 13%	01/06–31/10	Switzerland	69
Oberalp Pass	2045 m	east 22.0 km/west 11.5 km	east 10%/west 10%	15/05–15/10	Switzerland	62
Oberjoch Pass	1150 m	south 8.5 km/north 14.5 km	south 9%/north 8%	01/01–31/12	Germany	4
Ötztal and Timmelsjoch Road	2509 m	54.0 km	12%	15/06–15/10	Austria	13
Passo delle Palade	1518 m	north 24.5 km/south 14.0 km	north 9%/south 8%	01/01–31/12	Italy	38
Penser Joch	2215 m	south 53 km/north 16.5 km	south 12%/north 13%	15/05 or 01/06–31/10	Italy	37
Pordoi Pass	2239 m	east 9.0 km/west 11.0 km	east 8%/west 11%	01/01–31/12	Italy	27
Pragel Pass	1543 m	west 29.5 km/east 21.0 km	west 18%/east 14%	15/06–31/10	Switzerland	61
Predil Pass	1156 m	north 15.0 km/south 17.0 km	north 10%/south 12%	01/01–31/12	Italy/Slovenia	17
Riedberg Pass	1420 m	west 20.5 km/east 8.5 km	west 16%/east 16%	01/01–31/12	Germany/Austria	5
Rolle Pass	1980 m	west 19.5 km/east 21.0 km	west 9%/east 11%	01/01–31/12	Italy	34
Roßfeld Mountain Ring Road	1540 m	34.5 km	14%	01/01–31/12	Germany	1
Saanenmöser Pass	1279 m	west 45.5 km/east 16.5 km	west 9%/east 6%	01/01–31/12	Switzerland	72
Saastal and Mattmark Road	2197 m	34.5 km	13%	01/06–31/10	Switzerland	77
San Bernardino Pass	2066 m	north 9.5 km/south 23.0 km	north 9%/south 12%	01/05–31/10	Switzerland	75
St Gotthard Pass	2108 m	north 34.0 km/south 13.5 km	north 10%/south 10%	15/05–15/10	Switzerland	64
San Pellegrino Pass	1918 m	east 20.5 km/west 12.0 km	east 18%/west 14%	01/01–31/12	Italy	33
Savarenche High Valley Road	1960 m	27.0 km	12%	15/06–31/10	Italy	47
Schwägalp Pass	1305 m	west 10.5 km/east 20.0 km	west 10%/east 12%	01/01–31/12	Switzerland	59
Seiser Alm Pass	1900 m	20.5 km	15%	01/01–31/12	Italy	29
Sella Pass	2240 m	south 12.0 km/north 9.0 km	south 11%/north 10%	01/01–31/12	Italy	28
Silvretta High Alpine Road	2032 m	east 42.5 km/west 45.0 km	east 11%/west 12%	01/06–15/11	Austria	16
Simplon Pass	2005 m	north 22.5 km/south 41.5 km	north 9%/south 10%	01/01–31/12	Switzerland/Italy	74
Sölden Glacier Road	2829 m	13.0 km	13%	01/05–31/12	Austria	14
Sommet Bucher Mountain Road	2257 m	11.0 km	14%	01/01–31/12	France	90
Splügen Pass	2118 m	south 33.5 km/north 9.5 km	south 13%/north 11%	01/01–31/12	Switzerland/Italy	45
Staller Saddle	2052 m	west 24.0 km/east 28.0 km	west 13%/east 12%	01/06–31/10	Austria/Italy	19
Stelvio Pass	2757 m	north 28.0 km/south 22.0 km	north 12%/south 12%	01/06–31/10	Italy	40
Susten Pass	2224 m	west 28.0 km/east 18.0 km	west 9%/east 9%	15/-6–15/10	Switzerland	67
Tatzelwurm and Sudelfeld Saddle Road	1097 m	west 4.5 km/east 16.5 km	west 11%/east 14%	01/01–31/12	Germany	3
Timmelsjoch (southern side)	2509 m	29.5 km	13%	15/06–15/10	Italy	36
Tonale Pass	1884 m	east 27.5 km/west 11.5 km	east 10%/west 8%	01/01–31/12	Italy	42
Tre Cime di Lavaredo	2400 m	7.5 km	16%	01/06–30/09	Italy	20
Tre Croci Pass	1809 m	west 8.0 km/east 4.0 km	west 11%/east 12%	01/01–31/12	Italy	21
Turracher Mountain Road	1763 m	south 13.0 km/north 19.5 km	south 23%/north 12%	01/01–31/12	Austria	6
Umbrail Pass	2503 m	north 14.0 km/south 0.5 km	north 11%/south 8%	15/05–15/11	Italy/Switzerland	51
Valparola Pass	2192 m	north 14.0 km/south 1.0 km	north 10%/south 10%	01/01–31/12	Italy	24
Verdon Gorge Circuit	1406 m	122.0 km	14%	01/01–31/12	France	99
Vršic Pass	1611 m	south 30.0 km/north 11.5 km	south 14%/north 12%	01/05–31/10	Slovenia	18
Wildhaus Pass	1090 m	east 25.5 km/west 18.0 km	east 10%/west 10%	01/01–31/12	Switzerland	58
Winklmoos Mountain Road	1210 m	9.5 km	18%	01/01–31/12	Germany	2
Zillertal	2133 m	25.0 km	20%	01/06–31/10	Austria	11

INDEX

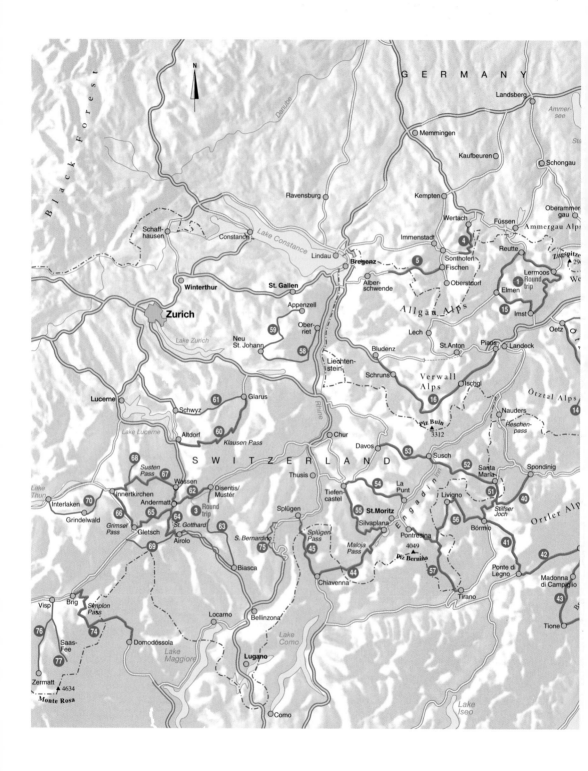

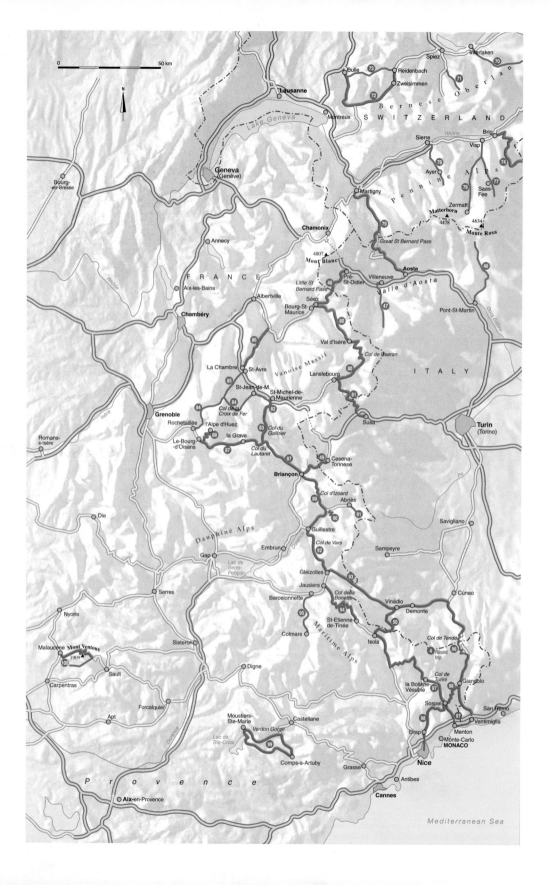